REVELATION: A COSMIC PERSPECTIVE

Revelation

A COSMIC PERSPECTIVE

Edward Reaugh Smith

SteinerBooks | 2016

2016 | SteinerBooks
An imprint of Anthroposophic Press, Inc.
610 Main Street, Great Barrington, MA 01230
www.steinerbooks.org

Cover image: *The Rainbow* © by Julia Tucker Franklin
Design: William Jens Jensen

LIBRARY OF CONGRESS CONTROL NUMBER: 2015952104

ISBN: 978-1-62148-143-0 (paperback)
ISBN: 978-1-62148-144-7 (eBook)

CONTENTS

A NOTE ON REFERENCES

References using the format styled, for example, **I-1**, **I-2**, **I-9** refer to the chart designations in *The Burning Bush*.

Bold type in the references indicates charts at the back of *The Burning Bush* that begin with a Roman numeral **I**, followed by a hyphen and an Arabic numeral. The Roman numeral signifies that the chart comes from the first volume of the series described as an anthroposophical commentary on the Bible addressing important biblical terms and phrases.

All biblical quotations are from the Revised Standard Version (RSV), 2nd ed. (1972).

LIST OF ABBREVIATIONS

AB	*Anchor Bible,* Garden City, NY, Doubleday, various volumes and dates
ABD	*Anchor Bible Dictionary,* New York (1992), editor in chief, David Noel Freedman, Garden City, NY, Doubleday, various volumes
ABRL	*Anchor Bible Reference Library,* New York, Anchor, various volumes
AP	Anthroposophic Press, Hudson, NY (Great Barrington, MA, after 2000)
ASJ	Rudolf Steiner, *The Apocalypse of St. John,* 4th ed., various translators, AP (1993) (CW 104)
BB	Edward Reaugh Smith, *The Burning Bush,* rev. ed., AP, 2001 (1st ed. 1997)
CW	Collected Works of Rudolf Steiner, various volumes, dates, and translators
DQWIM	Edward Reaugh Smith, *David's Question, "What Is Man?"* AP (2001)
IBJ	Edward Reaugh Smith, *The Incredible Births of Jesus,* AP (1998)
KJV–NIV, INT	Alfred Marshall, *The Interlinear KJV–NIV Parallel New Testament in Greek and English,* Grand Rapids, Zonderman (a division of HarperCollins) (1975)
MP	Mercury Press, Spring Valley, NY
NIB	*New Interpreter's Bible,* Nashville, TN, Abingdon Press, various volumes and dates
JPS	*The JPS Torah Commentary,* Philadelphia
OES	Rudolf Steiner, *An Outline of Esoteric Science*
PWA	Edward Reaugh Smith, *Pathways: An Autobiography,* SB (2014)
RPA	Rudolf Steiner, *Reading the Pictures of the Apocalypse,* tr. James H. Hindes, AP (1993) (CW 104a)
RSP	Rudolf Steiner Press, London
SB	SteinerBooks, Great Barrington, MA
SLJ	Edward Reaugh Smith, *The Soul's Long Journey,* AP (2003)
TL	Temple Lodge Publishing, London
TSRYR	Edward Reaugh Smith, *The Temple Sleep of the Rich Young Ruler,* SB (2011)

1

The Christian Mystery

In a 1939 radio address, Churchill characterized Russia as "a riddle, wrapped in a mystery, inside an enigma." He could scarcely have better described each of us as human beings. We are an "I Am" inside an astral body, inside an etheric body, inside a physical body. Stated differently, we are a body of senses, inside a body with life, inside a body of minerals. While we were yet in the spiritual realm, in the garden that "the Lord God planted...in Eden," he told us of two trees, one of knowledge and one of life, respectively the astral (sense) body and the etheric (life) body.

As the prodigal son, we disobeyed and began a very long journey from the spiritual realm into the pit of mineralization, in which we presently struggle. The Lord God Himself, the Word, as the one we call the Christ, "became flesh" for three years. By his crucifixion and the spilling of his blood, the carrier of His own "I AM," into the earth's etheric (life) realm, the dawning awareness of the significance of his resurrection in spiritual body has planted in us the recognition of our plight. There within our own I Am, always connected to the Christ I AM working within us, is born the inner craving to return to our spiritual home.

The Revelation of John is the vision, the uncovering or apocalypse, of that long journey of the prodigal son. For those, including those in the academic community, who have tried to understand it, Churchill's remark is a terribly apt description of John's book. "The book of Revelation [is] paradoxically the most veiled text of all in the Bible."[1]

---

1   Christopher C. Rowland, "The Book of Revelation," NIB, vol. 12 (1998), 505.

THE SUBMERGENCE OF THE FIRST INSIGHTS

The present undertaking is based upon the early twentieth century lectures and writings of Rudolf Steiner, termed by him Anthroposophy. Steiner does not claim to be the first initiate with anthroposophic vision, what can be called basic, or core, Anthroposophy. For that he gives credit to an individuality who lived several centuries earlier, Christian Rosenkreutz. However, Steiner not only intuited that such core insight came earlier to Rosenkreutz, but that such insight itself was true spiritual perception.[2] At a lecture on June 3, 1909, in Budapest, Steiner said, "One cannot be informed truly about Rosicrucianism by what is said about it in public. Nothing of what was cultivated in true Rosicrucianism is to be found in literature."[3]

What is presented in this writing is offered under the conviction that Christian Rosenkreutz was the reincarnated Lazarus/John (LJ) individuality. This was my position in *The Burning Bush* (*BB*) (543), where, however, I did not cite authority for the connection. Earlier in *BB* (484) I quoted Heidenreich's preface to Steiner's "Last Address" of September 27, 1924.[4] In that preface Heidenreich (9) said, "Although Rudolf Steiner spoke in the years after 1902 [when he published *Christianity as Mystical Fact*] of this event, and of the figure who passed through it, many times and from many different sides, he never referred to another incarnation of Lazarus *except on an intimate occasion, the content of which became known somewhat more generally only much later, after his death*" (emphasis added). In their book *Rudolf Steiner's Mission and Ita Wegman*, Margarete and Erich Kirchner-Bockholt offered the following passages:[5]

---

2   The archangel Michael is the ruler of the "divine" or "cosmic" intelligence. The last pre-Christian regency of Michael occurred from 602 to 248 BCE, the age in which Aristotle, through Michael's leadership, brought the elements of the ancient mysteries into an instructive philosophy that was useful in the outer world. Michael's first regency since the time of Christ began in 1879 and will run until about 2233 CE (*BB*, 574–575, chart **I-19**). It is far too soon in our script to bring in the role Aristotle plays in the "raising of Lazarus," the temple-sleep initiation of Lazarus/John. That must come much later in this account.

3   *Rosicrucian Esotericism*, AP (1978), 6 (CW 109/111).

4   *The Last Address*, RSP (1967) (CW 238); 3.

5   Kirchner-Bockholt, *Rudolf Steiner's Mission and Ita Wegman*, RSP (1977).

This Rosicrucian stream originated with the Initiation of an individuality who was the first to have been initiated by Christ Himself. After the later Initiation in the thirteenth century this individual bore the esoteric name of Christian Rosenkreutz. (99)

❧

It was a great tragedy for the Anthroposophical Movement that after the last Karma lecture (September 28, 1924) it was no longer possible for Rudolf Steiner to speak to the Members. Until then he had been describing the destinies of the group of human beings who at the time of the Mystery of Golgotha were in the spiritual world. In his Address on September 28, 1924 [The Last Address] he began to speak of the destinies of individuals who were living on the Earth when the Mystery of Golgotha actually took place. His intention, just as he had spoken about the first group, was to lecture about the Karma of this second Michael stream of individuals who were then working on the Earth. (121)

In a lecture at Neuchâtel, September 27, 1911, speaking of Rosenkreutz, Steiner said:

He was an individuality who had been incarnated at the time of the Mystery of Golgotha. In subsequent incarnations he had prepared himself for his mission through humility of heart and through fervent submission to the divine will. He was an exalted soul, a godly, deeply mystical man, one who had been born with these qualities and had not merely acquired them in the course of that life.[6]

In his Introduction to the Collected Works volume 284, Christopher Bamford, doubtless aware of the content of the statement by Steiner on the intimate occasion Heidenreich cited, which became "known somewhat more generally" after Steiner's death, referring to Rosenkreutz, said parenthetically, "in a previous incarnation, according to Steiner's research, he had been Lazarus/John."[7]

In Bamford's Introduction, he gives a synopsis of the brief thirteenth-century incarnation of the individuality of Rosenkreutz, around 1250 CE, followed by the incarnation in 1378 of that individuality as

---

6   *Rosicrucian Christianity*, MP (1989), 6 (CW 130).

7   *Rosicrucianism Renewed*, CW 284, SB (2007), xxix.

Christian Rosenkreutz, an incarnation that lasted 106 years. It was in the mid-fifteenth century when he experienced the spiritual infusion of what Steiner would later call Rosicrucianism, or Anthroposophy.

Some of the books about Rosenkreutz or Rosicrucianism other than those cited above have been considered and are worthy of mention.[8]

THE REEMERGENCE OF INSIGHTS

The thirteenth-century incarnation of the one who would later incarnate as Christian Rosenkreutz occurred in the Cultural Age of Aries that ended in 1414 CE.[9] Rosenkreutz, born in that same Cultural Age, expounded his intuitions, however, in the earliest years of the Cultural Age of Pisces. In both cases, humanity was not yet ready to receive them. Rosenkreutz recognized they would have to reemerge much later. What came to be known generally as Rosicrucianism was a materialistic perversion of the spiritual insight that was withdrawn till a later time.

The submergence of what Christian Rosenkreutz offered to humanity in the fifteenth century, in the earliest years of the Cultural Age of Pisces, reemerged in Anthroposophy as given us by Rudolf Steiner early in the twentieth century. The substance of what Rudolf Steiner tells us about the book of Revelation derives from the individuality who had the Apocalyptic Vision that we know as the book of Revelation.

Steiner has not been honored in the academy since his works involve intuition, an area outside the reach of the academy's methodology or means of verification. All writings, artifacts, or other items fixed in matter would seem to constitute, in the final analysis, graven images within the proscription of the second commandment of Moses. So suggests Paul, "the written code kills, but the Spirit gives life."[10] We are warranted, I judge, in understanding that the second

---

8   Steiner, *Theosophy of the Rosicrucian*, 2nd ed., RSP (1966) (CW 99); Steiner, *Esoteric Christianity and the Mission of Christian Rosenkreutz*, 2nd ed., RSP (1984) (CW 130); *A Christian Rosenkreutz Anthology*, 3rd ed., compiled and edited by Paul M. Allen in collaboration with Carlo Pietzner, Rudolf Steiner Publications (Garber), Blauvelt, New York (1981).

9   *BB*, 573, Chart **I-19**.

10   2 Cor 3:6.

commandment does not proscribe writing or sculpturing or fixing things in matter that are helpful; rather we may infer its intent to be that we "shall not bow down to them or serve them."[11] In this understanding, the Lord God, through Moses, is saying that He does not dwell in writings, even those he inspires. The Bible is and will continue to be a priceless religious document, an artifact no less, like a footprint in the human journey through the ages. That footprint is evidence of the journey. The book of Revelation is such a footprint, a helpful writing, but it is visionary and can only be understood by those of vision. Rudolf Steiner was, I suggest, preeminently one of those.

Since both John's Apocalypse and Rudolf Steiner's works are here termed "visionary," it is well to define the sense in which each is used here. On that, the visionary John was himself a turning point. He embodied the *metanoia* of the Baptist's message to repent, meaning to change one's way of thinking, or, as applied to the matter of spiritual vision, the very source of it. But to comprehend such turning point, we need first to examine, in some depth and several respects, who it is that was capable of filling such a monumental role.

For that purpose, see the positions espoused in the recent *The Temple Sleep of the Rich Young Ruler.*[12] There, the John who wrote the Gospel and the Revelation is the "rich young ruler" of Mark 10:17–22 and the Synoptic tradition, whose name was really Lazarus of the Johannine tradition (John 11). His name was changed to John as a result of his initiation through his "three days' journey" (three and a half days) in the mode of the ancient temple sleep. Under that name he also later became known as Elder John, of Ephesus.[13]

Near the end of his earthly ministry, to plant in humanity the seed for its development of understanding, Christ needed one who could go all the way to the cross with him in spiritual consciousness, something none of the Twelve was yet capable of doing. Christ initiated Lazarus in that ancient mode, which was also known as an initiation "under the fig tree."[14] The method of initiation had become dangerous by the

---

11   Exod 20:5.

12   *TSRYR*, SB (2011).

13   See note 1, page 18.

14   See Krishna's explanation of the Bhagavad Gita to Arjuna in *TSRYR*, 79–81, based upon *The Bhagavad Gita and the West*, CW 142, SB (2009), 64–66.

time of the Christ event. Lazarus had died in the sense that his etheric (life) body had left his physical body. But Christ was able to monitor the journey of the dead Lazarus for the necessary three and a half days (i.e., "four days" [John 11:39]) before bringing him back to earthly life through a return of his etheric body. For this period of time to expire, it was necessary that Christ delay his return to Bethany by two days (John 11:6), a delay that, without this understanding, seemed uncharacteristically callous and most puzzling.

In the Synoptic tradition, also enigmatically, Christ is said to have "cursed" the fig tree, such that no one would ever have fruit from it again. What was meant was that the raising of Lazarus, that is, his initiation in the mode of the ancient temple sleep, his experience "under the fig tree," was to be the end of that form of initiation.[15] Once the blood of Christ entered, and thus completely infused, the etheric realm of the earth, it inhered in the etheric bodies of all plant, animal and human creatures, being those three kingdoms whose etheric (life) bodies existed within their physical (mineral) bodies during earthly life. But it seems that we may infer, from what Steiner said, that for such indwelling life body of Christ, present in each such creature, to be effective in the further saving evolution of these kingdoms, it was important, if not actually essential, that at least one of his followers experience in full consciousness, the journey of Christ to his crucifixion on the cross.

Christ knew, and had foretold, that all of the Twelve would fall away from him on his journey to and through crucifixion. The "sweat…like great drops of blood" that fell to the ground as Christ prayed in Gethsemane was not from fear of his crucifixion, which he foretold and well knew he had to endure. Rather they were prompted by his divine anxiety that no follower would accompany him in full consciousness of the event.[16] He had "raised" Lazarus from the dead, initiating him into high levels of spiritual insight, an event that forthwith prompted the arrest of Jesus.[17] Here was one for whom Jesus

---

15 Steiner, *The Gospel of St. John*, rev. ed., SB (1962), lect. 4., 64 (CW 103); *TSRYR* 69–81, esp. 73–74.

16 Luke 22:44. *BB*, 2nd Ed., AP (2001), 478–479, quoting from *The Gospel of St. Mark*, AP (1986), Lect. 9 (Basel, Sept. 12, 1912), 168–169, to appear in CW 139.

17 John 12:9–11.

must surely have been praying in Gethsemane. It is suggested that the mysterious fleeing youth in Mark's Gospel (14:51–52) is an account of this conscious journey by John (Lazarus/John).[18]

Lazarus/John (hereinafter sometimes simply called John) had not only the experience in the spiritual world from his initiation by Christ, but he also had the astral body of Christ, that of Jesus of Nazareth as further perfected by the three years of burning purification by the Christ, that was handed down to John by Christ from the cross.[19] This is indicated, according to Steiner, by the words, surely of double meaning, "When Jesus saw his mother, and the disciple whom he loved, standing near, he said to his mother, 'Woman, behold your son!' Then he said to the disciple, "Behold, your mother!" And from that hour the disciple took her to his own home."[20] Though tradition has it that John took Mary with him to Ephesus, where they both died, the true mother of Jesus Christ that John took into his own being, his "home," was the Virgin Sophia, the immense spiritual wisdom in the fully purified astral body of the Christ. He was thus enabled eventually to write the Gospel and to experience, in his very old age, the vision, the Apocalypse, that we call Revelation. The true reference by this mother and son incident at the foot of the cross has to be to the Virgin Sophia, the Christ-purified astral body, for the Christ had no earthly mother.[21]

THE TWO WITNESSES

To appreciate a certain passage in Revelation we must carry the insight into this visionary John one step further. The Synoptic Gospels tell of the appearance of Elijah and Moses to Peter, James and John (the latter two being sons of Zebedee) at the Transfiguration of Jesus Christ

---

18   *TSRYR*, 155–176.
19   Compare the falling of Elijah's mantle upon Elisha; 2 Kgs 2:13–15.
20   John 19:26–27.
21   Mark 3:31–35; Matt 12:46–50; Luke 8:19–21; *BB*, 482; *TSRYR*, 111; Heb 7:3 (similarity of Melchizedek to the Son of God, both being "without father or mother or genealogy"); *SLJ*, SB, "Melchizedek," 142–154. Christ himself tells us that he was not "born of a woman" when he says, "Among those born of women there has risen no one greater than John the Baptist" (Matt 11:11), upon which see *TSRYR*, 111–112.

on the high mountain.[22] In Revelation John speaks of the voice telling him about "my two witnesses" who will be killed but be brought back to life after three and a half days.[23] Not only is the one who is writing this the one who was initiated by Christ in the three-and-a-half-day journey, called "the temple sleep," but I've previously made the case that Paul and John were also the embodiments of Moses and Elijah, the two witnesses who appeared at the Transfiguration, and that the two of them either wrote or directly influenced most of the books of the New Testament, thus being Christ's witnesses in that way also.[24] It is these two who were very specially initiated by the Christ himself, John during Christ's earthly ministry and Paul by the Risen Christ on the Damascus Road. Though contrary to current prevailing academic scholarship, anthroposophical considerations, not considered by such scholarship, seem to me to confirm Paul as the author of Hebrews.

No one else on the scriptural scene rises so high in spiritual sight directly administered by the Christ in explicit scriptural account as these two, Lazarus/John and Paul. Both of their names were changed through these high and spiritually enlightening events. These, together with the emphasis upon the "two witnesses" in Revelation itself, lend weight to their being the two witnesses in New Testament writings.[25] A case can be made that only the Gospel of Matthew and the letters of James and Jude were not written or significantly influenced by one of these witnesses; and on even these three books there were points of impact. Matthew's Gospel, following Mark, reports the instance of the rich young ruler as well as the appearance of the two witnesses at the Transfiguration.[26] James is one of only two with whom Paul conferred on his first post-conversion trip back to Jerusalem, and his brother Jude, i.e.,

---

22 Mark 9:4; Matt 17:3; Luke 9:30.

23 Rev 11:3, 7–11.

24 On the Moses–Paul individuality, see note 2 on page 20.

25 Since, as we shall see, Rev 11 involves a later Evolutionary Epoch (see **I-1**) than the Post-Atlantean, the Epoch when Moses and Elijah appeared, the extension of their influence that far will be discussed when we get to that chapter. That the Transfiguration must surely have involved the "More Perfect Astral Condition of Form," that extension may be warranted.

26 Matt 19:16–22; 17:3.

Judas (Mark 6:3), is the only NT writer, aside from Paul in his letters and Hebrews, who uses the phrase "once for all."[27]

PAUL AS THE AUTHOR OF HEBREWS

It seems fair to say that there is no consensus among scholars on who wrote Hebrews, when or where it was written, or to whom it was written.[28]

Koester traces the attitude toward Hebrews and its authorship in the following historical periods, early church to 600 CE; from 600 CE to 1500 CE; from 1500 CE to 1750 CE; and from 1750 CE to the present. During the third period, from 1500 to 1750, a shift was made from reliance upon the Latin Vulgate to the Greek text, but until the beginning of the nineteenth century the established tradition of Paul's authorship was not seriously challenged. Questions about it began to be voiced in the nineteenth century. Koester writes (43), "By the early twentieth century the theory that Paul wrote Hebrews had few supporters." No overpowering alternative was offered, and several of those put forward were close to Paul. Their writings would, therefore, have reflected Paul's immediate influence if not his recorded dictation.

Theories advanced in opposition to Paul as author included the fact that all of his other known works were letters to churches with established introductory format; seeming differences in style and vocabulary from that of his letters, as well as several different matters of emphasis.

Some scholars see in Hebrews a second century writing based upon the author's "what we have heard" (2:1), truth that "was declared at first by the Lord, and it was attested to us by those who heard him." They see this as inconsistent with Paul's words about the Gospel, "For I did not receive it from man, nor was I taught it, but it came through

---

27   Gal 1:19; Jude 3 and 5.

28   No claim is made as to exhaustive research. Principal authorities taken into account include George Wesley Buchanan, *To the Hebrews*, 2nd ed., AB, vol. 36 (1983); Raymond E. Brown, *An Introduction to the New Testament*, ABRL, chap. 32 (*Letter [Epistle] to the Hebrews*) (1997); 683–704; Fred B. Craddock, *The Letter to the Hebrews*, NIB, vol. 12 (1998), 3–173; Craig R. Koester, *Hebrews*, AB, vol. 36 (apparently replacing earlier).

a revelation of Jesus Christ."[29] Indeed, in Galatians, Paul indicates that after three years in Arabia he went to Jerusalem and visited there (only) with Peter and the Lord's brother James (1:18–19), and then after another fourteen years (2:1) he went again to Jerusalem where he was with Peter, James and John (the latter two being sons of Zebedee) (2:9), but he declared that they "added nothing to me" (2:6). Certainly we may assume that these he talked with "attested" to him the truth of his Gospel, as we would expect, but Galatians alone dissolves any inference from Hebrews 2 that Paul placed reliance for his Gospel upon the merely affirming attestations of those who heard Christ in person.

While Paul nowhere identifies himself by name, as John does in Revelation, and as every letter constituting the Pauline corpus does, the entirely different nature of this writing is a legitimate one for him to undertake near the end of his days, especially if directed to Jews, whether Christian or not, since, as we shall see later, there is a special connection of Hebrews to the Semitic race.

The ending of Hebrews does fit the style of Paul's letters, commending the "grace" of the Lord to his readers. Moreover, the penultimate sentence of Hebrews reads, "Those who come from Italy send you greetings," suggesting that there are those in Rome, where he is imprisoned, who will be coming, presumably to Jerusalem—but at least to a non-Italian destination.

Since the text has been the source of questions about authorship, let us now turn our attention to several textual comparisons, passages in Hebrews that, with few exceptions, are found only in Paul's other letters, and thus would seem to support his authorship.

1. "Once for all" (Rom 6:10; Heb 7:2; 9:12; 10:10; also in 1 Peter 3:18 and Jude 3 and 5).
2. "Vengeance is mine" (Rom 12:19; Heb 10:30).
3. "Without sin" (2 Cor 5:21; Heb 4:15; also in 1 Peter 2:22 and 1 John 3:5).
4. "First-born (Rom 8:29; Col 1:15, 18; Heb 1:6; 11:28; 12:23).
5. His unique focus upon "tents," by the tentmaker (2 Cor 5:1, 4; Heb 8:2, 5; 9:2–21; 11:9).
6. "Shadow" (Col 2:17; Heb 8:5; 10:1).

---

29   Gal 1:11–12.

7. Milk vs. solid food (1 Cor 3:2; Heb 5:12–14).
8. "Did not exalt himself" (Phil 2:5–9; Heb 5:5).
9. "Being changed" (1 Cor 15:35–40, 44: 2 Cor 3:18; Phil 3:21; Heb 1:12).
10. Emphasis and reliance upon faith (Rom, esp. 3 and 4; Gal 3; Heb 11).
11. Mysteries (Rom 11:25; 16:25–26; 1 Cor 4:1; 13:2; 15:51; Eph 1:9–10; 3:1–9; 6:19; Col 1:25–27; 2:2–3; 4:3; 1 Tim 3:16; Heb 5:11; 9:5; also in Rev 1:20; 17:5, 7). Anthroposophy has much to say about several of these, such as "once for all."[30] But in what follows, one who studies the scriptures with even a modest understanding of Anthroposophy must surely come to the deep conviction that only Paul could have been the author of Hebrews when the following connections are pondered:
12. The spiritual hierarchies as they appear only in Paul's letters and Hebrews.
13. The "first and second Adam" as they appear only in Luke's Gospel and Paul's letters.
14. The knowledge in Hebrews of how Melchizedek and Christ are alike.
15. The subject of trumpets as it appears in Paul's letters and Hebrews (and Matthew), especially as it relates to the meaning of the one hundred forty-four thousand in Revelation.

Some further word on each of these is in order, below.

The Spiritual Hierarchies (#12)

Chart **I-6** in *The Burning Bush* (556), derived from the several Steiner sources there listed, gives the nine levels of spiritual hierarchies above the human that are subject to the macrocosmic Christ.[31]

---

30 "An incarnation of the Christ-Being in a human body of flesh could take place only *once* in the course of the Earth-evolution. When people announce a repetition of the incarnation of this Being, it simply means that the Christ-Being is not understood." Steiner, *From Jesus to Christ*, RSP (1973), 170; Lect. 10 at Karlsruhe, Oct. 14, 1911; to appear in CW 131.

31 An Internet search under *Pseudo-Dionysius* (5th century) confirms the general accuracy of **I-6**, and is apparently the first reduction to writing of what was presumably taught by Paul to his convert Dionysius the Areopagite (Acts 17:34).

The second column gives the name of each according to "Christian Esotericism." In descending order they are seraphim, cherubim, thrones, dominions, powers, authorities, principalities, archangels, and angels. The seraphim appear only in Isaiah 6:2, 6. Cherubim appear in the NT only in Hebrews 9:5. Paul's letters speak of thrones, dominions, powers, authorities, principalities, archangels, and angels.[32] Aside from Paul's letters, the only NT appearance of the hierarchies from the thrones through the principalities is in 1 Peter 3:22, which says of Christ that he "is at the right hand of God, with angels, authorities, and powers subject to him." Peter had been exposed to Paul's Gospel, which mentions these hierarchies and makes them subject to the Christ, a position that Peter surely adopted from Paul's strong emphasis upon it.[33]

Hebrews does not speak of each of these five hierarchical levels (thrones through principalities) as such. Rather, it encompasses them generically by reference to the "angels," which should be considered inclusive of all the hierarchies—"When he had made purification for sins, he sat down at the right hand of the Majesty on high, having become as much superior to angels as the name he has obtained is more excellent than theirs."[34] The thrust is identical to that in all such hierarchical references in Paul's letters, namely, that Christ is above all of them. It is a theme that pervades both Paul's letters and Hebrews.

The "first and second Adam" and the similarity of Melchizedek and Christ (#13 and #14)

One of the seemingly few things upon which there is general consensus among scholars, clergy and laity alike is that there was a close

---

32 Thrones (Col 1:16), dominions (Col 1:16), powers (Rom 8:38; Eph 3:10; 6:12; Col 2:15), authorities (Col 1:16), principalities (Rom 8:38; Eph 3:10; 6:12; Col 1:16; 2:15), archangel (1 Thess 4:16; except for Jude 9, archangels are named, e.g., Michael and Gabriel, or are simply called angels, or such as "mighty angel" [2 Thess 1:7]); angels appear often in Paul and many other books. In its relationship to Romans 8:38, it appears that 1 Corinthians 15:24 is also referring to principalities ("rule"), authorities, and "powers." While Hebrews 6:5 refers to "powers of the age to come," it is not clear that he is speaking hierarchically.

33 Gal 1:18 and 2:2.

34 Heb 1:3b–4.

relationship between Paul and Luke.[35] The basis for this relative certainty is spelled out in most general writings on Luke.

What is not generally noted is that Luke's Gospel, Paul's letters, and the book of Hebrews constitute a triangle powerfully supporting not only Paul's authorship of Hebrews but also his completely preeminent qualification to serve, along with Lazarus/John, as one of Christ's "two witnesses," responsible, between them, for almost all of the New Testament.

What scholars who dismiss Anthroposophy miss on these two items, #13 and #14, is what makes each angle so essential to the relationship between them and how they so mutually support and reinforce each other in support of these conclusions.

What is vital to an understanding of how these three interrelate and support each other is to understand the Incarnation of Christ. Steiner's lectures, the first that I'm aware of to do so, make such an understanding possible. The complexity of that Incarnation is set out in great detail in the essay "The Nativity" in *The Burning Bush*, then in simpler version in *The Incredible Births of Jesus*.[36] More recently, a short and handy version is given in *The Temple Sleep*.[37]

The more extensive of the two Gospel accounts, and the one that is imperative if one is to comprehend both the first and second Adam interrelationship between Luke and Paul and the lack of earthly parents or genealogy of both Melchizedek and Christ in Hebrews, is Luke's nativity account. Essential, of course, to a deeper comprehension of all of this is some understanding of the basic Anthroposophy, for which the best single source is doubtless Steiner's *Outline of Esoteric Science* (the first four chapters).[38]

The "first and second Adam" phrase comes from Paul, succinctly in Romans, and more expansively in 1 Corinthians.[39] As to both "Adams," the first and the second, Paul refers to their respective etheric, or life,

---

35 Eckhard Plümacher, *Luke*, trans. Dennis Martin, ABD, vol. 4 (1992), Joseph A. Fitzmyer, *The Gospel According to Luke 1–9*, AB, vol. 28 (1981), 27–29; R. Alan Culpepper, *The Gospel of Luke*, NIV, vol. 9 (1995), 4–6.

36 *IBJ.*

37 *TSRYR*, 203–207.

38 Steiner, *An Outline of Esoteric Science*, tr. Catherine E. Creeger, AP (1997) (CW 13).

39 Rom 5:12–14 ; 1 Cor 15:21–22, 45, 47–49.

bodies. Before the first Adam and his wife descended, the creating Elohim, foreseeing the impurity that would infect such bodies from the Luciferic influence upon the astral body and the latter's influence upon the etheric, caused a part of the unspoiled etheric body (tree of life) to be withheld, thus maintaining its purity. The bodies of Adam and his wife were subject to "the fall," to what is called "original sin." The part held back remained pure. That pure part became the etheric or life body in both the infant and his mother in Luke's Gospel (but not in the child or mother described in Matthew's Gospel). This separation and endowment are described in *The Burning Bush*, more simply and clearly in *The Incredible Births*, and in *The Temple Sleep*.[40]

What evidence in Luke corroborates this connection? It is the leaping of the babe in Elizabeth's womb upon the approach of Mary. Elizabeth was carrying the fetus of the John who would become known as John the Baptist, a reincarnation of the first Adam, who lived in an etheric body soiled by the effect of the fall. Elizabeth's fetus was six months older than Mary's, and it "leaped for joy" at the approach of the other half of its own etheric being in Mary's womb that was free from original sin.[41] To understand the evidence in either Luke or Paul, it is necessary to understand them in connection with each other, both being based upon, and corroborating, by the power they offer, the fundamental truth of basic Anthroposophy.

Hebrews asserts that both Christ and Melchizedek were without earthly parents or ancestry. We have previously seen above how this is true of the Christ. But how is it true of Melchizedek? It is interesting that Paul, the author of Hebrews, tells his readers, in regard to Melchizedek, "About this we have much to say which is hard to explain, since you have become dull of hearing."[42] Melchizedek was an avatar. Steiner explains the connection, as related in the "Melchizedek" essay in *The Soul's Long Journey*.[43] Christ was the highest of the avatars. The two were alike in both being of that spiritual reality. The connection of Luke to this aspect of Hebrews is that without his Gospel it would not have been possible to comprehend that the Christ

---

40   *BB*, 42, 50; *IBJ*, 59–61; *TSRYR*, 205.
41   Luke 1:44.
42   Heb 5:11.
43   *SLJ*, esp. 150–154.

had no earthly parents or genealogy. The three bodies that he entered and, through his searing indwelling, transfigured into their spiritual counterparts were those of the child from Luke's Gospel, but as to the Ego element of Jesus Christ, it was not born of a woman and had no earthly genealogy. Steiner's descriptions make it clear that Melchizedek was an avatar for Abraham and his descendants; hence the book was uniquely for the Hebrews, a people for whom Paul had lamented in Romans and Galatians.

Paul recognizes the body of flesh that was prepared by the Hebrew people for the Incarnation of the Christ, for he says to them (emphasis added), "Sacrifices and offerings thou has not desired, *but a body [soma] hast thou prepared for me.*"[44]

The triangular relationship between Paul, Luke, and Lazarus/John is clear from one other detail. Lazarus had two sisters, Mary and Martha. There are several women named Mary in the NT (in the Old Testament the Hebrew version of the name is Miriam). In the canon, the name Mary appears in many places and applies to several different persons. Mary and Martha, the sisters of Lazarus, appear in John 11 and 12. This Mary and Martha appear also in Luke, but the name Martha appears nowhere else in the canon, and can only reasonably be understood as the sister of Lazarus.[45] This suggests both the influence of Paul upon Luke and the prominence of Lazarus/John among the earliest Christians, well before John wrote his Gospel, letters or Apocalypse.

The Subject of Trumpets (#15)

The (angelic) trumpet appears in the NT only in Matthew, Hebrews, and Revelation, and in 1 Corinthians and 1 Thessalonians.[46] Its meaning becomes crystal clear as we discuss the subject of the 144,000 in Revelation, when the connection between the use in Hebrews and Paul's letters will stand out starkly. The same could be said with respect to the appearance of the trumpet in Matthew's version of the "Little Apocalypse."[47] Steiner suggests that Matthew's Gospel

---

44   Heb 10:5.
45   Luke 10:38–41.
46   Matt 24:31; Heb 12:19; Rev; 1 Cor 15:52; 1 Thess 4:16.
47   Matt 24:31.

reflected Essene influence and was thus largely directed to the Essenes.[48] While the writer of Matthew is not suggested here as a probable author of Hebrews, the trumpet connection does suggest that its "To the Hebrews" title, added later, was based upon insight.

THE TWO WITNESSES: REPRISES

Two things stand out in the foregoing opening remarks that form a proper, and I felt necessary, foundational platform or perspective from which to go forward in our search for meaning in this most mystical book that concludes our Bible.

The first is that the human individuality who experienced the apocalyptic vision and wrote the book appeared again in the fifteenth century as Christian Rosenkreutz offering the Christ-centered substance of Anthroposophy into the spiritual realm from which Rudolf Steiner intuited and taught it early in the twentieth century. It is those teachings of Steiner of both the basic, or core, Anthroposophy, and its specific application to the meaning of John's vision that are the tools applied as we look below into such meaning.

The second is that two persons, Lazarus/John and Saul/Paul, the only two who were explicitly initiated to high spiritual level by the Christ, have given us essentially all of the New Testament, primarily through their own writing, but significantly also through their powerful influence upon others who wrote, such as Luke, Peter, Mark, and all of the Pauline corpus to the extent, if any, it was written by his followers. It is likely that Matthew, James, and Jude were not free from the significant influence of one or both of these two major witnesses.

We have focused above upon the triangular relationship between Lazarus/John, Paul, and Luke. We have also suggested that the spirit being within the former two were the "two witnesses" to the transfigured Christ on the "high mountain," then through the length and breadth of the NT, and then prophetically in their own transfigured appearance in Revelation 11.

Let us now turn back to the source Luke gives for his Gospel account, namely, the substance related to him "by those who *from the beginning* were *eyewitnesses* and ministers of the *Word*" (1:2 emphasis

---

48   *TSRYR*, 115–116.

mine). In its common meaning, "from the beginning" is meaningless in the sense that it lacks clarity of when "the beginning" started in regard to Christ's ministry. Moreover, Luke probably never met most of them, not having been a resident of Palestine. Yet, we must try to interpret the phrase in a way that gives it meaning, which we shall do. In common meaning, "eyewitnesses" would include everyone who had seen Jesus through their physical eyesight during his ministry. Luke uses the Greek term *logos* for "Word," the only Gospel writer other than Lazarus/John to start his Gospel by reference to that concept. Luke seems to be using it to refer to the same thing John did, "In the beginning was *the Word*." The phrase "Word of God" is more often used in a sense that seems to refer more to "the Gospel."

I do not find much scholarly effort devoted to these points, or to the collective meaning of the three italicized portions. But Steiner took them up many times, even before he got to his lectures on Luke's Gospel. In the first lecture of his cycle in Hamburg on John, illustrative of the "Word," the *logos*, he both cites and quotes this passage from Luke 1:2 ("those who from the beginning were eyewitnesses and ministers of the *Word* [*Logos*]" and indicates clearly that "from the beginning" goes back to when the Word first issued forth, as in John 1:1, "In the beginning was the Word." In the second Hamburg lecture, he returns to it again, this time as "servants of the Logos in the earliest times."[49] He returns to this again in the same way at the end of lecture 3 in Kassel (June 26, 1909), and then in lecture 7 (June 30) speaks of what it means to be a "witness," speaking of the initiation of Lazarus/John.[50] Then in his cycle on Luke he takes up this Luke 1:2 passage three times (lectures 1, 6 and 7 in Basle in September 1909) stating clearly that Luke got his information from seers initiated all the way back to the beginning indicated by Lazarus/John's Logos (John 1:1).[51]

In the first such lecture on Luke, Steiner says of the word *eyewitnesses* that "the term would be better translated as 'independent seers.'"

---

49   Steiner, *The Gospel of St. John*, rev. ed., AP (1962), 25–27, 41–42 (CW 103).

50   Steiner, *The Gospel of St. John and its Relation to the Other Gospels*, rev. ed., AP (1982), 57, 129 (CW 112).

51   Steiner, *According to Luke*, trans. Catherine E. Creeger, AP (2001), 23–24, 133–134, 155 (CW 114).

The Greek root word used is *autopt* (the source of our "autopsy"; [aut = self; opt = see]). According to my source, the word means "to see with one's own eyes;... esp. witness a divine manifestation."[52]

That Lazarus/John was such a seer and that Luke so recognized, is clear, at least through Paul and probably through meeting John personally in Ephesus, perhaps while journeying to Rome with Paul or later after Paul's death. Certainly Luke recognized Paul as having been initiated as a seer, being the one, in Acts, who narrates the account. Luke quotes Paul's testimony before Agrippa to the effect that the Lord Jesus had appeared to him and appointed him "to serve and bear witness to the things in which you have seen me."[53] Also, Ananias tells Paul that God has appointed him to be a witness.[54] Paul tells of having been "caught up to the third heaven" and receiving "things that cannot be told."[55]

Paul's reference to Luke as "the beloved physician" suggests a relationship between Paul and Luke like that of "the beloved disciple" to Jesus in John's Gospel.[56]

That Lazarus/John and Paul were Christ's two most special witnesses seems clear.

CHAPTER 1 ENDNOTES

Note 1, from Footnote 13

Somewhat relevant at this point is placing the age of Lazarus/John (LJ) when he had his vision on Patmos and then when he wrote his Gospel at Ephesus. Fixing these with certainty and giving the calendar year in which they happened is a bit of a challenge. That he was elderly when he wrote his Gospel in Ephesus is not particularly controversial. Nor is the fact that he was on Patmos as a result Emperor Domitian's persecution of Christians. For anthroposophists, his authorship of both Revelation and the Gospel is firmly established in Steiner's teachings.

---

52   Liddell & Scott, *Greek-English Lexicon*, 9th ed., 1996 Supp. New York, Oxford University Press (1996), 282.
53   Acts 26:12–18, esp. 16.
54   Acts 22:12–21, esp. 15.
55   2 Cor 12:2–4.
56   Col 4:14.

My own preferred view is that LJ was about two years older than Luke's Jesus child ("Nathan Jesus"), that Nathan Jesus was born in the lacuna between year 1 BCE and year 1 CE (there being no zero year between 1 BCE and 1 CE), and that Christ died in 33 CE when he was 33 years old. Since Christ was crucified very soon after the raising (initiation) of LJ (John 12:9–11), LJ would have been about 35 years of age in 33 CE. For the reasons set out in *TSRYR*, 143–144, my view here is based upon LJ having served for the very short period 16–17 CE, in his late teen years, as high priest of the temple (whose name was Eleazar, or Lazarus in Greek). Domitian's reign as emperor was from 81 to 96 CE and would likely have put LJ on Patmos in 95 CE, when he had his vision at 97 years of age. LJ returned to Ephesus soon after Domitian's death in 96 CE and wrote his Gospel during the reign of Trajan, which began in 98 CE when LJ turned 100 years of age.

References taken into account include:

1. Steiner, *How Can Mankind Find the Christ Again?*, 2nd ed., AP (1984), 41 (CW 187)—Christ died at 33 years of age.
2. *TSRYR*, 143–144.
3. James H. Hindes (Christian Community Priest), Introduction to Steiner,'s *Reading the Pictures of the Apocalypse*, AP (1993), 9 (CW 104a)—John was 97 at the time of his vision on Patmos, and was initiated ("raised") by Christ at age 33.
4. Steiner, *From Jesus to Christ*, RSP (1973), 99 (lect. 6) (CW 131)—LJ was in his 95th year when he wrote "Children love one another" (John 13:33–34).
5. René Querido, Introduction to Steiner, *The Book of Revelation and the Work of the Priest*, RSP (1998), 7 (CW 346)—LJ returned to Ephesus in 96 CE, where he lived for several more years and wrote his Gospel and died when over 100 years of age.
6. Brian W. Jones, *Domitian*, New York, Doubleday, *ABD*, vol. 2 (1991), 221–222, esp. 222—The persecution of Christians by Domitian was probably in 95 CE.
7. *TSRYR*, 139—Citing Irenaeus saying that John lived into the reign of Trajan.

Note 2, from Footnote 24

Sadly, from our perspective, Steiner was taken from us just as he was beginning to speak of the destinies and karmic relationships of persons incarnated at the time of Christ. He was able, essentially from his deathbed, to confirm that the spirit of John the Baptist entered into Lazarus down through the latter's consciousness soul. Lazarus then became known as John. Inasmuch as the individuality of John the Baptist was that also of Elijah, John became a conscious embodiment of the spirit of Elijah.

It is hard to imagine that Steiner, had he lived on, would not have dealt with the individuality of Paul. My conviction is that Steiner would have confirmed that Saul of Tarsus/Paul was Moses reincarnated. In any event, based upon things Steiner did say, I expressed in *BB*, "Pillars on the Journey," footnote 5, pages 543 to 544, my judgment that Paul was Moses reincarnated.

The primary foundation of this belief was based upon the following words of Steiner :

> It is an eternal cosmic law that each individual must perform a particular deed repeatedly. He must, above all, perform the deed twice—one time as though doing the opposite of the other time.[57]

This "eternal cosmic law" is a way of stating the law of karma. The Law came from Moses and was superceded by Paul. It is hard to even imagine an application of the "eternal cosmic law" that is as egregious as this one. Of course Christ actually superceded the Law—see "Karma as the Law Christ Came to Fulfill" in *SLJ*—but Christ is not subject to karma. It was Paul who bore that human karma and cleaned his Mosaic slate of it.

That Steiner would have confirmed this Moses-Paul individuality is further suggested to me by the fact that, immediately after he had pronounced this "eternal cosmic law," and after two paragraphs that connected the subject matter, he brings up Paul's acquaintance "with all that was inherent in the old Hebraic esoteric doctrine" as a basis for Paul's recognition of the Christ who appeared to him"—and this was

---

57   *The Reappearance of Christ in the Etheric,* 79, lect. 5, Stuttgart, Mar. 6, 1910 (CW 118).

in 1910, long before his *Karmic Relationships* series given toward the end of his life when he had begun to express to his wife that his etheric body was slipping way.

When the Lord appeared before Moses on Mount Horeb (Sinai) as the burning bush, Moses asked his name, to which first came to humanity the answer "I AM the I AM" (Exod 3). When the light flashed from heaven before him on the road to Damascus, Saul cried, "Who are you Lord," to which came the answer "I AM Jesus, whom you are persecuting" (Acts 9). One can feel the power that moves through the Moses-Saul individuality as these answers came to it.

By these things I am, and have from the early days of my study of Steiner been, persuaded that the thread of one individuality ran between these two giants in the human journey.

When Elijah and Moses appeared to Peter, James, and John at Christ's Transfiguration, the Mystery of Golgotha had not been consummated. After that consummation and Paul's conversion, they were respectively represented by, and existed within, Lazarus/John and Paul as Christ's "two witnesses."

2

THE GRAND SCHEME

While in John 1:1, Lazarus/John peers back to the earliest origins, and in Ephesians 1:9–10 and suggestively in Romans 8:19–23, Paul penetrates to the ultimate union, both meeting Steiner's description of Luke's "eyewitnesses," neither of the first and last books of the Bible go back, or reach forward, such distances. Those spirit regions are not the stuff of normal human consciousness during the Earth Condition of Consciousness.

Genesis opens as the Elohim approach the seven Evolutionary Epochs of the Physical Condition of Form of the Mineral Condition of Life of the Earth Condition of Consciousness, the fourth such Condition of Consciousness. The sun is about to separate from the rest of its solar mass as the Polarian Epoch opens.[1] Revelation takes us, according to Steiner into the Jupiter Condition of Consciousness, but in reality he makes a leap from the end of the seventh such Evolutionary Epoch over an enormous stretch returning through the last three Conditions of both Form and Life without elaboration. Both the beginning and end of our scriptures grow vague in detail, for their purpose is to help us make our way through the seven long Evolutionary Epochs of the Mineral-Physical state of human existence. The timeless spiritual realms lying beyond these extremes are perceived only by our most advanced seers, such as Lazarus/John, Paul, Christian Rosenkreutz, and Rudolf Steiner. We shall look a bit more closely at these lengths later.

Wisdom, Sophia, traditionally characterized as feminine, but existing so far back as to merge into that most ancient event when the emanation of the creative Word went forth is said to have hewn her

---

1   See **I-1** and **I-2**, as well as Steiner's *Genesis,* rev. ed., RSP (2002) (lect. 1), 6 and (lect. 9), 123 (CW 122).

house of seven pillars.[2] The first book of the Bible opens with seven ages ("days") of descending creation and the last book opens with seven ages of ascending departure therefrom. Both the first and last books progress into the realm of the twelve stars for the completion of their account.[3] The logarithmic spiral of Phi, the golden mean (1.618), is present in virtually the entirety of the sevenfoldedness of creation and, by the symbol of Cancer (the crab comprising interlocking spirals), the return journey from creation. As we shall see, that spiral that plays out such sevenfoldedness interlocks with twelvefoldedness first at twelve times twelve, or 144, and then again only at each succeeding multiple of twelve; reflected, it would seem, by the 12 by 12 by 12 ("length and breadth and height"), the dimensions of the Holy City.[4] The multiple intersections beyond 144 are probably indicated also by the twelve gates, twelve angels, twelve tribes, twelve foundations, and twelve names of apostles of the Lamb.[5]

The Wisdom Sophia that Christ passed down to Lazarus/John from the cross moved on through the latter's individuality into his Apocalypse, arose again in Christian Rosenkreutz in the fifteenth century, and reemerged through the intuition of Rudolf Steiner early in the twentieth century, who, from such reemergence, gave us the following schematic of humanity's long journey from, and back to, the unity of the high spiritual realm.

From the numerous charts at the end of *The Burning Bush*, the information contained in about a dozen are vital for the study of basic Anthroposophy. But among them, I have considered Chart **I-1** (on page 24) as the most critical and helpful of all; hence its priority in the list. Steiner stresses that it is an intellectual crutch, but also that for intellectual comprehension it is a helpful scheme. To the extent that it remains only an intellectual understanding, it will not be retained beyond one's present life inasmuch as the brain disintegrates. But if one comprehends, "at first in Imaginative pictures," what really happens, for which the seven seals prepared for the lecture cycle are

---

2   John 1:1–3; Prov 8:22; Prov 9:1.

3   Gen 15:5; Rev 12:1.

4   Rev 21:16.

5   Rev 21:12–14.

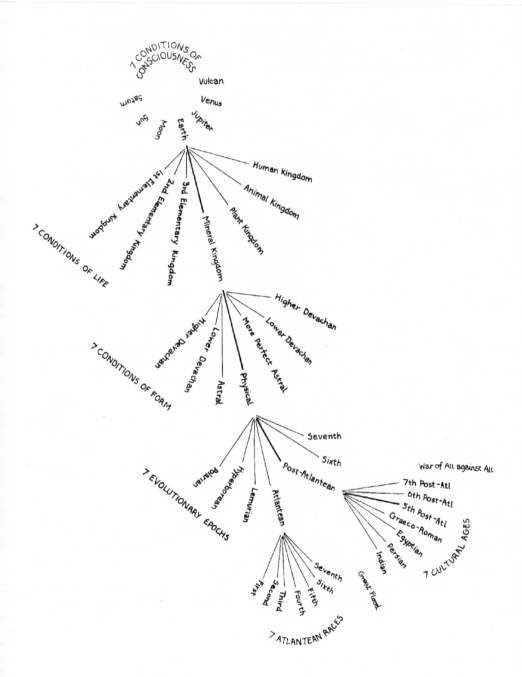

helpful contemplations, such imaginations, not created by physical thinking but from facts seen clairvoyantly, are not lost at death.

Such chart was presented on June 28, 1908, during the tenth of twelve lectures given in Nuremberg from June 17 to 30, and was attached at the end of the book, *The Apocalypse of St. John* (*ASJ*) along with the pictures of the seven seals.[6] An editorial comment on the chart in the *ASJ* quotes Steiner to the effect that "such a scheme is 'related to the full reality not even like the inner framework of a house to the complete building, but only the outer scaffolding...that has to be taken down when the building is complete.'"

Most readers will doubtless note the location of this lecture cycle that, a generation later became prominent in the rise of the polar opposite of Anthroposophy, Naziism. The Nazi party rally in 1923 was in Munich, then in 1926 in Weimar, but from 1927 on they were held only in Nuremberg. Fittingly, the inhumane Nazis were tried there.

This chart will be helpful company for us as we wend our way through Revelation.

---

6   Steiner, *The Apocalypse of St. John* (*ASJ*), esp. 177–181 (*CW* 104).

3

ONE LIKE A SON OF MAN

The first chapter of Revelation touches upon seven important introductory points, the central one of which is the "one like a son of man." The seven points are discussed below in the order of their appearance:

1. What must soon take place (Rev 1:1)

This first verse of Revelation, as it has traditionally been translated, presents an image that extends throughout the book and still pervades modern translations. It suggests that John's visions tell of events that will happen *soon*. Since the book was written 2,000 years ago, and the things that John saw have not come to pass, at least not in a way that has any meaningful application to our current or future time, for all but the most grievously misled the book has come to mean little to most during modern times and, except for a bare handful of hopeful-sounding passages, to be almost entirely disregarded by clergy.

Troubled by this, some modern scholars are moving away from the view that contemporary events of John's era and experience are the context in which the book is to be understood.[1] And one authority identifies the author as John the Baptist, which, standing alone, raises the eyebrows, for both herein and in *The Temple Sleep* the position is that Lazarus/John and John the Baptist were joined in consciousness from the time of LJ's initiation.[2] Yet none of these, nor the vast library of scholarly works on Revelation, so far as I have found, offer interpretation that presents a profound comprehension of John's vision capable of providing powerful meaning for humanity in our day and time.

---

1   Adele Yarbro Collins, *Revelation, Book of*, "Revelation of Other Ancient Literature," ABD, vol. 5 (1992), 704; Christopher C. Rowland, *The Book of Revelation*, "Introduction," Section A, NIB, vol. 12 (1998), 503–513 .

2   J. Massyngberde Ford, *Revelation*, AB, vol. 38 (1975), 28–30.

Rudolf Steiner, by lecture and writing early in the twentieth century, offers us both a foundational basis and specific suggestion for understanding the vision of John. Both that underlying basis and that suggestion must be applied as we examine the contextual meaning of "soon" as it appears eight times from Revelation 1:1 to 22:20.

Two excerpts from Steiner's 1908 lecture cycle in Nuremberg, *The Apocalypse of St. John* (*ASJ*), offer a starting point for us. The first, in lecture 1 (June 18, 1908), is as follows:

> Thus, in the very early days of Christianity the idea came into the exoteric stream that things which in the world's evolution first take place in the spiritual worlds...ought to take place externally in material life. And so it came about that while the writer of the Apocalypse expressed in his work the results of his Christian initiation, others only understood it exoterically; and their opinion was that what the great seer saw, what the initiate knows can be seen spiritually taking place over thousands of years, must happen in the very near future in external life and be visible to the senses. They imagined that the writer was indicating something like a speedy return of Christ Jesus, a descent from the physical clouds. When this failed to occur, they simply extended the period.[3]

The second, in lecture 12 (June 30, 1908), is as follows:

> At the beginning of the Apocalypse the writer says (I have tried to translate the first few words in such a way that they convey the true meaning): This is the revelation of Jesus Christ which God gave unto his servant, to show in brief what must needs come to pass. This is put in symbols [εσημανεν, *esēmanen*, Marshall translation, "he signified"] and sent through his angel to his servant John, who wrote these things. He wishes to describe it "in brief"; what does this mean? It means in other words: If I were to describe in detail all that will take place from now up to the goal of Earth evolution, I should have to write a very great deal, but I will show it to you in a short sketch. This the translators who could not penetrate into the spirit of the Apocalypse have translated as "to show what must shortly come to pass." They thought that what is described in the Apocalypse was to happen

---

3   *ASJ*, 31–32

in the near future. It it ought to read: I will briefly describe what will take place. (223–224)

Recently one scholar has noted that a translation such as Steiner's "briefly describe" is possible, "The phrase *en taxei* [εν ταχει] can in some cases mean suddenly speaking of how something will happen," but then he discounts that interpretation as being wrong since Revelation 1:3 says "for the time is near."[4] The quoted words in Greek are καιρος εγγυς (*kairos eggus*), which should better, in this instance, be translated as "time is short, or limited," referring to John's time or circumstances and the massive demands of a fuller esoteric explanation. Indeed, Marshall himself translates εν ταχει (*en tachei*) as indicating the action, "with speed," rather than any time to which it refers ("time is near").[5]

Steiner specifically addressed only this first occurrence of "soon" in 1;1, but such reasoning should be carried forward into each of the other seven instances, for the critical Greek word ταχει (*tachei*) is used, with such grammatical variation as the context requires, in each of the other seven instances, as follows:

> 2:16: ερχομαι σοι ταχυ *erchomai soi tachu*
> Marshall—I am coming to thee quickly
> 3:11: ερχομαι ταχυ *erchomai tachu*
> Marshall—I am coming quickly
> 11:14: ερχομαι ταχυ *erchomai tachu*
> Marshall—is coming quickly
> 22:06: γενεσθαι εν ταχει *genesthai en tachei*
> Marshall—to occur quickly
> 22:07: ερχομαι ταχυ *erchomai tachu*
> Marshall—I am coming quickly
> 22:12: ερχομαι ταχυ *erchomai tachu*
> Marshall—I am coming quickly
> 22:20: ερχομαι ταχυ *erchomai tachu*
> Marshall—I am coming quickly

Simply by carefully observing the Grand Schematic of Revelation presented in chapter 2, the reader should see the massive scope of the

---

4   Ben Witherington III, *Revelation*, New York, Cambridge University Press (2003), 67.

5   The Greek text that I am using is in KJV-NIV—INT.

evolutionary journey through the seven Conditions of Consciousness reflected there. The application of that schematic will become clearer as we proceed through the Apocalypse.

What becomes immediately apparent, however, is that whether the words εν ταχει (*en tachei*) are still translated as "soon" or as alternately suggested above, the result should be the same, for in evolutionary times "soon" can stretch over vast periods of time, thousands of years, as the schematic suggests, or indeed into the portion beyond the blowing of the last trumpet (the end of the seventh Evolutionary Epoch) when time shall exist no more because matter, an essential component of time, ceases to exist. "Soon" or "quickly" are then words without meaning as we understand them in our material state. Our long human journey from and back to the spiritual realm only encounters matter during the seven Evolutionary Epochs of the Physical Condition of Form of the Mineral Condition of Life of the Earth Condition of Consciousness. Just as objects entering the earth's atmosphere encounter increasing density of matter that dramatically slows them down, so also does time progress much more slowly during the deepest descent into matter, represented by the Atlantean and Post-Atlantean Evolutionary Epochs. In the words of the Psalmist (23:4), these are the regions most appropriately called "the valley of the shadow of death." A passage in the so-called "Little Apocalypse" passages of Mark and Matthew speaks of the speeding up that will increasingly occur as we begin the long journey of reascent, "And if the Lord had not shortened the days, no human being would be saved."[6]

When we begin to see how John's vision truly peers into the long Evolutionary periods and Conditions in the journey each of us is making, then that vision can generate powerful meaning that should be a most helpful guide for us as it seeps slowly into our conscious being.

2. Servant John, who bore witness... (Rev 1:1–2)

Notable because John considers himself a witness. He had said of John the Baptist, "He came for testimony, to bear witness to the light, that all might believe through him," and we have seen that the spirit of John the Baptist cohabited Lazarus/John all the way down through the

---

6   Mark 13:20; Matt 24:22.

latter's consciousness soul. Lazarus/John is thus the Elijah being, who had reincarnated as the Baptist.[7]

3. "Seven churches... seven spirits... seven lampstands... seven stars" (Rev 1:4–20)

These four subjects, *churches, spirits, lampstands,* and *stars,* are listed in the order in which they first appear; churches (1:4), spirits (1:4), lampstands (1:12), and stars (1:16).

The *seven churches* represent the first of three sevenfold progressions of humanity that follow the fourth Great Epoch, the Atlantean. Each such progression represents an Evolutionary Epoch of the Mineral Physical Condition of Form of the Earth Condition of Consciousness, as follows:

Seven Churches: Our present Post-Atlantean evolutionary epoch
Seven Seals: The sixth Evolutionary Epoch
Seven Trumpets: The seventh and last Evolutionary Epoch

The realm of matter is moving in each such Epoch toward its own dissolution. When the seventh Evolutionary Epoch ends, except in the more complex discussions much later herein, humanity moves out of the realm of matter and into the More Perfect Astral Condition of Form of the Mineral Condition of Life of the Earth Condition of Consciousness. Time for such humanity will cease to exist as its connection with matter ends. A fourth sevenfold progression is that of the bowls of wrath (Rev 16), which will be part of the more complex discussions later.

Steiner tells us that the seven churches are John's esoteric representation of the seven Cultural Ages of our present Post-Atlantean Epoch, each such Age being of 2,160 years. In this, he breaks completely with academia, which identifies them with seven historical cities in the Roman province of Asia. It is well to see what is perhaps the leading theory about these seven churches.

The *seven churches* are identified literally by John as those located, in sequence, in Ephesus, Smyrna, Pergamum, Thyatira, Sardis, Philadelphia, and Laodicea. Some have wondered why only seven are mentioned, when there were others in the province, such as Troas,

---

7   John 1:7; Mal 4:5; Mark 9:12–13; Luke 1:17.

Colossae, and Hierapolis.[8] There is no clear evidence that any of the three letters of John were to a given church. The first bears strong resemblance to his Gospel. The second and third are both explicitly by "the elder," suggesting a person who had dwelt in Ephesus for a good while and was advanced in years. Perhaps all three were to "the church" generally, as particularly seems true of the first.

On why these seven, and only seven, were chosen remains unresolved in the academy though one approach has gained wide approval. Duane F. Watson, writing in the *Anchor Bible Dictionary*, describes it:

> The explanation of William Ramsay (1904: 171–96) has received wide support. He proposed that these church cities were selected because, in their given order, they are the postal and judicial (tribunal) districts which a courier from Patmos would encounter and from which his letter could be distributed most effectively throughout the province of Asia. From Patmos, the letter courier would arrive at Ephesus, travel N to Smyrna and Pergamum, and then turn SE to Thyatira, Sardis, Philadelphia, and Laodicea. This forms a circular route through the west central portion of the province. Other church cities not mentioned are located beyond the main circular route and could easily be reached on a secondary route from one of these seven cities.[9]

The explanation is an exceptionally good one, though, quite aside from that, it is the uniquely appropriate rationale Lazarus/John (LJ) used to cloak a far deeper esoteric account. The word *apocalypse* means a removal of what conceals, thus revelation. However, the revelation to John was so profound that, as an initiate to the highest levels he would seek to put his message in settings that were familiar to all of his time and thus conceal the deep inner meaning he was leaving for others, then or later, who could see the vast spiritual panorama that he was describing. It is one that has baffled and misled Christendom and its scholars, until Rudolf Steiner brought forth the anthroposophical insights of Christen Rosenkreutz. Paul would doubtless have understood its deeper meaning, but Paul died

---

8   Troas (Acts 20:5–12; 2 Cor 2:12), Colossae (Col 1:2; 2:1), and Hierapolis (Col 4:13).

9   Duane F. Watson, *Seven Churches, ABD*, vol. 5, 1143–1144; Watson cites Ramsay, W. 1904. *Letters to the Seven Churches*. London.

long before John had his vision on Patmos, and doubtless long before John became known as an "elder."

LJ's ingenious use of these particular seven becomes ever more evident in our discussion of the lampstands and the son of man. John uses the phrase *seven spirits* four times.[10] It is possible that he meant the angels of the seven churches, but it seems far more likely that he was speaking of much higher spirits. They were before the throne of the Alpha and Omega (1:4); they are the instruments of the one giving instruction to the angel of the church in Sardis (3:1), they seem to be above the twenty-four elders (4:5), being described as "spirits of God" (the 24 elders representing the 24 Conditions of Life that had preceded the Mineral Kingdom Condition of Life); and they are the "eyes of the Lamb" sent out to all the Earth, the Condition of Consciousness that precedes Jupiter. My sense is that they are the spirits of the seven Conditions of Consciousness, acting in the Mineral Kingdom Condition of Life of the Earth Condition of Consciousness (5:6).[11]

Finally, the "seven stars" are the angels of the seven churches (1:20). The lowest triptych of the nine spiritual hierarchies comprises the angels of individual human beings, the archangels of folk groups, and the Archai of ages. It seems to me that the seven angels of the churches are the seven Archai, for they each deal with a Cultural Age. Daniel, in the passages that deal with the "son of man," calls them Ancient of Days.[12]

4. He is coming with the clouds, and every eye shall see him (Rev 1:7)

This coming in, upon or with the clouds is not a new apocalyptic theme, but that it appears so frequently postures it as the type

---

10   Rev 1:4; 3:1; 4:5; and 5:6.

11   In *ASJ* (lect. 5), 101, Steiner explains the "twenty-four elders" as "the guides of evolution, the directors of time." Each pertains to one Condition of Life. The Mineral Condition of Life of the Earth Condition of Consciousness was preceded by 24 prior Conditions of Life, seven in each of the three Conditions of Consciousness (Saturn, Sun, and Moon) that preceded the Earth Condition, and three in the Earth Condition that preceded the Mineral Kingdom of Life (see the Grand Schematic).

12   Dan 7:9, 13, 22. This chapter also seems to relate to the 3½-day event in Rev 11:9–11, for in Dan 7:25 he speaks of "a time, two times, and half a time" during which the beast shall rule.

of "coming" that must be considered as having some credibility. In the seventh chapter of Daniel, we find much that parallels parts of John's vision. Pertinent on this passage is Daniel's, "I saw in the night visions, and behold, with the clouds of heaven there came one like a son of man."[13] Chronologically, Paul takes up the theme next, "with the sound of the *trumpet* of God... [both those who have died and those who are alive] shall be caught up... in the clouds to meet the Lord in the air."[14] In their so-called Little Apocalypse passages, Mark and Matthew both speak of this, "And they will see the Son of man coming in clouds with great power and glory," followed by Matthew at the "loud *trumpet* call.[15] When Pilate asks Jesus if he is "the Christ, the Son of the Blessed," Jesus replied, "I am; and you will see the Son of man seated at the right hand of Power, and coming on the clouds of heaven," followed by Matthew, except that the questioner there is the high priest.[16] In John's "coming with the clouds" passage he shortly thereafter puts the *trumpet* with it.[17] Beyond his 1 Thessalonians passage, Paul had firmly established the connection between the trumpet call and this "coming on the clouds."[18] We shall see the immense significance of this trumpet call when we get to the section on the seven trumpets, especially the last.

5. *"I am the Alpha and the Omega" (Rev 1:8)*

"The Alpha and the Omega" belongs to the book of Revelation, appearing in its first chapter and in the last two, and nowhere else in the canon, though Isaiah says the same thing in "I am the first and I am the last," as does John in Revelation.[19]

Interestingly, the passage "who is and who was and who is to come" appears twice in rapid succession.[20] It has only a whiff of similarity to Isaiah 44:6, "I am the first and I am the last," and literally is not its equivalent, nor is it the equivalent to the Alpha and

---

13 Dan 7:13.
14 1 Thessalonians 4:16–17.
15 Mark 13:26; Matt 24:30–31.
16 Mark 14:61–62; Matt 26:63–64.
17 Rev 1:7, 10.
18 1 Corinthians 15:52; Hebrews 12:19.
19 Rev 21:6; 22:13; Isa 44:6; also 41:4; Rev 1:17.
20 Rev 1:4, 8.

Omega, for one could have been both before and after without being the first and the last. But why the repetition? My rhetorical question, to which I have no answer. Something about the passage calls to my mind the wide variety of interpretation of God's simple "I Am the I Am" in Exodus.[21]

6. *"In the midst of the lampstands one like a son of man" (Rev 1:13)*

Since we will consider the son of man in point 7, immediately following, only a brief comment, though a very important one, is needed here. What means so much in this short passage is that it places the one like a son of man in the middle of the lampstands (churches; 1:20), the Cultural Age in which the Christ event, the Mystery of Golgotha, occurred, the Greco-Roman.[22] It directly fore-shadows his description of the seven ages (churches), pointing to the fourth, that he calls Thyatira.

7. *"One like a son of man" (Rev 1:13)*

This complete phrase appears three times in the canon, the two passages in Revelation doubtless taking their cue from its appearance in Daniel.[23] It would seem that "one like a" tells us that it is speaking of the human being who, in the far distant future, will have spiritualized the three bodies (physical, etheric, and astral) into their three higher counterparts (manas, buddhi, and atma); or in Steiner's terminology, Spirit-Self, Life-Spirit, and Spirit-Man.[24] Such ninefold character is described by Revelation 1:13–16 in the following three threefold group-ings: 1. long robe—golden girdle—white wool; 2. Flame of fire—bur-nished bronze—many waters; 3. seven stars—two-edged sword—sun shining in full strength.

Except in Ezekiel, the OT's prolific use of the "son of man" phrase is never capitalized, and in the New Testament, except in the two instances in Revelation cited above and Paul's quotation in Hebrews 2:6 from Psalms 8:4, it is always capitalized as a reference

---

21   Exod 3:14. See *BB*, 244–246.

22   *BB*, 591–592, chart **I-25**.

23   Dan 7:13; Rev 1:13; 14:14.

24   *BB* chart **I-9**.

to the Christ.[25] Since the New Testament is largely the work of Christ's "two witnesses," and since John's Gospel prologue spoke of the *"power to become* children of God," which, as we will see, is part of the process of becoming a "son of man," the "one like a" seems clearly to be pointing to what a human being can become through its long journey to the new Jerusalem as outlined in John's vision, the Revelation.[26]

One might easily challenge the view that *"one like a* son of man" speaks primarily of the human being, for verses 17 to 20 that follow it lend themselves more readily to the Christ, the Son of Man. Still, the "first and the last" does seem to also describe the eventually perfected human being as a "son of man"—a human entelechy. It is perhaps best to remain open to it continuing to have a prophetic and mystical double meaning. The human beings who eventually become perfected do so only because, over their long journey through many incarnations, they follow the Christ Spirit that always dwells within them, even when they fall back.

Admittedly, in most of what follows it will be easier to imagine the Risen Christ, the Lamb, as the one who emerges from the image in chapter 1. On the other hand, the Christ has perfected the earthly Jesus of Nazareth (now Master Jesus) who, like Christian Rosenkreutz of the "White Brotherhood," continues to work in the progress of evolution from the spiritual realm and clearly falls into the son of man realm, without displacement of the Son of Man. We shall see more of this Son of Man. It is an image of what was being fulfilled, perfected, in the bodies of Jesus of Nazareth on Earth during the three years that the Christ completed the perfection of those bodies, Jesus of Nazareth having perfected his Ego by withdrawing from those bodies and yielding them to entry of the Christ Spirit at his Baptism in the Jordan.

---

25 The "son of man" passage appears in the OT in Job, Psalms, Isaiah, Jeremiah, Ezekiel and Daniel, as follows: Job 25:6; 35:8; Ps 8:4; 144:3; 146:3; Isa 51:12; 56:2; Jer 50:40; 51:43; Ezek 92 times over all but 8 chapters (9, 10, 19, 41, 42, 45, 46, and 48); Dan 7:13; 8:12. In the non-canonical but influential book of Enoch, the phrase is used with great frequency, sometimes apparently in a late pre-Christian period and sometimes in seemingly clear reference to the Christ, its dating thus not entirely clear.

26 John 1:12–13.

Even though the academy has not embraced Steiner, since his work is primarily intuition-based, and thus not subject to verification by the academy's methodology, there is merit in having some awareness of academic positions on scriptural meaning. Noted to that end is Nickelsburg's article.[27] That said, the academy is thus bereft of the vast and powerful insights from Steiner's work that give a depth of meaning to the biblical message that, for this writer, has greatly reduced the relevance of the prevalent theology within modern Christendom. In no book of the Bible is there greater exegetical (interpretational) contrast between the academy and Anthroposophy than in this book of Revelation.

Let us now consider what Steiner's lectures tell us on the meaning of son of man, Son of Man, and Son of God.

A powerful description of the Son of God and its relationship to the Son of Man, is in a lecture Steiner gave in Munich on February 11, 1911. Another lecture was given in Munich on the same date that has been published in English. The lecture I have in mind, so far as I have yet been able to determine, is only in an unpublished English typescript (UET) titled *The "Son of God" and the "Son of Man."*[28] Here is a pertinent portion of it:

> What is it that must now be fulfilled in the course of the evolution of humanity? What is the one and only way in which to achieve it? This can most easily be expressed by the two concepts that in earlier times designated these two beings within us. The one is the concept of the being of spirit-and-soul in the first three years of childhood, the being who is now no longer really adapted to the external nature of man and is, moreover, unable to unfold ego-consciousness: this being of spirit-and-soul was called in olden times the *Son of God*. And the being whose physical body today is so constituted that ego-consciousness can awaken within it was called the *Son of Man*—the Son of God within the Son of Man. The conditions prevailing today are such that the Son of God can

---

27 George W. E. Nickelsburg, *Son of Man, ABD* (vol. 6), 137–150.

28 It is cited in footnote 5, page 2 of *DQWIM* and is in the bibliography of *BB*, 693. As yet I have been unable to determine if it is included in Steiner's archive and has been published in English and will thus be in the collected works (CW). It was loaned to me in the early 1990s by the Rudolf Steiner Library (now in Philmont, NY) for me to copy and may still be available there.

no longer become conscious in the Son of Man, but must first be separated if the ego-consciousness of today is to arise. It is the task of man, through conscious absorption of the realities of the spiritual world, so to transform and make himself master of his external sheaths that the Son of Man is gradually permeated by the Son of God. When the earth has reached the end of its evolution, man must have consciously achieved what he has no longer been able to achieve from childhood onward: he must have completely permeated what he is as Son of Man with the divine part of his being. What is it that must completely permeate the flow through his human nature? What is it that must pour into every part of the physical, etheric and astral bodies, so that the whole Son of Man is permeated with the Son of God? It is that which lives in the first three years of life, but permeated with the fully conscious ego— this it is that must spread through the whole of man.

Let us imagine that a being were to appear before us as an Ideal, a model of what man should be. What would have to be fulfilled in this being? The soul nature of such a being cannot penetrate the outer sheaths of an ordinary man of present-day development, for he would not be able to realize the human Ideal of earthly evolution, would not be able to make it manifest. We should have, as it were, to tear the soul out of him and put in its place a soul such as is present in the first three years of life, but permeated with full ego-consciousness. In no other way could an Ideal of earth-evolution stand before us. And for how long would such a soul be able to endure a physical human life? The physical body is capable of bearing such a soul for three years only; then, if it is not to be shattered, it is bound to overpower that soul. The whole karma of the earth would have to be so organized that after three years the physical body is shattered. For in man as he is today, the being who lives in him for three years is overpowered; if, however, it were to remain, it would overpower and shatter the physical body. The Ideal of man's mission on the earth can therefore be fulfilled only if, while the physical body, etheric body and astral body remain, the ordinary soul nature is ejected and the soul nature of the first three years, plus ego-consciousness, is inserted in its place. Then this soul would shatter the human body; but during these three years it would present a perfect example of what man can achieve.

This Ideal is the Christ-Ideal; and what took place at the Baptism in Jordan is the reality behind what has here been described.

The human Ideal was once actually placed before mankind on the earth. Through the Baptism in [the] Jordan, the soul with which we are connected during the first three years of childhood—but in this case completely permeated by the ego and in unbroken connection with the spiritual world—entered into a human body from which the earlier soul had departed. Then, after three years, this soul from the spiritual worlds shattered the bodily sheaths. Therefore we have before us in the first three years of life a faint image, an utterly inadequate image, of the Christ-Being Who lived for three years on earth in the body of Jesus. And if we try to develop in ourselves a manhood whose nature is that of the soul of childhood but fully permeated with the reality and content of the spiritual world, then we have a picture of that Egohood, that Christhood, of which St. Paul is speaking when he calls upon men to fulfill the "Not I, but Christ in me." This is the childlike soul, permeated with full and complete egohood. Thereby the human being is able to permeate his Son of Man" with his "Son of God" and to fulfill his earthly Ideal, to overcome his external nature and once again to find the connection with the spiritual world.

But how can this be achieved? In sacred records every utterance has more than one meaning. If we are to look into the kingdom of Heaven we must become as children, but with the full maturity of the ego. That is the prospect before us until the earth's mission has been fulfilled. We may well be moved when we realize on the one hand that our physical body is actually facing a withering process and takes into itself the spiritualizing process by overcoming that which is tending to wither. The inner nature must be so strengthened from the spiritual worlds that the opposing outer nature is brought into conformity with it. When this is achieved, we stand, as men, in harmony with the evolutionary process of our earth.

All of this is by way of explaining the depth of meaning in a single sentence Christ is said to have spoken, as reported in all three Synoptic Gospels, "Truly, I say to you, whoever does not receive the kingdom of God like a child shall not enter it."[29] What Steiner tells us about the Kingdom of God in us in this Munich lecture is not an isolated content. In two other lectures, one shortly before and the other soon

---

29   Mark 10:15; also see Matt 18:3 and Luke 18:17.

after, both clearly published in English, he presents versions that con-
vey in some detail the same substance.[30] In at least two other lectures,
in 1909, he presents shorter versions of the same thing, with specific
reference to the cited scriptures.[31]

One reading the many "son of man" passages in the OT must
surely notice that they seem to carry a different meaning from how
the passage is used in the NT, one in which the fact of incompleteness
is evident. The initiates of the OT could see that One was coming who
would make it possible to attain completion, and that one would be
the Christ they foresaw. In his lecture on "The 'I AM'" in the cycle
on John's Gospel in Hamburg, Steiner explains what the "son of man"
meant in the OT.[32] These initiates were aware of the evolution that had
resulted in the difference between the waking and sleeping states of
consciousness. During sleep, as they knew, the astral body and Ego
left the part that remained in bed, the physical and etheric bodies. Of
this state, Steiner explained:

> They [the physical and etheric bodies] gave birth to that which
> dipped down into the physical senses and looked out into the
> physical world during the day, but which at night sank down into
> a state of unconsciousness, because it had severed itself from
> that condition in which it previously existed. In occult language,
> the part remaining in bed is called the real earth-man. That was
> "man." And that part in which the ego remained day and night,
> that part born out of the physical and ether bodies was called
> the "child of man" or the "son of man." The "son of man" [was]
> the ego and astral body born out of the physical and ether bodies

---

30 Steiner, *Background to the Gospel of St. Mark*, 3rd ed., AP (1968), lect. 6 (Berlin,
Jan 16, 1911), 104–113 (CW 124) and *The Spiritual Guidance of Man*, ed. Henry
B. Monges, AP (1950), lect. 1 (Copenhagen, June 6, 2011), 7–18, esp. 10–11 (CW
15)—the content of all three lectures given by Steiner in Copenhagen June 6, 7
and 8, 2011, according to his preface dated August 20, 2011, were written by him
from the transcript of their oral presentation, stating, "in general my opinion [is]
that the form of work intended for reading should be quite different from that
used in speaking."

31 *Rosicrucian Esotericism*, AP (1978), lect. 4 (Budapest, June 6, 1909), 38–39
(CW 109/111) and *According to Luke*, AP (2001) lect. 10 (Basel, Sept 26, 1909),
210–211 (CW 114).

32 Steiner, *The Gospel of St. John*, rev. ed., AP (1962), lect. 6 (May 25, 1908), 105
(CW 103).

in the course of earthly evolution. The technical expression for [this] was the "son of man."

Then comes the question, for what purpose did Christ Jesus come to earth; what was imparted to the earth through His Impulse?... Through the force of the Christ Who came upon the earth, the son of man will again be raised to his divine estate. Previously, after the manner of the ancient Mystery initiation, only chosen individuals could perceive the divine-spiritual world.... Therefore, in ancient times only a prophecy of the "I AM" teaching could gain a footing.

Collected Works volume 104a contains sixteen lectures on pictures from the Apocalypse. *Reading the Pictures of the Apocalypse* contains all of them.[33] The first four were lectures in Munich in the spring of 1907. The last twelve were in Kristiania (Oslo) in May of 1909. *RPA* contains the Munich lectures in its Part 1 and the Kristiania lectures in Part 2. Lecture 1 in Part 2 says that the initiates in the ancient mysteries were able to perceive developments in the spiritual world and anticipate that a savior-being was descending and would enter the earth's etheric body that worked upon the physical.[34] The same was true with the initiates of the OT, but they also experienced what Moses had experienced on the mountain. From that they understood that "Christ would arise in the future. Paul, as a Jewish initiate, knew all of this; nevertheless, before the Damascus event he could never have believed that the one who died on the cross was the same one as the Messiah."[35] Steiner then distinguishes the perceptions of the Hebrew initiates:

But the ancient Hebrew initiates always saw the physical human being spiritualized and placed in the spiritual world as its crowning, and such people understood the Christ to be the first real human form that could be seen in the spiritual world from the point of view provided by the physical world. In this way those receiving the Hebrew initiation saw how, in the distant future, the "Son of Man," the Christ, would heal and purify the physical form. For this reason

---

33 *RPA.*
34 *RPA*, 68–70.
35 *RPA*, 69–70.

Paul knew that what appeared to him before Damascus in human form could be none other than the Christ.

The writer of the Apocalypse describes the same thing to us when he speaks of the "Son of Man." He calls the seven communities the "seven stars," and he saw the "Son of Man" as the spiritualized, purified form of the physical body, not only the etheric body, but the spiritual-physical form of "Man," the human being, now purified and sanctified.[36]

We return now to the Master Jesus, none other than Jesus of Nazareth, as he hung dying on the cross, crying out "My God, my God, why has thou forsaken me?"[37] The Christ Spirit that entered the three bodies of Jesus of Nazareth as the latter's Ego sacrificially withdrew at his baptism, was departing. That Spirit, though experiencing the death process, could not itself die. It had perfected all three of this great earthly initiate's three bodies, and entered the earth's etheric realm to stay until not only the physical but also the etheric body were spiritualized as humanity entered into the More Perfect Astral realm. Gradually the powers of Jesus, enabled by the presence of that Spirit, waned as the three years ran their course, the searing power of the Christ destroying the greatly weakened physical body that hung dying on the cross. All that was left as that Spirit departed was the cosmic element it had implanted in the earth. It was escaping. "This is what makes the whole episode so soul-shattering," Steiner says (174).[38] Jesus of Nazareth, as he died upon that cross, became, in the fullest sense, a Son of Man. As previously stated, he is now referred to in his spiritual capacity in the guiding White Brotherhood as the Master Jesus—not the Christ, but the one fully Christ-imbued who works as a guiding master for creatures below.

Steiner identifies the mysterious fleeing youth in Mark 14:51–52 as this youthful cosmic spirit that "fled naked" away (175). In chapter 3 of *The Temple Sleep*, I take the position that such fleeing youth was Lazarus/John, but do so while being in full agreement with

---

36 *RPA*, 70–71.

37 Mark 15:34.

38 Steiner, *The Gospel of St. Mark*, AP (1986), lect. 3 (Basel, Sept. 23, 1912), 173–177 (CW 139).

41

Steiner's conclusion. The passage has more than one meaning, and mine was complementary, not contrary, to Steiner's.[39]

Steiner gives an interesting insight into the OT meaning of the son of man in lecture 11 of *The Gospel of St. Matthew*.[40] He had explained that "there must always be some who are in advance of their generation, who already bear within them in an earlier epoch the knowledge and potentialities of a later one" (189). These, he said, were "sons of men," and that "it behooved the disciples...to recognize and learn to understand the nature of these leaders." To test their abilities in this regard, "Christ Jesus asked them [to tell him] of which human beings it can be said that they are 'Sons of Men' in this generation?" My Revised Standard Version has Jesus posing the question to his disciples, "Who do men say that the Son of man is?"[41] But Steiner says that according to the meaning of the original Aramaic text, "We must picture Christ Jesus...asking them: Which individuals of the previous generations in the Greco-Latin epoch are held to have been 'Sons of Men'? The disciples then spoke of Elias, John the Baptist, Jeremias and other prophets."[42] Of course, Christ then asked them "Who do you say that I am?" While Peter gave a correct answer, it did not come from his own consciousness, as his later actions demonstrate, for Christ's mission was not yet complete and until then the human capacity to assimilate the true I Am did not exist.[43]

Other Steiner lectures speak of the son of man, always consistently with the above, but deal with applications that can here be simply given by reference.[44]

---

39 *TSRYR*, 155–178, esp. 159.

40 Steiner, *The Gospel of St. Matthew*, 4th ed., AP (1965) (CW 123).

41 Matt 16:13.

42 Matt 16:14.

43 On this, see also *According to Luke*, 209.

44 See the concluding paragraphs of lect. 5 in the November 1907 cycle on the Gospel of St. John at Basel (Nov 20, 1907) (CW 100); *Building Stones for an understanding of the Mystery of Golgotha* (*BSU*), 2nd ed., RPA (1972) (lect. 7, Berlin, Apr 19, 1917), 142–159, esp. 149 (CW 175) on Julian (called "the apostate"); and *The Temple Legend*, RSP (1985) (lect. 13, 3rd lecture in Berlin on May 29, 1905), 164–166 (CW 93) on the sons of Cain, the physical temple builders (Masons), as sons of men and the sons of Abel/Seth as sons of God.

In summary, chapter one of Revelation gives an expansive view of much that follows. It opens with a declaration that the vision is of vast importance, not myopic but far-reaching, perceiving into and through countless ages ahead. Noting Christ's "coming with the clouds," it sees beyond the realm of matter and into the timeless spiritual paths beyond, even to the "son of man" state.[45] The body of the chapter is directed to the "seven churches," though the vision to be presented to them extends far beyond their time frame. In closing, it opens the portal into the first of the three creative series of seven, for which John appropriates the names of seven well-known regional churches, themselves discreet cloaks that carry deeper meaning for the initiate, the more spiritually perceptive, than for the authorities and those of less spiritual development.

---

45   Rev 1:7.

4

FROM TIMELESSNESS TO TIME TO TIMELESSNESS

Or we could use a different double phrase, from spirit to matter to spirit, to say the same thing. What is "time"? Uniformity of definition hardly exists.[1] The simple definition of time is how long it takes an object, at a certain velocity, to move from one item of matter to another. Sometimes the concept of space is connected to the idea of time, but space cannot, it would seem, exist other than as something that separates one bit of matter from another, such as in galaxies or the universe itself. If, for the purpose of discussion, our entire universe were to cease to exist, could the absolute void of any materiality within it be called space? Perhaps the question is only semantic. Spirit is not spatial, for it knows no limits of space, though it pervades the latter and affects the evolutionary processes that take place in space and time. Steiner often dealt with the profound relationship between the human being and not only our solar system and galaxy (zodiac), but implicitly the entirety of the universe.

Our sun makes life within our world of matter possible, but it also destroys that matter. We have seen, from Steiner's teachings, that the searing power of the Christ could only live in an earthly body for three years, during which it progressively destroyed the materiality of the bodies of Jesus. The crucifixion accomplished nothing that the Christ Spirit itself had not by then essentially completed, but it established for us the spiritual reality that over the course of our human journey we must also overcome the material body, that is, through moral perfection we must crucify it. The Master Jesus, by housing that Christ Spirit, assented to its own crucifixion, but the Master Jesus lives and

---

1   Consider www.en.wikipedia.org/wiki/Time and www.en.wikipedia.org/wiki/Spacetime.

guides from the realm of spirit. One who approaches the book of Revelation from any other direction must come away without comprehending its meaning, as we shall see as we work our way through it.

We must conceive that spirit and matter are mutually exclusive domains, and that spirit is negative matter. Here I must invite my reader to read, or to read again, the final essay, itself entitled "What Is Man?" in my book *David's Question, "What Is Man?"* (*DQWIM*), or at least the concluding portion (pages 430–435) that deals with the polarities between the stars and other bodies in the universe, the polarities of matter and negative matter, as Steiner sets them out, and my concluding reflections thereon.

As wonderful, and, for me, deeply satisfying, as these reflections are, the human journey is that of the Alpha and the Omega. Inasmuch as the Revelation, and essentially the full scope of the Bible itself, falls within the Earth Condition of Consciousness, this greater scope of our human journey would carry us too far afield.[2]

As we move back to our journey through time in the realm of matter, let us recognize that there does appear to be a relationship between space and spirit. To the extent that the journey of our spirit between lives is a journey of spirit, we must say that at least part, if not all, of it is space related. For a capsulized version of that journey, see *BB*, chart **I-33**, entitled "Course of the Ego between death and rebirth: Regions of soul and spirit worlds," and the sources in Steiner's works from which it is drawn.

---

2   For those who would like to peer into that greater scope, the following assortment of Steiner references has been helpfully assembled and privately provided to me by Paul V. O'Leary: *The Spiritual Hierarchies and their Reflection in the Physical World*, AP (1970), lect. 5 (April 14, 1909), esp. 56–68 (CW 110); *True and False Paths in Spiritual Investigation*, 3rd ed., RSP (1985), lect. 10 (August 21, 1924), 202 (CW 243); *Karmic Relationships*, vol. 5, 2nd ed., RSP (1984), lect. 2 (March 30, 1924), 29 (CW 239); *Man as Symphony of the Creative Word*, 2nd ed., RSP (1945), lect. 6 (October 28, 1923), 98 (CW 230); *Spiritual Beings in the Heavenly Bodies & in the Kingdoms of Nature*, AP (1992), lect. 5 (April 7, 1912), 95 (CW 136); *The Inner Aspect of the Social Question*, RSP (1974) (CW 193). To these, he added words of Christopher Bamford, "The human being is not a little cosmos [although, by another approach, it would seem to be]; the cosmos is a big human. Cosmic evolution is therefore the progressive unfolding, transformation, and mutation of the seeds planted in the original human archetype." Bamford, *An Endless Trace*, New Paltz, New York, Codhill Press (1993), chap. 1, 22.

But consideration of how our spiritual journey progresses through time and materiality seems most advisable before we get into Revelation's description of that journey. The following passage from Steiner is descriptive and relevant:[3]

> A fact which will play a certain role...concerns the speed with which the development on the different planets [Conditions of Consciousness] takes place. For this is not the same on all the planets. Life proceeds with the greatest speed on Saturn, the rapidity then decreases on the Sun becomes still less on the Moon and reaches its slowest phase on the earth. On the latter it becomes slower and slower, to the point *at which self-consciousness develops.* Then the speed increases again. Therefore, today [1904] man has already passed the time of the greatest slowness of his development. Life has begun to accelerate again. [Emphasis added.]

It was in 1904 that Steiner published the above. He speaks as though the acceleration had but recently then begun, the point at which "self-consciousness develops." Our present Cultural Age, from 1414 to 3574 CE, is the age for development of the consciousness soul.[4] "What flowed into humanity's evolution through the appearance of the Christ worked within it like a seed that could only ripen gradually. Until now, only the very smallest part of this profound new wisdom has flowed into physical existence, which is only at the very beginning of its Christian evolution."[5] As we saw in the first chapter, the substance of what was later to become Anthroposophy was presented in the human stream by Christian Rosenkreutz at the very threshold of the age of the consciousness soul, but it had to submerge until brought forth in the early twentieth century by Steiner. Steiner identified the year 1840 as the year when the slowness gave way to the reversal of direction and the beginning of the gradual acceleration in development of the consciousness soul.[6]

---

3   Steiner, *Cosmic Memory*, New York, Harper & Row (1959), chap. 13, 171 (CW 11).
4   *BB*, Charts **I-19** and **I-24**.
5   Steiner, *OES*, 2nd ed., AP (1997), 274–275 (CW 13).
6   Steiner, *Materialism and the Task of Anthroposophy*, AP (1987), lect. 11 (Dornach, April 30, 1921), 191–210 (CW 204).

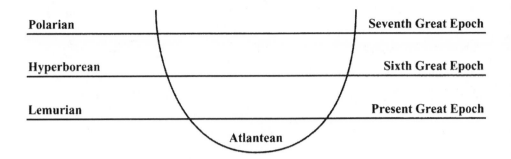

Polarian	Seventh Great Epoch
Hyperborean	Sixth Great Epoch
Lemurian	Present Great Epoch
Atlantean	

The Seven Evolutionary Epochs

So, we have clear indication from Steiner that the impulse of the Mystery of Golgotha in the Greco-Roman Cultural Age only planted the seed that would not reverse the downward trajectory of humanity's journey until the European age. At the same time Steiner makes it clear that within the European Cultural Age, the reversal did not come until approximately the year 1840 when the slowing speed finally came to an end and began to accelerate.

The central core of my book, *David's Question, What Is Man?* (*DQWIM*), comprises three long essays entitled "Fire," "Light," and "Blood." Because of their respective lengths, each such essay is preceded by its own separate table of contents; and each such topic title is structurally immanent within John's Apocalypse. Particularly relevant to our present discussion is the section in the "Fire" essay captioned "Christ, the J-Curve and the Right Time" (175–181). The J-Curve describes the situation "where an impulse calculated to bring a change of direction actually causes an increase in the original direction for a time before the reverse sets in."[7]

The chart above reflects the parabola of the human journey through the seven Evolutionary Epochs of the Physical Condition of Form of the Mineral Condition of Life of the Earth Condition of Consciousness.[8] The chart on the next page represents the human journey through the seven Post-Atlantean Cultural Ages.

---

7   *DQWIM*, 178.

8   *DQWIM*, 177; the chart following it, from *DQWIM*, 178, reflects the same parabolic human journey through the seven Cultural Ages in the Post-Atlantean Evolutionary Epoch of such Conditions of Form, Life, and Consciousness.

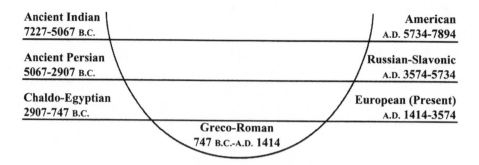

Ancient Indian	American
7227-5067 B.C.	A.D. 5734-7894
Ancient Persian	Russian-Slavonic
5067-2907 B.C.	A.D. 3574-5734
Chaldo-Egyptian	European (Present)
2907-747 B.C.	A.D. 1414-3574

Greco-Roman
747 B.C.-A.D. 1414

The Seven Cultural Ages

The J-curve is clearly evident in the Evolutionary Epochs and the Cultural Ages. We may ask if the same might be true that what was planted during the Earth Condition of Consciousness, with the development of the Ego, was as the seed that could only perfect the astral body into manas (Spirit-Self) in the Jupiter Condition of Consciousness. The fractal nature of creation suggests that such is the case.[9] If a similar parabola was prepared for the seven Conditions of Consciousness, we would see that the astral body implanted in humanity during the Ancient Moon Condition of Consciousness was only to be perfected into manas (Spirit-Self) during the Jupiter Condition of Consciousness, humanity traversing in an upward direction in the Fifth Condition of Consciousness what it moved through in a downward direction during the descending portion in the third such Condition.

What the Earth Condition of Consciousness, the fourth, was to implant in humanity was the Ego, the fourth element of the fourfold human being. If we reflect upon Chart **I-9** in *BB*, it is obvious that the Ego represents more than the bottom half of both the sevenfold and ninefold human being. This indicates that to perfect the human Ego it is necessary during the course of the Earth Condition of Consciousness that the Ego work on the higher components, manas (Spirit-Self), buddhi (Life-Spirit), and atma (Spirit-Man):

> In a sixth culture-epoch man will develop still further and his soul nature will grow in a certain way into manas, the Spirit-Self; in a seventh period—the last Post-Atlantean culture-epoch—man will grow into Life-Spirit or buddhi; and what has been able to grow

---

9   See *DQWIM*, "As Above, So Below", 98.

into atma will actually unfold only after the great catastrophe by which the whole Post-Atlantean epoch will be brought to an end.[10]

While humanity will live in the astral realm in the Jupiter Condition of Consciousness, its goal there is to perfect the astral (passion and desire) body into manas, and thus redeem the Animal Kingdom. In the Venus Condition, we will work to perfect the etheric (life) body, and thus redeem the Plant Kingdom. Finally, on Vulcan we will work to perfect the physical body, and thus redeem the Mineral Kingdom. What Paul spoke will have been consummated:

> For the creation waits with eager longing for the revealing of the sons of God; for the creation was subjected to futility, not of its own will but by the will of him who subjected it in hope; because the creation itself will be set free from its bondage to decay and obtain the glorious liberty of the children of God. We know that the whole creation has been groaning in travail together until now.[11]

Thus, we find the J-Curve existing in all of the relevant levels. Even though the term itself first arose in the financial realm, it has been applied in other fields and seems to be a natural phenomenon that occurs in everything that evolves, as it evolves. It describes the situation "where an impulse calculated to bring a change of direction actually causes an increase in the original direction for a time before the reverse sets in."[12]

The phenomenon can be seen in the lag between the commencement of each Cultural Age of the Post-Atlantean Epoch and the Astrological Age for which it is named.[13] It is these Cultural Ages that become so relevant in comprehending what John means by the seven "Churches" in Revelation 2–3, to which we shall immediately turn in the next chapter.

It has been deceptively difficult for me to find Steiner's explicit approbation for the precise tabulations in Chart **I-19**. Apparently

---

10 Steiner, *Occult History*, RSP (1982), lect. 3 (Stuttgart, December 29, 1910), 48–49 (CW 126).

11 Rom 8:19–23; cf. also Eph 1:9–10.

12 *DQWIM*, 178.

13 Witness the tabulation of each of these "Age" groupings in *BB's* Chart **I-19**, at 573. See also the related Chart **I-25**, at 591.

Robert Powell, whose work is cited as the source of Chart **I-19**, had this same experience, for he cites Steiner's *Ancient Myths*, where, in lecture 7 (Dornach, January 13, 1918), he relies upon Steiner's statement that the end of the Lemurian Evolutionary Epoch (and thus presumably the beginning of the Atlantean) lies "approximately 25,900 years before our epoch" [2,160 X 12 = 25,920]; this assumes that Atlantis comprised seven "Cultural Ages" of 2,160 years and that we are in the first such time span in the Post-Atlantean Epoch.[14] Because of the changing speed of the different segments of our parabolic journey, I become increasingly uneasy about applying the same time frame for each Epoch either before or after our own, although both the Atlantean and Post-Atlantean are in the lower portion of the parabola and thus may not be greatly different in this respect. Since time is only a phenomenon of the lower portions of the parabola, perhaps we need not fret about whether the "shortening of days" (Mark 13:20; Matt 24:22) applies to time or distance [speed or space], or a combination of both.

Everything Steiner said about our seven Cultural Ages is consistent with the time periods given, or at least not inconsistent with them. He recognized the length of the great solar year, the period it took the sun, in its precession of the equinoxes (one degree every seventy-two years) to travel around all twelve signs of the zodiac, thus a period of 25,920 of our years, with an average length of 2,160 years in traversing each zodiacal realm. In his lectures on the Apocalypse, he gave approximate time periods for the first two Post-Atlantean Cultural Ages. Lecturing in June, 1908, he placed the Ancient Indian "at a time which now lies more than eight or nine thousand years behind us" (literally, though obviously roughly, sometime before 6150 or 7,150 BCE), and the Ancient Persian as "about five thousand years back" (literally, though again roughly, about 3092 BCE).[15]

It is these seven Cultural Ages of the Post-Atlantean Evolutionary Epoch that are the focus, respectively, of the seven "churches" in chapters 2 and 3 of John's Apocalypse, as presented in chapter 6.

---

14 Robert Powell, *Hermetic Astrology*, vol. 1, Kinsau, West Germany, Hermetika (1987), 67, note 20.

15 *ASJ*, 59–60.

5

Basic Structure of Revelation

What must "soon" take place; coming with the clouds; One
   Like a Son of Man (Rev 1)
Seven Letters (Rev 2–3)
Interlude for Evolutionary Panorama and Reflection (Rev 4)
The Seven Seals (Rev 5–8:1)
The Seven Trumpets (Rev 8:2–11)
Portent of woman, and Michael's heavenly battle (Rev 12)
The two beasts (Rev 13)
The 144,000 (Rev 14:1,3; 21–22; 7:4)
Seven Bowls of Wrath (Rev 15–16)
The judgment and doom of Babylon (Rev 17–18)
Heavenly marriage of the Lamb and Bride; the "new name"
   known only to its holder (Rev 19)
The "thousand-year" reign and its sequel; the "second death"
   (Rev 20)
The new Jerusalem and its twelvefold dimension; the Jupiter
   Condition of Consciousness (Rev 21–22)

The Grand Scheme, the Structure of Revelation, and the Limitations of Consciousness

Within the overall "Grand Scheme" of the human journey, the structure of Revelation is front-loaded. Its focus is more delineated in the portions that are close to us, both in the recent past and the nearer future. No matter how much we yearn to conceptualize the more distant realms through which we have journeyed, and will journey, it is only the portions near to us where any clear picture can be drawn. The immensity of our "trip" is utterly beyond our ability to conceptualize it meaningfully, save in such tools as the "Grand

Scheme." The two witnesses, Elijah and Moses, moved forward in and through Lazarus/John and Saul/Paul, respectively, thence LJ reincarnated as Christian Rosenkreutz, essentially all of whose gloriously elevated level of consciousness opened anew later in our own Cultural Age through the capacity of Rudolf Steiner's intuition. The salience of divine intelligence in these spiritual outriders has given us, in the Grand Scheme, a road map on the scale of the universe itself.

Within that schematic, the vision of Lazarus/John, as presented in Revelation, wisely focuses upon the portions nearest to us, growing less distinct in its farther reaches both before and after our material existence. Whatever we might have wished, from our hungering curiosity, is still increasingly veiled the farther from our present existence it reaches, just as is the phenomena of our physical vision.

Why must this be so? Why could these great human seers not have spelled out the more distant ranges in more detail for our understanding. To even ask this question is to jump over the deep meaning of "Conditions of Consciousness." In our incarnated form, and in a large part of our journey between lives depending upon our individual spiritual development, we exist only within the Earth Condition of Consciousness. This means that we do not yet, and will not for a very long time, have the capacity to comprehend anything in those Conditions of Consciousness that lie distantly ahead of us, and only hazily of those equidistantly behind us. Even if the great spiritual leaders just mentioned were able to peer into these more distant realms, they have recognized that what they perceive there is not cognizable for humanity embroiled in the depths of spiritual darkness that requires bodies of matter remaining to be purified.

"The light shines in the darkness, and the darkness comprehends it not."[1] As the prodigal son, we presently exist at the deepest level of darkness our journey has taken us, the deepest point in "the valley of the shadow of death."[2] Steiner's above translation of John 1:5, rendered "the darkness comprehends it not," was in accord with the major translation then existing, the King James Version (KJV).[3]

---

1   John 1:5.

2   Ps 23:4.

3   Steiner's usage on this specific word is at *The Gospel of St. John and Its Relation to the Other Gospels*, 2nd ed., AP (1982), lect. 3; 57 (CW 112).

Later versions have varied between "comprehends" and "overcome." The authorities are essentially unanimous in recognizing the literal correctness of each usage, and whichever has been adopted by any new version of the Bible is usually accompanied by a note indicating the alternative. Since comprehension of anything seems generally to be a requisite for overcoming it, while the reverse seems generally not to be true, I prefer "comprehends." Human science has yet to come to a deep understanding of light, a deficiency bemoaned by Einstein himself.

Christ came at a time of "deep darkness," in the midst of humanity's virtually total loss of understanding, a darkness that would not be lifted until "the Lord removes men far away."[4] Thanks to the J-Curve effect, we are even more deeply enmeshed in darkness today than at any other time in our human journey, and we seem destined to "descend ever more and more deeply.[5] Revelation, as John's vision, presents the process of the "removal far away" that Isaiah prophesied. Yet, Revelation seems to deposit humanity only into the Jupiter Condition of Consciousness, "the holy city, new Jerusalem," introduced as "a new heaven and a new earth; for the first heaven and the first earth had passed away, and the sea was no more," a place where "death shall be no more."[6] Steiner identifies this stage as the Jupiter Condition of Consciousness, speaking of the "Jupiter man."[7]

By definition, humanity does not, during our long Earth Condition of Consciousness, have a consciousness capable of comprehending in higher Conditions of Consciousness. An aspect of this limitation is expressed by Steiner, "The conditions prevailing today are such that the Son of God can no longer become conscious in the Son of Man, but must first be separated if the ego-consciousness of today is to arise."[8] The best we can do is strive for some glimmer of these dimly lit distant portions of our journey. We shall strive to that end. The attempt to

---

4   Isa 9:2 ("deep darkness"); 6:9–10 (loss of understanding); 6:12 (moved "far away").

5   *ASJ*, lect. 3; 64–66 (CW 104).

6   Rev 21:1–4.

7   *ASJ*, lect. 12; 211.

8   Taken from excerpt, quoted at length earlier, from the typescript of a lecture by Steiner entitled, *The "Son of God" and the "Son of Man"* (Munich, February 11, 1911).

bring anthroposophic insight into the latter portions of John's vision is a challenging undertaking, which we shall attempt by suggestion. The magnitude of the leap can be contemplated on the Grand Schematic by observing all we must pass through during the Earth Condition of Consciousness after the seven Evolutionary Epochs as we move toward the Jupiter Condition.

6

THE CHURCHES

In Revelation chapters 2 and 3, John addresses letters to the "seven stars," which he identifies in 1:20 as "the angels of the seven churches." Steiner's main contribution on the Apocalypse is his major lecture cycle (*The Apocalypse of St. John [ASJ]*) in Nuremberg in June 1908. His earliest publication commentary on John's vision was in 1902 in the original version of *Christianity as Mystical Fact (CMF)*.[1] In the most recent version of that, he says of the seven churches in Asia Minor:

> This cannot mean actually existing communities. Rather, the number seven is a sacred symbol and must have been chosen because of what it represents; there must in reality have been a number of other communities in Asia. Moreover, the way in which John receives the revelation equally suggests an esoteric significance. (123–124)

In his Nuremberg cycle, lecture 3, he considers the seven churches to be the seven Cultural Ages of the Post-Atlantean Epoch. In view of what he wrote in *CMF* on the matter, it is clear that Steiner does not mean that there was anything in these actual churches that was truly representative of what was said about and to them, other than the fact, discussed in chapter 3, "One Like a Son of Man," that these churches did lay in a meaningful postal and tribunal sequence at the time of John's vision. This latter physical reality served well John's purpose of concealing meaning from those not able to recognize the deeper esoteric message in his vision.

---

1   The most recent edition of *Christianity as Mystical Fact* was published by Anthroposophic Press in 1997, to which references herein are made.

John wrote in the middle Age of the Post-Atlantean Epoch; hence he was obliged to present what humanity was in the middle of by going back to the first Age and proceeding through the seventh. While it is important for a significant portion of humanity in our time to conceptualize the journey through this Epoch, what we are facing now and for a very long time yet is right here in this Cultural Age. Our vision is clearest with regard to it, which is our immediate setting in time. One is reminded of Christ's words from the Sermon on the Mount, "Therefore do not be anxious about tomorrow, for tomorrow will be anxious for itself. Let the day's own trouble be sufficient for the day" (Matt 6:34).

We can best appreciate the relevance of this bit of wisdom by reflecting upon the following periods (Cultural Ages) of time spanned by the Post-Atlantean Epoch:

CULTURAL AGE	DATES	CIVILIZATION	REVELATION	CHURCH
Cancer	7227–5067 BCE	Indian	2:1–7	Ephesus
Gemini	5067–2907 BCE	Persian	2:8–11	Smyrna
Taurus	2907–747 BCE	Chaldo-Egyptian	2:12–17	Pergamum
Aries	747 BCE–1414 CE	Greco-Roman	2:18–29	Thyatira
Pisces	1414–3574 CE	European	3:1–6	Sardis
Aquarius	3574–5734 CE	Russian-Slavonic	3:7–13	Philadelphia
Capricorn	5734–7894 CE	American	3:14–22	Laodicea

This current Post-Atlantean Epoch reaches out to 7894 CE, and even our Fifth Cultural Age does not end until 3574 CE, some 1560 years from now.

We must look at what Steiner says about each of the seven Cultural Ages in our Post-Atlantean (Fifth) Evolutionary Epoch.

Here is the message Christ gives "to the angel of the church in Ephesus":

Ancient India (7227–5067 BCE)

"I know your works, your toil and your patient endurance, and how you cannot bear evil men but have tested those who call themselves apostles but are not, and found them to be false; I know you are enduring patiently and bearing up for my name's sake, and you have not grown weary. But I have this against you, that you have abandoned the love you had at first. Remember then from what you have fallen; repent and do the works you did at first. If not, I will come to you and remove your lampstand from its place, unless you repent. Yet this you have, you hate the works of the Nicolaitans, which I also hate. He who has an ear, let him hear what the Spirit says to the churches. To him who conquers I will grant to eat of the tree of life, which is in the paradise of God."[2]

In *ASJ*, he gives us the setting for the message:

The culture of which we are now speaking stood directly under the influence of the Atlantean Flood, or the great ice age, as it is called in modern science. The engulfing of Atlantis by the Flood was a gradual process, and there then lived upon the earth a strain of men of which some members had worked their way to the highest attainable stage of development. These constituted the ancient Indian people, a strain that then dwelt in distant Asia, and lived more in the memory of the ancient past than in the present. The greatness and might of the culture of which written descriptions such as the Vedas and Bhagavad Gita are only echoes, lies in the fact that the people lived in the memory of what they themselves had experienced in the Atlantean epoch. You will remember that in the first lecture of this course we said that most human beings of that epoch were capable of developing a certain dim kind of clairvoyance. They were not limited to the physical sense-world; they lived among divine spiritual beings; they saw these divine spiritual beings around them. In the transition from the Atlantean to the Post-Atlantean epoch, man's vision was cut off from the spiritual, astral, and etheric worlds and limited to this physical world. In the first Post-Atlantean age of culture men were possessed by a great longing for what their ancestors had seen in ancient Atlantis, on which, however, the door had closed. Our ancestors saw most ancient wisdom with their own spiritual eyes, though dimly. They dwelt among spirits, they had intercourse with gods and spirits. And so the feeling of those who belonged to that ancient sacred Indian culture was that they longed with every fiber of their being to look back and see what their forefathers had seen, that of which the ancient wisdom

---

2   Rev 2:2–7.

spoke. And thus the land which had just appeared before the physical vision of man—the rocks of the earth, which had just become visible, which previously had been seen spiritually—all this external world seemed of less value to them than what they could remember. All that the physical eyes could see was called *maya*, the great illusion, the great deception, from which they longed to escape. And the most advanced souls in that first age were to be raised to the stage of their ancestors by the method of initiation of which a few remnants remain in yoga. From this proceeded a fundamental religious mood which may be expressed in the words: What surrounds us here in external sense-appearance is a worthless and vain deception; the real and true is above in the spiritual worlds which we have left.—The spiritual leaders of the people were those who could transpose themselves into the regions in which man had formerly lived.[3]

It might help in imagining the soul condition of the Ancient Indian to contemplate the birth of an infant today. Having passed through the higher realms between lives, it is forcefully pushed out of the intervening nurture of the womb through the stressful birth canal. Its loud protestations contrast with its family's joy. Save when sleeping or cradled in the mother's arms and nurtured by her breast, its moments of contentment come slowly. As we have seen, for three years it is a child of God. It seems a fitting metaphor for the Ancient Indian.

Later (68), having laid the above excerpt as background, Steiner addresses the core of the letter "to Ephesus," the first Post-Atlantean Cultural Age.

Man never works according to evolution if he hates external works, if he ceases to love external works. The community at Ephesus (the Cultural Age) forsook the love of external works. So it is quite rightly said in the Apocalypse of John: Thou hatest the deeds of the Nicolaitanes. 'Nicolaitanes' is nothing but a designation for those who express life merely in a material sense. In the time referred to in this letter there was a sect called the Nicolaitanes, who considered the external fleshly sensual life as the only valuable thing

---

3   *ASJ*, 59–60.

for man.[4] The one who inspires the first letter says: This you shall not do. And he also says: But do not forsake thy first love, for inasmuch as you love the external world you quicken it, you exalt it to spiritual life.

In the *CMF* chapter on the Apocalypse (126), Steiner identifies one's "first love" as a love that is "greater than all other loves." But we might also recall that it was Lucifer who led the human astral body to succumb to the urge to eat of the "tree of knowledge" (Gen 2–3), prompting the descent into materiality. In this sense, the primordial, and thus immanent, "first love" was to get down to earth and into matter. Having taken that step, humanity was obliged to spiritualize that matter before it could return, regaining the "tree of life" through the application of its "knowledge" gained through pain, toil, and death. The Ancient Indians of the first Post-Atlantean Cultural Age seemed desirous of repudiating that fateful choice, thus launching them on the path of the "tree of knowledge" while separating them from the precious "tree of life" and putting them on that long path of "pain, toil, and death."[5]

Ancient Persia (5067–2907 BCE)

One of the two taproots for the incarnation of the Christ Spirit can be traced back to the leader who symbolized the Ancient Persian culture. This leader, the ancient Zarathustra, after many intervening embodiments, incarnated in the Solomon Jesus child of Matthew's Gospel and, when the purer Nathan Jesus child of Luke's Gospel was twelve years old, this Zarathustra Ego left its own bodies, which then withered and died, and entered the Luke child who before then did not have anything but a "provisional Ego." From the time of that entry, the Jesus child could be identified as Jesus of Nazareth until, at thirty years of age the Zarathustra Ego sacrificially withdrew and the Christ Spirit descended as the Word became flesh.[6]

The Christ Spirit began withdrawing as Jesus, whose three bodies had already truly been inexorably crucified by the searing power of

---

4   See the discussion of the Nicolaitanes in the discussion of the third letter (Pergamum) below.

5   Gen 3:16–19.

6   See "The Nativity" in *BB* for a fuller narration of these momentous events.

the Christ Spirit, was left hanging alone at the end. Surely the great Zarathustra spirit reclaimed what was left on the cross and uttered the words "My God, my God, why has thou forsaken me?"[7] It was this Zarathustra that entered what Steiner calls "the Great White Brotherhood of mankind," taking his place there, as the Master Jesus, among the great spirits that included the Individuality of Adam–Elijah–John the Baptist–Lazarus/John–Christian Rosenkreutz.

We owe Steiner's Intuition for the bulk of what can be known about this major prehistoric Personality Zarathustra. Steiner's most extensive description of this ancient Personality is in a major lecture on him given in Berlin on January 19, 1911. That lecture will be included in Collected Works volume 60. It is the first of six lectures that Steiner's widow, Marie, soon after Steiner's death, selected from his massive oeuvre, each lecture focusing upon a Personality "whose life and work constituted a turning point in the spiritual life of humanity." These six lectures were published within the first decade after Steiner's death under German title which, in English translation, was *Turning Points in Spiritual History*. An English printing in 1987 went out of print by the mid-1990s, but from early in the 1990s, not having known of that 1987 printing, I began to instigate for a reprinting. Its importance was recognized by the management of SteinerBooks, but resources were under heavy constraint. Since the lecture on Elijah was the primary source for the deep and new insights Steiner had given on him, my instigations became ever more pressing. Finally, upon indicating that our contributions would be directed toward that reprinting, it was done. In the process SteinerBooks invited me to write the introduction for the new publication, which I accepted as an honor.[8]

As stated, my urgency in seeking the new publication was based upon the information about Elijah. But as we look at the message "to the angel of the church in Smyrna" (2:9–11), it is the lecture on the first of those six personalities, Zarathustra, which draws our immediate attention.[9]

---

7   Mark 15:34.

8   Steiner, *Turning Points in Spiritual History*, SB (2007). The quoted words in this paragraph are at page ix of the Introduction.

9   *Turning Points*, 1–32.

It was Zarathustra who reversed, for his Cultural Age and all that were to follow, the position taken by the Ancient Indian civilization in regard to the "first love." Zarathustra perceived the great shining spirit in the sun. The following excerpt, from Steiner's fuller elaboration, is helpful:

A further matter of interest lies in the fact that Zarathustra actually taught his disciples to recognize in detail the hidden workings of the spirit in all material things, and from this starting point the whole of his gifts to culture emanated. He emphasized that it was not sufficient for humankind merely to say: "There before us spreads a material world, behind which ever works and weaves the Divine Spirit." Such a statement might appear at first sight full of significance, but it leads only to a general pantheistic outlook and means nothing more than that some vague nebulous spirit underlies all material phenomena. Zarathustra, like all other great personalities of the past who were exalted and had direct contact with the spirit world, did not present these matters to his followers and the people in any such indefinite and abstract manner; he pointed out that in the same way as individual physical happenings vary in import, so is it with the latent spiritual factor, it being sometimes of greater and sometimes of lesser moment. He further stated that the sun, regarded purely from the physical point of view as a member of the stellar system, is the source of all earthly phenomena, life, and activity, while concealed within is the center of spiritual existence insofar as we are immediately concerned.

These things Zarathustra impressed earnestly and clearly upon his disciples. Using simple words, we can picture him as addressing them somewhat as follows: "When you regard human beings, you must realize that they do not consist only of a material body—this is but an outer expression of the spirit that is within. Even as the physical covering is a manifestation in condensed and crystallized form of the true spiritual human being, so is the sun that appears to us as a light-giving mass, when considered as such, merely the external manifestation of an inner spiritual sun." In the same way as we term the human spirit element, as distinguished from the physical, the Aura, to use an ancient expression, so do we call the all-embracing hidden spiritual part of the sun, the Great Aura (Aura Mazda), in contradistinction to the

61

human being's spiritual component, which is sometimes called the Little Aura. Zarathustra named all that lies hidden within and beyond the human being's mere apprehension of the physical sun "Aura Mazda" or "Ahura Mazda" and considered this element as important to our spiritual experiences and conditions, as is the physical sun to the well-being of plants and animals and all that lives upon the face of the earth. There behind the physical sun lies the Spiritual Master, the Creator, "Ahura Mazda" or "Aura Mazda"; from "Ahura Mazda" came the name "Ormuzd," or "the Spirit of Light."

While the Indians mystically searched their inner being to attain to Brahma—the Eternal—who shines outward as a point of light from within the human essence, Zarathustra urged his disciples to turn their eyes upon the great periphery of existence and pointed out that there within the body of the sun dwells the great Solar Spirit—Ahura Mazda, "the Spirit of Light." He taught them that in the same way as human beings strive to raise their spirit to perfection, so must they ever battle against the lower passions and desires, against the delusive images suggested by possible deception and falsehood and all those antagonistic influences within, which continually oppose spiritual impulses. Thus must Ahura Mazda face the opposition of "the Spirit of Darkness"—"Angra Mainyus," or "Ahriman."[10]

The letter to the angel of the church at Smyrna is the shortest of the seven letters. Its substance is a mere three verses (9–11), from which we derive the two deceivers, Satan and the devil (*diablos*). Though each of these often appears in other scripture, the Apocalypse is unique in using them together, the first combination being in this letter (2:9–10), and appearing later in 12:9 and 20:2. They often seem to be used interchangeably, or even wrongly when the other would have been more appropriate.[11] But it was the ancient Zarathustra who first recognized Ahriman as the Spirit of Darkness working in opposition to the great, or shining, Light, Ahura Mazda or Ormuzd. Perhaps it is that recognition from which his own name derived, for Zarathustra (Persian) or Zoroaster (Greek) means shining star, the

---

10 *Turning Points*, 12–14.

11 For a broader discussion of the two and how they relate to each other, see chart I-32 (Lucifer and Ahriman) in *BB*.

star that, in its descent to incarnation in Matthew's Gospel, led the Persian Magi to the place of Jesus' birth.

The ancient Zarathustra was a major turning point, calling for his people to love the world of matter and to impress their spirit upon it. That message is one that we shall have to return to when we come to the message for our own Cultural Age.

Chaldo-Egyptian (2907–747 BCE)

Again in the letter to the angel of the church at Pergamum we have a continuation of the cloak provided by using current terminology while at the same time inserting items that have a clear connection with the Chaldo-Egyptian Cultural Age. Both Antipas and the Nicolaitanes carry a contemporary connotation consistent with the existence of churches at the seven named cities in the province of Asia.

The martyr Antipas appears in the canon only in Revelation 2:13. Described as a faithful witness, legend has it "that Antipas was slowly roasted to death in a brass bull during the reign of Domitian."[12] John was exiled to Patmos ca. 96. If Antipas was martyred during the reign of Domitian ca. 92, the martyrdom would have been quite current at the time of John's vision.

The Nicolaitanes appear in both the first and third letters. In discussing the first letter, Steiner says of them that they are "those who express life merely in a material sense." He immediately follows that with the somewhat ambiguous sentence, "In the time referred to in this letter there was a sect called the Nicolaitanes, who considered the external fleshly sensual life as the only valuable thing for man."[13] The question is, does "the time referred to" point to the time of John's vision and the church at Pergamum, or does it refer to the earliest Post-Atlantean Age? It has to refer to the period of the church at Pergamum. During the first Cultural Age the emphasis was not on the material world or "the external fleshly sensual life," which both those of that earlier Age as well as the "one who holds the seven stars" hate. In the third letter there is a clear sequence to

---

12 ABD, vol. 1, 272; see also www.antipas.net/whois.htm and www.en .wikipedia.org/wiki/Antipas_of_Pergamum which gives the date ca. 92.

13 *ASJ*, 68.

the teaching of Balaam and the Nicolaitanes.[14] One who reads the account of Balaam in Numbers 22–24 might find it hard to comprehend how it is that Balaam represented such an immoral influence as the third letter clearly asserts. Jo Ann Hackett opens her account of Balaam with the statement, "Our sources for the story of Balaam are varied and often conflicting." The prevailing sources, however, connected the apostasy of the Israelites with the Midianites at Peor, as described in Numbers 25, to the sorcery of Balaam.[15]

Balaam was a personality of the Chaldo-Egyptian Cultural Age. We can hardly pass the significance of Lazarus/John's association of Balaam with that Age, for it is in Numbers 25 when Phinehas appears and eradicates the immoral element from Israel. We note the significance of the Individuality that appeared in Phinehas; the chain of significant incarnations of this Individuality comprises Adam, Phinehas, Elijah, and John the Baptist (followed by Raphael and Novalis).[16] We know from Steiner's deathbed pronouncement that upon the raising of Lazarus the soul/spirit of Elijah penetrated the being of Lazarus down through the consciousness soul.

Manna first appears in Exodus 16 and Numbers 11, as food from heaven. Clearly this is during the wandering in the wilderness during the Chaldo-Egyptian Age. We know from our studies that manna is the purified astral body.[17] Steiner says of it, "The good in this culture consists in the possibility for man to begin purifying and transforming his astral body. This is called the 'hidden manna.'"[18]

Even more significant is the "white stone, with a new name written on the stone which no one knows except him who receives it" (2:17). The "white stone" implies the purified astral body, or manna, and can be related to the first of the three stages of the

---

14 Rev 2:14–15.

15 Jo Ann Hackett, "Balaam," *ABD*, vol. 1, 569–572. See also Christopher C. Rowland, "Revelation," NIB, vol. 12, 578–579.

16 *BB*, 543. In lecture 8 of his cycle on the Gospel of St. Mark (Basel, September 22, 1912), Steiner says, "Esoteric teaching and occult research reveal that the same soul lives in the body of Phinehas that was later present in Elijah.... In Aaron's grandson we have one soul that is of concern to us, the soul that lives in Phinehas. The same soul appears again in Elijah-Naboth and then in John the Baptist." (Steiner, *The Gospel of St. Mark*, AP (1986), 153)

17 *BB*, chart **I-9**.

18 Rev 2:17; *ASJ*, 70.

giving of the law to Moses on Mount Sinai.[19] Still more significant is the first reference to the name "which no one knows except him who receives it." This is the first biblical appearance of the "I Am," and it is to Moses on the mountain, again, clearly in the Chaldo-Egyptian Age.[20]

Most of Steiner's comments on this Age in *ASJ* have to do with the increasing application of the Chaldean astronomers and the Egyptian geographers to their earthly existence, when "man comes still nearer to the external sensible reality," as compared with the two earlier Cultural Ages.[21]

Greco-Roman (747 BCE–1414 CE)

Steiner begins his description of this age by reference to the "prophetic art of the Egyptians" through which "they divided the next age into seven parts" prescribing their contents.[22] He speaks of "the origin of the ancient Roman civilization" emerging from the journey of Aeneas, from "Troy, a place belonging to the third age, coming at length to Alba Longa" (Italy) and a "city of a priestly culture, from which the culture of Rome was to proceed." He refers to the "reigns of the seven Roman kings [which] were outlined beforehand" by the Egyptian priests. Not the time to go into details regarding the seven kings, he says that they correspond "exactly to the consecutive cultural ages according to the seven principles which present themselves in such different domains." From the standpoint of history, the records of which were destroyed, the seven kings have become legendary; their time span, however, started with Romulus in 753 and ended with Lucius Tarquinius Superbus in 510 BCE, a total of 243 years for an average reign of 34.7 years.[23]

Our present postulate is that the Greco-Roman Age began in 747 BCE. This relates positively to the Romulus reign and the salient vision of Isaiah "in the year that King Uzziah died" (6:1). Whether Uzziah's death was in 742 BCE or some six years later, as some contend, the

---

19   See *BB*, item 2(a) on page x (Preface to the Revised Edition).

20   Exod 3:14.

21   *ASJ* 61–63, 69–70.

22   *ASJ*, 63.

23   See "King of Rome," http://en.wikipedia.org/wiki/King_of_Rome.

difference is not significant for our purposes.[24] The historical documentation of the year 747 BCE as the beginning of the Age is cited in *TSRYR* (198).

As we approach the most meaningful Greco-Roman Cultural Age, the words of Steiner are helpfully descriptive of the situation:

> So in the third age man has been able gradually to permeate *maya* with the human spirit. This was completed in the fourth cultural age, the Greco-Latin, when in wonderful works of art man produced a perfect image of himself in the outer material world, and portrayed in dramas...pictures of human fate. Observe in contrast how in the Egyptian culture men still sought the will of the gods. The conquest of matter such as we see in the Greek age signifies another stage, in which man made a step further in love of material existence; and finally in the Roman age he completely stepped out upon the physical plane. One who understands this knows also that in this we must recognize the full appearance of the principle of personality. Hence in Rome first appears what we call the conception of justice where for the first time man appears before us as a citizen. Only a confused science is able to trace jurisprudence back to all sorts of previous ages. What was previously understood as justice was something quite different.... It is absurd in our age to try to trace back the ideas of law to Hammurabi and so on.[25] True law and the idea of man as a citizen was first brought to recognition in Rome. In Greece the citizen was still a member of the city-state. It was in Rome that the individual first became a citizen.... What we now call a testament or will did not exist in this sense before Roman times. A will or testament in its present meaning first originated at that time, because only then did the separate human being

---

24 At least twice before I have assigned 742 BCE as the year of King Uzziah's death; *DQWIM*, 184n65 and *TSRYR*, 86. Scholars are not all agreed. 742 BCE is recognized as the year Uzziah's reign ended. The year 742 BCE seems to be suggested as the year of his death by R. B. Y. Scott in 5 *Interpreter's Bible*, 161, but as "uncertain " and only "approximate" by G. G. D. Kilpatrick at 207 of the same volume. Joseph Blenkinsopp prefers a date no earlier that 736 BCE; *Isaiah 1–39, AB* vol. 19, 224 (2000); while Brevard S. Childs, in his commentary on Isaiah, Louisville, Westminster John Knox Press (2001), 54, recognizes divergent views as between 742 and 736 BCE.

25 In my first year of law school, the one-hour course on the history of Jurisprudence did just that, ascribing origins to the Code of Hammurabi.

become determinative in his egoistic will, so as to impose his will upon his successors.... Thus...man stepped out upon the physical plane.[26]

The "hidden manna" (astral body) from the third age had to be made possible in the fourth age. "Man...has created his image even in the media of external culture. The period has now come when the deity himself becomes man, becomes flesh, becomes person...this age had to receive an impulse through the divine appearing in human form. Man, who had descended, could only be saved through God himself appearing as a man. The 'I Am,' or the 'I,' in the astral body had to receive the impulse of Christ Jesus. What earlier only existed as a germ, the 'I,' or the 'I Am,' was to appear in history in the outer world.... And all the churches shall know the 'I Am,' which searcheth the reins and hearts (Revelation 2:23). Stress is here laid upon the 'I Am.'"[27]

And then we come to Revelation 2:26–28, "He who conquers and who keeps my works until the end.... I will give him the *morning star*" (emphasis added).

Which planet is the morning (and evening) star? Clearly, in astronomy, it is Venus. In "The Innermost Planets as Bright Stars" we read:

Venus and Mercury, the innermost planets in the solar system, always appear only a small distance away from the Sun in the sky.

Mercury is so small and so close to the Sun (always within 28 degrees) that it is difficult to see from Earth, since it is usually lost in the Sun's glare. The innermost planet can be seen with the naked eye only at twilight, very low in the sky, near the horizon.

From Earth, Venus can appear up to 47 degrees away from the Sun. During these times, when it rises or sets a few hours before or after the Sun, it can be seen just before sunrise or just after sunset as a bright morning or evening star. At these times, Venus is up to 15 times brighter than the brightest star, Sirius, and can even cast shadows.[28]

---

26 *ASJ*, 63–64.

27 *ASJ*, 70–71.

28 "Windows to the Universe" (see www.windows2universe.org/venus /morning_star.html.

Even though in astronomical reality our "morning star" is Venus, in esotericism, more fully discussed below, it is called Mercury. From ancient times the names of the days of our week are taken from bodies in our solar system in the following order, Saturn, Sun, Moon, Mars, Mercury, Jupiter and Venus.[29] These also constitute the order of our Conditions of Consciousness in the grand scheme, except that in order to have seven, where Vulcan is the octave of Saturn, the Earth Condition of Consciousness is divided into two halves, the first being called Mars and the second, brought about by the Incarnation of Christ, is called Mercury. Steiner suggests that John's calling it the "morning star," at the time when he wrote, would have been to "mask against those who would only have misused" spiritual knowledge.[30] It was the Ptolemaic system, which was "geocentric," as distinguished from our present "heliocentric," that "gave the order of spheres from Earth outward" as follows: Moon-Mercury-Venus-Sun-Mars-Jupiter-Saturn.[31] The Ptolemaic system dominated astronomy for 1,500 years (and still has some limited applications; the geocentric system was also known to the Greeks); Ptolemy was a second century astronomer, thus somewhat following the time of John's vision.

In the soul's journey between lives, it expands outward from Earth through Lower devachan (which follows the Moon Sphere) passing first through the Venus Sphere, but it is called the Mercury Sphere based upon the reversal.[32]

Emerging from all this confusion is the reality that the "giving" of "the morning star" was the gift of Christ that enabled the reversal of the downward path and the beginning of the upward path of evolution.

European (1414–3574 CE)

It is presently the summer of 2014. We are exactly 600 years into this Fifth Cultural Age of the Post-Atlantean Epoch. Another 1,516 years have yet to unfold before we move into the sixth such age, the

---

29   See *BB*, 558; chart **I-8**. See also Steiner's lecture in Munich on May 21, 1907, in *Rosicrucianism Renewed*, SB (2007), CW 284, at 81.

30   *ASJ*, 71.

31   "Geocentric model" (see www.en.wikipedia.org/wiki/Geocentric_model (note 15).

32   For the course of the soul between lives see *BB*, chart **I-33**, at 605.

Russian–Slavonic, the Age John's vision reveals as Philadelphia. The assessment of John's vision for our Age is austere and sobering. What one sees of it thus far, particularly in its most recent phenomena, suggests that there is not any widespread recognition of our plight, nor any prevailing momentum revealing the moral strength to deal responsibly with the *morning star's* message for us in our Age. In his concluding remarks on our Age, Steiner says:

> If there is to be a spiritual movement and if it is to agree with the Revelation of John, it must fulfil what the speaker, this great inspirer, demands of this age. What does he demand and who is he? Can we know him? Let us try.
>
> [The message comes from "him who has the seven spirits of God and the seven stars" (3:1a). The seven "spirits of God" are the guides of the seven Conditions of Consciousness, Saturn through its octave Vulcan. The "seven stars" are those seven Conditions, which relate to the sevenfold nature of the human being, the three bodies and their three spiritually attained counterparts, with the Ego in the midst of the seven.]
>
> If we understand the call of the spirit who has these seven stars and the seven Spirits of God, the sevenfold nature of man[,] in his hand, then we shall be practicing Anthroposophy in the sense of the writer of the Apocalypse. To practice Anthroposophy is to know that the writer is here referring to the fifth age of man's evolution in the Post-Atlantean epoch, it is to know that in our age, when man has descended most deeply into matter, we are again to ascend to spiritual life by following the great individuality who gives for our guidance the seven Spirits of God and the seven stars, so that we may rightly follow our path.[33]

Before we react to John's assessment of us, we need to reflect on who it is that sees, or gives, this picture of us. The first chapter of this book indicated that it was the reincarnated Lazarus/John who, as Christian Rosenkreutz, worked at the threshold of our Age, but submerged from our consciousness only to resurface through Steiner in what he gave us as Anthroposophy.

Steiner's description of the phenomena of our Age came first. Speaking of it, he says:

---

33   *ASJ*, 72–73.

We are now living in an age when man is the slave of outer conditions, of his milieu. In Greece the mind was employed to spiritualize matter; we see spiritualized matter in the form of an Apollo or a figure of Zeus, in the dramas of a Sophocles, and so on; there man has emerged as far as to the physical plane but has not yet descended below the level of man. Even in Rome this was still the case. The deep descent below the sphere of the human has only now come about. In our age the mind has become the slave of matter. An enormous amount of mental energy has been used in our age to penetrate the natural forces in the outer world for the purpose of making this outer world as comfortable a place as possible for man....

Think of all the conveniences of civilization man has achieved up to the present day! What an enormous amount of spiritual energy was expended to invent and build the steam engine, to think out the railway, the telegraph, the telephone, and so on! Enormous forces of spiritual life had to be used to invent and construct these purely material conveniences of civilization—and to what end are they used? Does it make any essential difference to the spiritual life, whether in an ancient civilization a man crushed his grain between two stones, for which naturally very little mental power was needed, or whether today we are able to telegraph to America and obtain thence great quantities of grain that we grind into flour by means of ingeniously constructed mills? The whole apparatus is set into motion simply for the stomach. Try to realize what an enormous amount of spiritual life-force is put into purely material culture. Spiritual culture has not yet been advanced very much by these external means.... If you were to make a statistical comparison between what is used for material culture and what benefits spiritual life, you would understand that the spirit has plunged below the human level and has become the slave of material life.

Thus we have a decidedly descending path of culture up to our age..., and it would descend ever more and more deeply. For this reason, mankind must be preserved by a new impulse from slipping completely into matter. The being of man has never before descended so deeply into matter.[34]

This lecture was given 106 years ago, in June, 1908. The descent into matter seems to have accelerated since then at a geometric rate.

---

34 *ASJ*, 64–66.

Change was accelerating, but in what direction? It is important to realize that Steiner elsewhere made it clear that mastery of the material world was essential, but only so that it could all be spiritualized. In short, our working with matter had to change direction, from the enhancement of economic wealth and personal comfort to the accomplishment of the perfection of the soul and spiritualization of the lower aspects of our sevenfold human structure. The Sermon on the Mount has been considered an idealistic and basically unattainable goal by any practical human being, yet it stands there as a guide to the upward path. It is sobering to contemplate that the end of our Fifth Post-Atlantean Epoch will come about, as we shall see as we journey further into Revelation, by what Steiner calls "the War of All against All." Lest this is too draconian to ponder, consider the Little Apocalypse remark of Jesus, "When you hear of wars and rumors of wars, do not be alarmed; this must take place, but the end is not yet."[35] On this, see the grand scheme in chapter 2.

Anthroposophy is still only a struggling spiritual light in our day. The vast horde of humanity still think, individually, that they need not be concerned about anything yet so far away. What Anthroposophy, and the Bible in anthroposophical insight, tells us is that each of us has made, is making, and will continue to make, on earth, our way toward and through this period of War, and for most, the consequences, in an earthly sense, will not be pretty, though in a spiritual sense necessary.[36]

But let us approach the most momentous aspect of this message for our Age. Our "works" are known (3:1). We "have the name of being alive, [but we] are dead." Aside from what exists in much of the rest of the world, America, particularly portions of it, have churches on every corner with congregations that come assuming that they are spiritually "alive." We have "the name of being alive," but we are told that is not the case. We received "the morning star," the Incarnation, crucifixion, and Resurrection of Christ about the same distance into the Age that preceded us as we are into our Age. The Age of Aries, the Lamb of God, ended and ours, the Age Pisces, the "two fish," the Fifth Age, that of the "five loaves" and the "two fish," is fully

---

35   Mark 13:7; see also Matt 24:6.
36   See *SLJ*.

engaged.[37] Lacking perfection we are told to "remember what [we] received," and that "If [we] will not awake, I will come like a thief, and you will not know at what hour I will come upon you."

This last has to be the most critical part of the message to us. What does it signify? That the second coming of Christ will begin, and, more importantly, has begun, without our being aware of it. It has "come like a thief, and [we have] not know[n]" when it has occurred, or even that it has occurred. Its occurrence was one aspect of perhaps the greatest polarity in human existence. The second coming was contemporaneous with the immense evil in the ascent of Naziism in the 1930s. Both occurred during that decade, probably centered on the year 1933.

Steiner's most important series of lectures dealing with the second coming took place in eight lectures in seven different cities (sequentially, in Karlsruhe, Heidelberg, Cologne, Stuttgart [2], Munich, Palermo, and Hanover) between January 25 and May 10, 1910. This series, along with other lectures, was published by SteinerBooks in 1983 as the first portion of a book entitled *The Reappearance of Christ in the Etheric*.[38] The following excerpt is from the first lecture:

[Speaking of the Incarnation of Christ] Indeed, it is true, not everyone realized that something of the utmost importance had taken place, an event which, striking into the unearthly darkness as divine light, was capable of carrying human beings over Kali Yuga![39] The possibility for further evolution was given to humanity through the fact that there were certain souls who comprehended that moment in time, who knew that Christ had walked upon the earth.

If you were to imagine yourselves for a moment in that period, you could then easily say, "Yes, it was quite possible to live at that time and yet know nothing of the appearance of Christ Jesus on the physical plane! It was possible to dwell on earth without taking this most significant event into one's consciousness." Might it not then also be possible today that something of

---

37 John 6:9.

38 Steiner, *The Reappearance of Christ in the Etheric*, AP (1983), 1–115, at 14–16, to appear in CW 118. The later lectures in the same volume will appear in CW 130 and 178.

39 That is, "over the remainder of the 5,000-year "Dark Age," known as the Kali Yuga, that would end in 1899.

infinite importance is taking place and that human beings are not taking it into their consciousness? Could it not be that something tremendously important is taking place in the world, taking place right now, of which our own contemporaries have no presentiment? This is indeed so. Something highly important is taking place that is perceptible, however, only to spiritual vision. There is much talk about periods of transition. We are indeed living in one, and it is a momentous one. What is important is that we are living just at the time when the Dark Age has run its course and a new epoch is just beginning, in which human beings will slowly and gradually develop new faculties and in which human souls will gradually undergo a change.

It is hardly to be wondered at that most human beings are in no way aware of this, considering that most human beings also failed to notice the occurrence of the Christ event at the beginning of our era. Kali Yuga came to an end in the year 1899; now we must adapt ourselves to a new age. What is beginning at this time will slowly prepare humanity for new soul faculties.

The first signs of these new soul faculties will begin to appear relatively soon now in isolated souls. They will become more clear in the middle of the fourth decade of this century, sometime between 1930 and 1940. The years 1933, 1935, and 1937 will be especially significant. Faculties that now are quite unusual for human beings will then manifest themselves as natural abilities. At this time great changes will take place, and Biblical prophecies will be fulfilled. Everything will be transformed for the souls who are sojourning on earth and also for those who are no longer within the physical body. Regardless of where they are, souls are encountering entirely new faculties. Everything is changing, but the most significant event of our time is a deep, decisive transformation in the soul faculties of man.[40]

In a lecture in Dusseldorf in the midst of the above eightfold series, Steiner said:

---

40   These words were spoken in Karlsruhe on January 25, 1910. Robert Powell writes that, "In Stockholm, on the evening of January 12, 1910, he had proclaimed for the first time the imminent return to the Earth's aura of the Risen One in etheric form" (*Hermetic Astrology II*, which he published in English in Kinsau, West Germany in 1989). Insofar as I can ascertain, this lecture has never been published in English. Assuming that it is a part of the Steiner Archive, perhaps it will appear in CW 118.

In the course of 2,500 years a sufficiently large number of human beings will develop etheric sight. This is the beginning of the clairvoyance that will be an added faculty of the Ego. Those who understand it will be able to convince themselves of the truth of the Christ Event exactly as Paul became convinced of it at Damascus. When men have developed etheric sight they will be able to behold Christ in an etheric body. This is Christ's new descent to the men of Earth.[41]

I deal far more extensively with all of this in my essay entitled "Second Coming" first published in 1997.[42]

As we dwell in the depths of materiality, we are working our way more and more deeply into it. Great wealth accumulates in some hands, while poverty is the lot of so many others. Our courts have extended the sacred domain of human personality to the soulless corporation. Surely we must contemplate that spiritually, save for those who have not "soiled their garments" and are "worthy" (3:4), we are "on the point of death" with no inkling of the unfolding of the second coming. The spiritual callousness, the darkness, of materiality has us in its grip. But let us "awake, and strengthen what remains and is on the point of death." May we commence to use matter in service of the spirit rather that exploiting it for the enhancement of earthly comfort and power. May we yearn for the development of these spiritual faculties that will create the vision to behold the second coming of Christ as it is now unfolding. John's vision of our destiny in this Age is indeed sobering.

Preface to What Follows our Current Cultural Age

For the last two, of the seven, letters to the churches, we deal with Cultural Ages that, in evolutionary terminology, are in the "near-distant" future, meaning many hundreds and, for the second, many thousands of years away as yet. What those letters, including ours in Sardis, say to us should, however, alert us to the situation we, individually and collectively, face if we do not soon reverse the ever-deeper descent into materiality that grips us and our Age.

---

41 Steiner, *The Sermon on the Mount and the Return of Christ*, unpublished English typescript, translated by D. S. Osmond from notes (in German) of Steiner's lecture. This lecture in Dusseldorf on February 20, 1910 is also to be included in the publication of CW 118.

42 *BB*, 213–243.

In lecture 3 Steiner dealt with the letters to the churches.[43] He devotes a brief single paragraph near the end of this lecture to each of the last two, Philadelphia and Laodicea.[44] Right at the first he speaks of what will bring the Post-Atlantean Evolutionary Epoch, which started with the Atlantean Flood, to a close at the end of the seventh, the Laodicean Age, "Our epoch will come to an end through what we call the War of All against All, by frightful, devastating moral entanglements."[45]

Before we look at these two paragraphs that cover, respectively, the Cultural Ages of Philadelphia and Laodicea, let us consider the fractal-like pattern of evolution that has existed in our past and how it will continue to play out in the future, as is affirmed by the Apocalypse. Even though lecture 4 is focused upon the seven seals, in it Steiner prepares his hearers by a review of how we and our lower kingdoms have evolved from the beginning. It is well for us, even now, to consider the pattern. I have elsewhere described the descending part of our long journey as one of fission and the ascending part as one of fusion. But the fusion does not happen uniformly to all human souls and spirits, and we must recognize that there is the possibility of ultimate failure—though it is not the intent of our Father and the Christ that any fail as the parable of the ninety and nine seems to suggest.[46]

The pattern in the descent was established in all three Conditions of Consciousness that preceded our Earth Condition. All four of our "kingdoms," mineral, plant, animal, and human, started out on Ancient Saturn in a condition of equality. Each of the lower three kingdoms failed in one or more of the three preceding Conditions of Consciousness to attain the goal of that Condition and thus remained behind. What on Earth is mineral failed in all three prior Conditions; what is plant failed in two; and what is animal failed in one. Each lower kingdom serves human needs in our Mineral-Physical Condition, and each lower kingdom is present in each of us. Paul envisioned the time when all three lower kingdoms would be redeemed through the efforts of the

---

43   *ASJ*, 56–74.

44   *ASJ*, 73–74.

45   *ASJ*, 57.

46   Matt 18:12–13; Luke 15:4–7).

redeemed in the human kingdom.[47] But the redemption of these lower kingdoms only occurs progressively in the Jupiter, Venus, and Vulcan Conditions of Consciousness. It is only the first of these that appears at the end of Revelation.

The descent has continued during our Earth Condition. The entry of the Christ into the Earth assured the *possibility* of our reascent, but humanity has continued even yet to embed itself in ever-greater materiality with its spiritual decline into Ahriman's grasp. It is hard for most to realize how enslaved we are, or that, eventually, we must surrender not only our material wealth but even our bodies of matter, for by the end of the Evolutionary Epochs those who would move on to the Jupiter Condition must have been able to relinquish both their physical and etheric (life) bodies and live in the astral realm.

In lecture four, Steiner carries the descent on into the period of Earth evolution, noting that those elements that descended into matter left the main stream of evolution and became fixed in bodies that would proceed to degenerate from their more pristine original condition. Only those that remained to "come last" would be "first" and descend into bodies that would accommodate an indwelling Ego (I Am) capable of progressing, or regressing, spiritually. It is the challenge of our Fifth Cultural Age, to "Awake," recognizing that we are "on the point of death," and that there are only "a few names" among us "who have not soiled [our] garments." Separations will continue, and those who fail to recognize and sacrificially endeavor to overcome our present enslavement in matter will remain behind when many of the dire things ahead of us in John's Apocalypse will create much hardship. Those falling behind will be separated from the more advanced souls. They will still have opportunity, but with ever greater hardship to overcome.

It seems well to move the earlier part of what Steiner said in lecture 4 regarding the cycle of the seven seals (the Sixth Evolutionary Epoch) into our discussion of where we are today, in the fifth, or European, Cultural Age of the Fifth Evolutionary (Post-Atlantean) Epoch. It behooves us, in understanding our situation, to bring forward to our time a realization of what the consequences of our lives in our Age are for the Ages in front of us. The following seems pertinent:

---

47   Eph 1:9–10; Rom 8:19–23.

Our cycle [Post-Atlantean Evolutionary Epoch], which embraces seven ages, was preceded by the Atlantean cycle [Epoch], during which were developed the races whose echoes still exist. When the seventh age of our present cycle is at an end, it will be followed by another cycle again consisting of seven parts. The present cycle is preparing indirectly for the next one, so that we may say our age of culture will gradually pass over into one of brotherly love, when a comparatively small part of mankind will have understood the spiritual life and will have prepared the spirit and attitude of brotherly love (literally, in Greek, Philadelphia). That culture will then again divide off a smaller portion of human beings who will survive the event that will have such a destructive effect upon our cycle, namely the War of All against All. In this universal destructive element there will be everywhere individuals who lift themselves above the rest of warring humanity, individuals who have understood the spiritual life and who will form the foundation for a new and different epoch, the epoch of the sixth period.

Something similar also took place during the transition from the fourth epoch to ours. When one who with spiritual vision can review the course of time has passed back through the [past Cultural Ages], he comes into the Atlantean epoch. We need not now consider it in detail but we must at least understand how this Atlantean civilization passed over into our own. There, too, the greater part of the Atlantean population was not sufficiently mature to develop further[;] it was incapable of coming over into our times. A smaller part, living in a region near to present-day Ireland, developed to the highest flowering of the civilization of Atlantis and then journeyed toward the East.... eventually settl[ing] down as a very small tribe of chosen individuals in Central Asia. From this point, the colonists migrated to the various regions of culture mentioned, to ancient India, to Persia, Egypt, Greece, etc.

You might now be inclined to say: Is it not an extremely bitter thought that whole bodies of peoples remain immature and unable to develop their capacities; that only a small group becomes capable of providing the germ for the next culture?— This thought will no longer disquiet you if you distinguish between race-development and soul-development, for no soul is condemned to remain in one particular race. The race may fall behind; the community of people may remain backward, but the souls progress beyond the individual races. If we wish to form

a true conception of this we must say that all the souls now living in bodies in civilized countries were formerly incarnated in
Atlantean bodies. A few developed there in the requisite manner,
and did not remain in Atlantean bodies. As they had developed
further they could become the souls of the bodies that had also
progressed further. Only the souls that as souls had remained
backward had to take bodies which as bodies had remained at a
lower stage. If all the souls had progressed, the backward races
would either have decreased very much in population, or the bodies would have been occupied by newly incoming souls at a low
stage of development. For there are always souls that can inhabit
backward bodies. No soul is bound to a backward body if it does
not bind itself to it. . . .

Let us imagine race following race, civilization following
civilization. The soul going through its Earth mission in the right
way is incarnated in a certain race; it strives within this race,
and acquires the capacities of this race in order next time to be
incarnated in a higher one. Only the souls that sink down into the
race and do not work their way out of the physical materiality are
held back in the race by their own weight, as one might say. They
appear a second time in the same race and possibly a third time in
bodies in similarly formed races. Such souls hold back the bodies
of the race.[48]

This last paragraph illustrates the principle that failure to progress
in a soul development that is appropriate for the Age means a dividing
off from those that do progress upward spiritually speaking. In other
words, those in our age who enjoy their satisfactions with enslavement to the material aspects of life will be left behind in the evolution
applicable to our time. When they reincarnate, it will be at a level
retarded from that where it should have been, and they will be thus
separated off, as is described by Steiner and the Apocalypse itself. But
there is one major problem with Steiner's usage of the term *race* if, as
assumed, he is talking in this last paragraph about our Post-Atlantean
Epoch; at least it is inappropriate to recent Cultural Ages. It is also
directly in conflict with what he has given us in other lectures contemporaneous with this one.

For instance, on June 1, 1908, in Berlin, he said:

---

48   *ASJ*, lect. 4, 76–78.

We stand today at a transitional point; race will gradually disappear entirely and something else will take its place. Those who will again grasp spiritual truth as it has been described will be led together of their own free will...uniting in groups with those of similar ideas while retaining their complete freedom and individuality.[49]

Again, on August 16, 1908, in Stuttgart:

When people speak of races today they do so in a way that is no longer quite correct....

Thus everything that exists today in connection with the [different] races are relics of the differentiation that took place in Atlantean times. We can still speak of races but only in the sense that the real concept of races is losing its validity. But what new concept will replace that of race?

Mankind will be differentiated in the future even more than in the past; it will divide itself into certain categories but these categories will not be externally imposed. Out of their own inner spiritual insight [men] will realize that they must work together for the whole body social. There will be categories and classes, but...divided according to differences in intellect and morality.[50]

In an earlier book published in 1904 he said, "That which deserves to be called 'race' also *comes into being* and *perishes*. One should only use the expression 'race' for a certain span in the development of mankind. Before and after this, there are evolutionary forms which are something totally different from 'races.'"[51]

Then in his second lecture on June 4, 1907 in Munich: "There is...active in the human being an ancient feminine principle as group-soul and a new masculine principle as individualizing element. It will come about that all connections of race and family stock will cease to exist, men will become more and more different from one another, interconnection will no longer depend on the

---

49   Steiner, *The Influence of Spiritual Beings Upon Man*, AP (1961), lect. 9; 155, to appear in CW 102.

50   Steiner, *Universe Earth and Man*, RSP (1987), lect. 11; 158–159, to appear in CW 105.

51   Steiner, *Cosmic Memory*, New York, Harper & Row (1981), chap. 17, 222, to appear in CW 11 under the title *From the Akasha Chronicle*.

common blood, but on what binds soul to soul. That is the course of human evolution."[52]

Speaking near the end of his life to anthroposophists in Dornach, Steiner said, "Human beings who in the present incarnation receive the [Archanglic] Michael impulses through Anthroposophy, are thereby preparing their whole being in such a way that these Michael impulses enter even into the forces that are otherwise determined merely by the connections of race or nation.... [One] who stand[s] with full intensity within the Anthroposophical Movement... [must] know that... as [an] anthroposophist his karma will be harder to experience than it is for other men. And if [he tries] to pass this harder experience by... it will surely take vengeance on [him] in one direction or another. We must be anthroposophists in our experience of karma too... able to observe our own experience of karma with constant wide-awake attention. If we do not, then our comfortable, easy-going experiencing of our karma—or rather our desire to experience it so—will find expression and take vengeance in physical illnesses, physical accidents and the like."[53]

From these various expressions, we must gather that our spiritual growth, stagnation, or slippage will relate to the level or group in which we find ourselves in the incarnation in question. If we hear the progressive content of John's vision, the proportion must be substantial of those who fail to progress, and thus, in effect, regress. The message to the church at Sardis closes with the admonition, found in each of the seven letters, "He who has an ear, let him hear what the Spirit says to the churches" (3:6). This warning is, in this instance, for each of us in our present Cultural Age.

In Steiner's third lecture of the *ASJ* cycle in Nuremberg, he gave only broad-brush treatment to the sixth and seventh cultural ages. We cannot be satisfied with just that. Nor, indeed, was he, for in lectures seven and eight he speaks of things that treat of the sweep through the last three Cultural Ages, that of our present fifth through the sixth and the seventh that concludes with the fearsome War of All against All.

---

52 Steiner, *Theosophy of the Rosicrucian*, 2nd ed., RSP (1966), lect. 12; 130, to appear in CW 99.

53 Steiner, *Karmic Relationships*, vol. 3, 2nd ed., RSP (1977), lect. 9, August 3, 1924, 140–141, to appear in CW 237.

Threads are woven together from our present time through the last two Ages till the end of our Post-Atlantean Evolutionary Epoch. We have already borrowed, for the present "preface," from his fourth lecture that is dedicated to the seven seals and their opening in the Sixth Evolutionary Epoch. Let us now consider some of his further elaboration in the seventh and eighth lectures that is appropriate for this "preface."

In our descent in the higher worlds, those who are now human beings withstood the various animal passions as the latter descended to earth as the various genera and species of animals, all having come from us who waited till we could descend into bodies of matter that could stand fully upright and nurture a soul and spirit capable of communication with higher worlds, while adapting to the conditions to be mastered, over the ages, in spiritualizing matter. But all the animal phases that we passed through are still in us to be purified. They are all in our astral body awaiting purification by the Christ element in each of us. Steiner continues:

> Imagine [that] man [is] not fertilized by the Christ power; he springs back into the animal form. Thus it will happen to those who fall back. They will afterward form a world beneath the present world, so to speak, a world of the abyss, where man will again have assumed animal shape.[54]

Thus we learn to understand the direction evolution will indeed take. What is now being prepared will come out again bit by bit in the future, just as what was laid down in the Atlantean epoch has come out bit by bit in our epoch. I have said that in the last third of the Atlantean epoch a small colony was formed from which our cultures have been derived, and from which the two following ones still to come will also originate. It will be somewhat different in the next epoch, which will succeed all these cultures. There will not be a colony limited to one place, but from the general body of mankind will everywhere be recruited those who are mature enough to form the good, the noble, the beautiful side of the next civilization, after the War of All against All. This again is a step forward compared

---

54 Note the marking of those who assume an animal shape; see Rev 14:9,11; 16:2; 19:20, and 20:4; though the location of these verses in Revelation seems to apply to Epochs after the War of All against All. Nevertheless, the foundation for them is being built during our Post-Atlantean Epoch, especially in our current Cultural Age and the two to follow.

with the earlier Atlantean epoch when the colony developed in one small place, while with us there is the possibility that from all races of the world will be recruited those who really understand the call of the Earth mission, who raise up the living Christ within themselves, who develop the principle of brotherly love over the whole Earth; and indeed in the true sense, not in the sense of the Christian confessions, but in the sense of true esoteric Christianity which can proceed from every culture. Those who understand this Christ-principle will be there in the period following the great War of All against All. After our present purely intellectual culture, which is now developing in the direction of the abyss of intellect...there will come a time when man will be the slave of intelligence by which his personality will be submerged. Today there is only one way of preserving the personality, and that is to spiritualize it. Those who develop the spiritual life will belong to the small band of the sealed from all nations and races that will appear in white garments after the War of All against All.

We are now beginning to comprehend the spiritual world from our immediately present intellectual civilization. It is the aim of true Anthroposophy to comprehend the spiritual world from out of the present intellectual standards and to gather together those who can understand the call to spiritualize the world. These will not form a separate colony but will be gathered from every nation and will gradually pass into the sixth age, that is to say, not yet beyond the great war, but to start with into the sixth age, for necessities still exist which are connected with old race ties. In our epoch, races and cultures are still intermingled. The true idea of race has lost its meaning but it still plays a certain part. It is quite impossible at present for every mission to be carried out equally by every people. Certain nations are predestined to carry out a particular mission.

The nations that today are the vehicles of Western culture were chosen to lead the fifth age to its zenith; they were the nations who were to develop the intellect. Hence wherever this Western culture extends we have predominantly the culture of the intellect, which is still not yet finished. This intelligence will spread still further; people will exercise still more of their spiritual forces in order to satisfy their bodily needs; to slay one another they will employ much greater spiritual forces before the great War of All against All. Many discoveries will be made in order to be able the better to carry on war; an endless amount of intelligence will be exercised in order to satisfy the lower impulses. But in the midst of it something is being prepared, with which certain nations of the East, the Northern part of the East, are gifted. Certain nations are preparing to emerge from a certain dullness and bring in a spiritual impulse with mighty force, an impulse which will be the opposite pole to intelligence. Before the sixth age, represented by the community of Philadelphia, we shall experience something like a mighty marriage of peoples, a marriage between intelligence and intellect and spirituality. At the present time we are only experiencing the dawn of this marriage and no one should mistake what is here said for a song of praise to our age; for one does not sing songs of praise to the sun where there are only the first signs of dawn. But we find remarkable phenomena when we compare East and West when we look into the depths and foundations of the different nations.

Here Steiner dedicates a paragraph to illustrate the point just made. Passing over the first third of the paragraph, he goes on:

In Western Europe, one makes spiritual culture with the intellect; one chisels out certain details and puts them together to form something that is supposed to make the world comprehensible, and the achievements of Western European civilization in this respect will never be surpassed. But if you understand such a book as Tolstoi's *On Life*, you will often find condensed into ten lines what in these Western European libraries it takes thirty volumes to say. Tolstoi says something with elemental force, and in a few lines of his there is the same amount of energy as is assembled in thirty such volumes. Here one must be able to judge what comes forth from the depths of the spirit, what has a spiritual foundation, and what has not. Just as overripe cultures contain something that is drying up and withering, so do rising cultures contain within them fresh life and new energy. Tolstoi is a premature flower of such a culture, one that came far too soon to be fully developed. Hence he has all the faults of an untimely birth. His grotesque and unfounded presentations of many Western European things, all that he brings forward in the way of foolish judgment, show that great personalities have the faults of their virtues and that great cleverness has the folly of its wisdom.

This is only mentioned as a symptom of the future age when the spirituality of the East will unite with the intellectuality of the West. From this union will proceed the age of Philadelphia. All those will participate in this marriage who take into themselves the impulse of Christ Jesus and they will form the great brotherhood which will survive the great war, which will experience enmity and persecution, but will provide the foundation for the good race. After this great war has brought out the animal nature in those who have remained in the old forms, the good race will arise, and this race will carry over into the future what is to be the spiritually elevated culture of that future epoch. We shall also have the experience that in our epoch, between the great Atlantean Flood and the great War of All against All, in the age represented by the community at Philadelphia, a colony is formed, the members of which will not migrate but will be everywhere; so that everywhere there will be some who are working in the sense of the community of Philadelphia, in the sense of the binding together of mankind, in the sense of the Christian principle.

Peering ahead into his eighth lecture in the *ASJ* cycle, we get a broad look from another perspective in the chapter that deals with the seals and trumpets of the last two Evolutionary Epochs. This glimpse actually covers the broad period from our own cultural age through the end of our Epoch with the War of All against All. Steiner tells us:

We have repeatedly said that our seven cultural ages will end with the War of All against All; now this War must really be pictured quite differently from the way we have been accustomed to think of wars. We must bear in mind the foundation, the real cause of this War. Its foundation or cause is the increase of egoism, of self-seeking and selfishness on the part of man. And we have now progressed so far in our considerations that we have seen what a sharp two-edged sword this ego of man is. Those who do not fully realize that this ego is a two-edged sword will scarcely be able to grasp the entire meaning of the evolution of mankind and the world. On the one hand this ego is the cause that man hardens within himself, and that he desires to draw into the service of his ego his inner capacities and all the outer objects at his disposal. This ego is the cause of man's directing all his wishes to the satisfaction of this ego as such. Its striving to draw to itself as its own possession a part of the earth which belongs to all, to drive away all the other egos [sic] from its realm, to fight them, to be at war with them, is one side of the ego. But on the other hand we must not forget that it is the ego that at the same time gives man his independence and his inner freedom, which in the truest sense of the word exalts him. His dignity is founded in this ego, it is the basis of the divine in man.

⊛

Thus the ego will be the pledge for the highest goal of man [i.e., perfect love, described in the omitted paragraph]. But at the same time, if it does not discover love, if it hardens within itself, it is the tempter that plunges him into the abyss. Then it becomes what separates men from one another, what brings them to the great War of All against All, not only to the War of nation against nation (for the conception of a nation will then no longer have the significance it possesses today) but to the War of each single person against every other person in every branch of life; to the war of class against class, of caste against caste, and sex against sex. Thus in every field of life the ego will become the bone of contention; and hence we may say that it can lead on the one hand to the highest and on the other hand to the lowest. For this reason it is a sharp two-edged sword. And he who brought full ego consciousness to man, Christ Jesus, is, as we have seen, symbolically and correctly represented in the Apocalypse as one who has the sharp two-edged sword in his mouth.

We have represented it as a high achievement of man that just through Christianity he has been able to ascend to this concept of the free ego. Christ Jesus brought the ego in all its fullness.... And the fact that this sharp two-edged sword proceeds from the mouth of the Son of Man is also comprehensible, for when man has learnt to utter 'I' with full consciousness it is in his power to rise to the highest or sink to the lowest. The sharp two-edged sword is one of the most important symbols met with in the Apocalypse.[55]

Now if we understand what was said at the close of our last lecture, that after our present cultural age will follow the one that is characterized in the letters to the churches as the community of Philadelphia, we must particularly notice that from the sixth age will be taken those human souls who have to pass over into the following epoch. For, after the War of All against All... there will be expressed in man's features all that is in our age being prepared in men's souls. The so-called seventh age will be of very little importance. We are now living in the fifth age of culture; then follows the

---

55   See Rev 1:16; 2:12,16; 19:15,21; see also Isa 49:2a and Heb 4:12.

sixth, from which will proceed a number of people full of understanding for the spiritual world, filled with the spirit of brotherly
love, which results from spiritual knowledge. The ripest fruit of our
present culture will appear in the sixth age. And what will follow
will be what is lukewarm, neither warm nor cold; the seventh age is
something like an overripe fruit, which will outlast the War of All
against All, but contain no principle of progress.

After a three-paragraph review of the Atlantean Epoch and its
most advanced race which carried the fruits of the Epoch over into the
Post-Atlantean Epoch, he continues.

Just as it happened at that time with the fifth [Atlantean] race, that
it provided men who were capable of development and with the
sixth and seventh, they experienced a descent, so will it also be in
our epoch. We are now looking with great longing toward the sixth
cultural age, to what must be described as developing out of the
spiritual marriage between the West and East. The sixth cultural
age will be the foundation for the new cultures that will arise after
the great War of All against All; just as our cultures arose after
the Atlantean epoch. On the other hand, the seventh age of culture will be characterized by the lukewarm. This seventh age will
continue into the new epoch, just as the sixth and seventh races of
the Atlantean epoch continued into our epoch as races hardened
and stiffening. After the War of All against All, there will be two
streams in mankind: on the one hand the stream of Philadelphia
will survive with the principle of progress, of inner freedom of
brotherly love, a small band drawn from every tribe and nation;
and on the other hand the great mass of all those who will be lukewarm, the remains of those who are now becoming lukewarm, the
stream of Laodicea. After the great War of All against All, gradually the evil stream will be led over to good by the good race, by
the good stream. This will be one of the principle tasks after the
great War of All against All; to rescue what can be rescued from
those who after the great War will only have the impulse to fight
one another and allow the ego to express itself in the most external egoism. Such things are always provided for in advance in the
spiritual guidance of mankind.

Do not consider it unduly severe in the plan of creation, as
something which should be disputed, that mankind will be

divided into those who will stand on the right and those who will stand on the left; consider it rather as something that is wise in the highest degree in the plan of creation. Consider that through the evil separating from the good, the good will receive its greatest strengthening. For after the great War of All against All, the good will have to make every possible effort to rescue the evil during the period in which this will still be possible. This will not merely be a work of education such as exists today, but occult forces will cooperate. For in this next great epoch men will understand how to set occult forces in motion. The good will have the task of working upon their brothers of the evil movement. Everything is prepared beforehand in the hidden occult movements, but the deepest of all occult cosmic currents is the least understood. The movement which is preparing for this says the following to its pupils: Men speak of good and evil, but they do not know that it is necessary in the great plan that evil, too, should come to a peak, in order that those who have to overcome it should, in the very overcoming of evil, so use their force that a still greater good results from it.—The most capable must be chosen and prepared to live beyond the period of the great War of All against All when men will confront those who bear in their countenances the sign of evil; they must be so prepared that as much good force as possible will flow into mankind. It will still be possible for those bodies that are to a certain extent soft to be transformed after the War of All against All by the converted souls, by the souls who will still be led to the good in this last period. In this way much will be accomplished. The good would not be so great a good if it were not to grow through the conquest of evil. Love would not be so intense if it had not to become love so great as to be able even to overcome the wickedness in the countenances of evil men. This is already being prepared for and the pupils are told; Therefore you must not think that evil has no part in the plan of creation. It is there in order that through it may come the great good.

One who reads digestively the foregoing paragraphs and then reads with an open mind what is revealed by John in his Apocalypse must surely see their correspondences in instance after instance. Especially will one be impressed with the similarity in reflecting on the premise presented earlier herein that the one who had the apocalyptic vision is the one who laid down the principles of Anthroposophy.

Having considered the contents of this preface, let us now return to the short account Steiner gives on the last two Cultural Ages to conclude his lecture three on the seven "churches."

Russian-Slavonic (3574–5734 CE)

First, the message from the angel, the "true one, who has the key of David, who opens and no one shall shut, who shuts and no one opens":[56]

[8] "'I know your works. Behold, I have set before you an open door, which no one is able to shut; I know that you have but little power, and yet you have kept my word and have not denied my name. [9] Behold, I will make those of the synagogue of Satan who say that they are Jews and are not, but lie—behold, I will make them come and bow down before your feet, and learn that I have loved you. [10] Because you have kept my word of patient endurance, I will keep you from the hour of trial which is coming on the whole world, to try those who dwell upon the earth. [11] I am coming soon; hold fast what you have, so that no one may seize your crown.[57] [12] He who conquers, I will make him a pillar in the temple of my God; never shall he go out of it, and I will write on him the name of my God, and the name of the city of my God, the new Jerusalem which comes down from my God out of heaven, and my own new name. [13] He who has an ear, let him hear what the Spirit says to the churches.'"

Verse 9 speaks of those who "lie" and those who are "loved." Embodied in this one verse is a lot of the content from John's first letter, which focuses throughout on those who, and what is a, "lie" and the importance of "love." It is in this letter where we encounter the three powerful words "God is love" (1 John 4:16). In his one paragraph of comment on this Sixth Cultural Age, Steiner says:

And if we follow this path [ascending from our slavery to materiality and again ascend to spiritual life] we shall bring into the sixth age the right spiritual life of wisdom and of love. Then

---

56 Rev 3:7.

57 See the discussion of the meaning of "soon" in chapter 2, "One Like a Son of Man."

the anthroposophical wisdom we have acquired will become
the impulse of love in the sixth age, which is represented by
the community expressing itself even in its name as the community of brotherly love, Philadelphia.... Man will develop his
ego to the necessary height, so that he will become independent
and in freedom show love toward all other beings in the sixth
age... This is the spiritual life that is to be prepared for the sixth
cultural age. We shall then have found the individual ego within
us in a higher degree, so that no external power can any longer
play upon us if we do not wish it; so that we can close and no one
without our will can open, and if we open no opposing power can
close. This is the key of David.... That is the ego that has found
itself within itself.[58]

In the conclusion of this letter, "the holy one... who has the key
of David" says that... he will write on the one who perseveres in
this brotherly love "my own new name."[59] This is the middle one of
the three times in Revelation where the name "which no one knows
except him who receives it" appears.[60] The deep meaning in this
"name" laid undisclosed until revealed by Steiner. In the Introductory lecture in the *ASJ* cycle on June 17, 1908, in Nuremberg (21),
he revealed it:

We remember how when *Moses* was to lead his people he received
the command: Say to thy people that the Lord God has said unto
thee what thou shalt do. Then Moses asks: How will the people
believe me, how can I convince them? What shall I say when they
ask who has sent me?—Read it again and compare as exactly as you
can with the original text and you will see its significance. The "I
am," what does that mean? The "I am" is the name for the divine
Being, the Christ-principle of man—the Being of whom man feels a
drop, a spark within himself when he can say "I am." The stone cannot say "I am," the plant cannot say "I am," the animal cannot say "I
am." Man is the crown of creation inasmuch as he can say "I am" to
himself, inasmuch as he can utter a name that does not hold good for

---

58 *ASJ*, 73.

59 Rev 3:12.

60 Rev 2:17; 3:12; and 19:12. See also *BB*, "I Am," 252–253.

anyone but the one who utters it. You alone can call yourself "I"; no one else can call you "I."

Over and over again in his Gospel, John has Christ saying of himself "I Am."[61] Each of us can easily say "I am," but to rise to the "I Am" which is the name of Christ is something far above that. Its three uses in Revelation as "the name that no one knows except him who receives it," each indicates that it lies at the end of a long journey to a very high level of spiritual perfection, of being Christ-like, worthy of Christ's bestowing his own name upon us.

American (5734–7894 CE)

Those of us who are native-born Americans, having resided only here in America, may find the characterization of this degenerating Cultural Age disquieting, to say the least. However, before we harbor resentment or otherwise take offense by it, perhaps it behooves us to examine our souls in the light of what has been said. Most especially should we do so since we have, from the founding of our country, made quite a thing about claiming to be a Christian nation and relying upon the Bible. While the intensity of these attitudes may be lessening with the passage of time, inasmuch as we have characteristically, as a people, advanced claims to the various avenues of religiosity, primarily Christian religiosity, perhaps as the very Bible people we have professed to be we should take seriously the writings of Lazarus/John, especially those in the Bible's concluding book, his Apocalypse, or Revelation. The very fact that we might have the foregoing reaction perhaps suggests, more than anything else, our collective need for serious reflection. It would be hard to gainsay that, more than any other nation in world history, we have expended enormous spiritual and intellectual energy in the accumulation, enjoyment, and development of matter, not the least of which has been in the development and production of efficient means of killing, and its frequent application. We are not the only nation to participate, but we have excelled and led the way. It was all, of course, foreseen by Steiner, and the process had to run its course. But the path it paves, described in the letter to the angel of

---

61   See *BB*, "I Am" at 266–267.

the church in Laodicea, leads away from the brotherly love of the sixth age, whose congregation will carry over to the Sixth Epoch and beyond.

But in all this line of reasoning, we have lost sight of the issue, which is not nationalism, but purely and distinctly the perfection of Egos, of the "I Am" of individuals, who will compose the colony of brotherly love. All nationalism, racism, or other group-soul nature will have disappeared from that congregation. It will comprise all those from every nation, tribe or group who have risen, as individual "I Ams" into the communion of Philadelphia (even those brought over into it in the decadent 7th Age), the realm of pure brotherly love of all human beings and other creatures, including the evil ones. America must surely have its share of these Philadelphians, but they will not then be called Americans nor carry the flag or uniform of any nation.

Let us then hear what the letter to the angel of the church of Laodicea says:

[15] "'I know your works: you are neither cold nor hot. Would that you were cold or hot! [16] So, because you are lukewarm, and neither cold nor hot, I will spew you out of my mouth. [17] For you say, I am rich, I have prospered, and I need nothing; not knowing that you are wretched, pitiable, poor, blind, and naked.

[18] Therefore I counsel you to buy from me gold refined by fire, that you may be rich, and white garments to clothe you and to keep the shame of your nakedness from being seen, and salve to anoint your eyes, that you may see. [19] Those whom I love, I reprove and chasten; so be zealous and repent. [20] Behold, I stand at the door and knock; if any one hears my voice and opens the door, I will come in to him and eat with him, and he with me. [21] He who conquers, I will grant him to sit with me on my throne, as I myself conquered and sat down with my Father on his throne.

[22] He who has an ear, let him hear what the Spirit says to the churches.'"

Steiner's closing comment on the seventh Age at the end of his third lecture, paraphrased, says only, that it is the "great leader," around whom the community of Philadelphians will flock, the one who is identified as "the Amen, the faithful and true witness, the beginning of God's creation."[62] Here Lazarus/John, most significantly it would seem, reverts to the substance of the first two verses of his Gospel, "In the beginning was the Word, and the Word was with God, and the Word was God.[63] He was in the beginning with God."[64] He was "the beginning of God's creation."

---

62 Rev 3:14.

63 On at least one occasion or in one instance, not here identified, Steiner rendered the latter portions of John 1:1 as follows (emphases added), "and the Word was with God, and the Word was *a* God." It is hard to argue with that characterization, but I also remain comfortable with the rendition of the verse in the text, that is, "was God."

64 John 1:1–2.

7

INTERLUDE FOR EVOLUTIONARY PANORAMA AND REFLECTION

John's Apocalypse purports to show what is still to take place in the long human journey. Its essential character is Promethean, that is forward-looking, rather than Epimethean, or backward-looking. But inasmuch as the past is prologue, what is to occur depends very greatly on what has already taken place. Thus, there is a very important element in the Revelation that reflects back upon what has gone before in order to project what still must be accomplished.

The letters to the angels of the first three Churches, or Cultural Ages, at the time of John's vision, were looking back, and in our time so also is the fourth. The rest of the seven letters were forward-looking.

The first verse in Revelation 4 invites John to "Come up hither, and I will show you what must take place after this." It reveals that the human journey will rise to a higher spiritual state as it moves from the last Cultural Age of the Fifth Evolutionary Epoch into the Sixth Epoch. But in order to lay the essential foundation for showing what lay ahead, the rest of chapter 4 is a reflection of what has gone before.

We note that the voice of the speaker in 4:1 is "like a trumpet," suggesting that already, at the beginning of the Sixth Evolutionary Epoch, the speaker is at the hierarchical stage that will be attained by those hierarchical beings who will have risen to the level of blowing trumpets during the Seventh Evolutionary Epoch.[1] This speaker may well have been one of the Elohim, the lowest hierarchical level to have attained its human status *prior to* the Ancient Saturn Condition of Consciousness.[2]

---

1   Rev 8:2–11:15.
2   See *BB*, charts **I-15** and **I-6**.

We immediately encounter a barrage of words, none of which can be considered to be without significant meaning. At the outset, the "throne" that appears in 4:2 is one of the hierarchical rank just below the Seraphim and Cherubim. We risk missing the vision if we assume less, for he who sat upon it "appeared like jasper and carnelian, and round the throne was a rainbow that looked like an emerald," and round that one throne sat the twenty-four elders on other thrones.[3] We shall consider these elders, but clearly the one on the throne they surrounded was of very high rank. The fact that this is one of only three places in the Bible where a rainbow appears packs meaning that we will later explore.

Let us consider also the meaning of the three precious stones; jasper, carnelian and emerald. The first two describe the appearance of the one on the throne. "Jasper is a precious stone with a greenish shimmer; but for the ancients it was the jasper with the nearly white, diamond-like radiance, whose pure white light bears only a distant shimmer of green, that was the most precious one," while "carnelian is a precious stone of blood-red color."[4] The new Jerusalem coming down out of heaven has a "radiance like a most rare jewel, like a jasper, clear as crystal."[5] Clearly the emerald is green. It may be helpful on the meaning of these colors to consider some of Steiner's indications.[6]

The "twenty-four elders" appear next. We saw earlier, in "One Like A Son of Man," that they represented the twenty-four Conditions of Life that had preceded our own. But a bit deeper examination of who they are is needed. They appear frequently in Revelation.[7] Steiner refers to them as "twenty-four human beings [who] look down upon

---

3   Rev 4:2–4.

4   Emil Bock, *The Apocalypse*, Edinburgh, Floris Books (1957), 41, cited by Friedrich Benesch, *Apocalypse: The Transformation of the Earth; An Occult Mineralogy*, SB (2015), 172. For fuller reference to this Benesch book, see its citation in chapter 14.

5   Rev 21:10–11.

6   See, for instance, *BB* Chart **I-83**, 663–665. Note the relative positions of white and green and their significance on the circular chart, while red, not on the chart itself, is "the luster of the living." One can hardly consider these things without remembering that he, Lazarus/John, who had this vision spoke of the Christ, the Word of God, as embodying *life* that was the *light* of men, though not comprehended by them; John 1:4–5.

7   Rev 4:4, 10; 5:8; 11:16; 19:4.

the present man.... beings whom... we have called the guides of evolution, the directors of time. Time is connected with evolution. [They] meet us in the Apocalypse of John."[8] Elsewhere I refer to them somewhat differently as "twenty-four members of the spiritual Hierarchies who attained their respective 'human' [i.e., consciousness] states in the twenty-four successive Conditions of Life that have preceded our present one."[9] This is, I'm confident, what Steiner meant. I suggest that as they attained that consciousness, they were at the hierarchical level of Principalities, or Archai, this latter name seemingly being synonymous with the term *elder*.[10] Since the hierarchies advance with the progression of the Conditions of Life, the attainment of human status of all of the twenty-four would have been when they were at the Archai level, hence their name and function, the administrators of the march of evolution through the ages.

We are told that before the throne stood the "seven spirits of God," which we also saw in "One Like A Son of Man" were the spirits of the seven Conditions of Consciousness, and these were before the throne of the Alpha and the Omega (1:4), higher than the twenty-four "elders."[11]

Revelation 4:6 tells us that before this high throne "there is as it were a sea of glass, like crystal." Steiner says, "This 'sea of glass' is to indicate the bursting forth, the budding forth of the mineral kingdom in its primary form."[12]

Immediately there follows in John's vision the four animals that had first appeared to Ezekiel in a vision remarkably similar to John's, yet slightly different in a meaningful way. Perhaps that most significant difference is in the number of their wings. Each animal in Ezekiel's

---

8   *ASJ*, Lect. 5, p. 101.

9   See the narrative part of *BB*, chart **I-1**.

10 The hierarchical attainment of "human" status is the subject of *BB*, chart **I-15**. It can be seen there, in conjunction with chart **I-6**, that the rank that attained human status on Ancient Saturn were the Archai (Principalities) and that all beings higher than that level attained their human status *prior* to Saturn.

11 While the terms *Alpha* and *Omega* appear only in Revelation, and thus perhaps suggest that the meaning of "him who is and who was and who is to come," the language of 4:1 and 4:8, is intended to be a synonymous identification, I point out in item 5 of "One Like a Son of Man" that they are not literally identical in meaning.

12 *ASJ*, Lect. 5; 102; see also Lect. 4 (80).

vision had four wings, while those in John's had six. Ezekiel lived in the early part of the Fourth Cultural Age, as did John.[13] However, in John's Revelation, the appearance of these four occurs as humanity moves from the seven Cultural Ages of the Churches into the Sixth Evolutionary Epoch. Both visions have eyes that appear to look forward and back.[14] This suggests an immense evolution, both past and future, rendering the vision inappropriate to a stationary condition of short duration such as would exist if the spirit of a human being lived only once on earth.

The four creatures have been assigned, in Christian tradition, respectively to the four Gospels, variously by different early Christian leaders, most likely generally following Jerome, namely, Matthew = Face of Man, Mark = Lion, Luke = Ox (Taurus, the bull), and John = Eagle (and its polar opposite, scorpion, the symbol thus seemingly akin to the two-edged sword). Not only are the four creatures traditionally related to the four Gospels but each of them is also a member of the animal circle called the zodiac.[15] In that circle they stand at ninety degree intervals, thus perhaps suggesting that they are the "four corners of the earth."[16]

As we shall see later in our discussion of the beast with seven heads and ten horns, these four creatures were the human being, its group-soul, in the first four ages of the Atlantean, or Fourth, Evolutionary Epoch.[17] They are also collectively portrayed in the mysterious sphinx, suggesting a degree of memory of the Atlantean times even into the days of ancient Egypt (the third Cultural Age of the Post-Atlantean Epoch).[18]

Chapter 4 closes with the four creatures singing a paean unto the Lord, recognizing the Lord as being "worthy...to receive glory and honor and power," paving the way for the worthiness in chapter 5 to open the seals of the Sixth Evolutionary Epoch.[19]

---

13 *BB*, chart **I-19**, 573.

14 Ezek 1:18; 10:12; Rev 4:6.

15 See *BB*, chart **I-62**, 640.

16 Rev 7:1.

17 *ASJ*, lect. 9; 163

18 See *TSRYR*, 165 and Steiner's works there cited.

19 Rev 4:8–11.

8

THE SIXTH EVOLUTIONARY EPOCH
AND THE OPENING OF THE SEVEN SEALS

Lazarus/John's Apocalypse occurred on Patmos a bit past the thirty-ninth percentile of the fourth Post-Atlantean Cultural Age (Greco-Roman 747 BCE–1414 CE). But today, all of humanity has lived through all of that fourth Cultural Age and slightly less than twenty-eight percent of the fifth Post-Atlantean Cultural Age (European 1414–3574 CE). The first four Cultural Ages are thus history. They are a part of the karma of humanity and of each of us.

The "Seals" and "The Valley of the Shadow"

John's vision speaks of seven seals. What is such a "seal"? In its various grammatical forms it can be found in Wisdom literature (Job 41:15; Song 4:12b), the Prophets (Isa 8:16; Dan 8:26; 9:24; 12:4), John's Gospel (3:33; 6:27), and Paul (Rom 4:11; 1 Cor 9:2; 2 Cor 1:22; 2 Tim 2:19), but it is most prominent in John's Apocalypse.[1]

As used in the Bible, whatever is sealed is hidden from normal human consciousness, accessible only to those with more advanced spiritual vision, those generally known as seers or prophets.[2] One of

---

1   The book of Daniel is classified with the major prophets in the Septuagint (LXX), the Greek version of the Hebrew Bible. But in the Hebrew Bible's three main sections, the Pentateuch, the Prophets, and the Writings, Daniel is listed near the end of the Writings, suggesting its late date in relation to those included in the Prophets, and perhaps also that it belongs in the genre of the apocalyptic or revelatory rather than the prophetic. ABD, vol. 2 (1992), 31.

2   Steiner spoke of three kinds of seership or prophecy: clairvoyance (seeing), clairaudience (hearing), and Intuition (understanding), which one recognizes in the their seminal appearance in Isaiah 6:9–13 where the loss of these was envisioned, an encroaching development recognized also by other prophetic

the effects of this loss of vision was the loss, for at least two or three thousand years of the certain knowledge that the spirit of human beings reincarnated over and over on the evolutionary journey of humanity and of their own individualities. The Eleusinian Mysteries of the Greeks called this loss the crossing of the "River Styx" (see *BB* 418, n. 6) and the Romans the "River Lethe" (see *BB* 262, n. 12; 268; 309; 418, n. 6; and 432), beautifully and allegorically portrayed in Ezek 47:1–12. This loss of spiritual perceptiveness grew with the increasing immersion of humanity in the denser world of matter. Bodies of matter die. Humanity was destined to "walk through the valley of the shadow of death" (Ps 23:4a) in "deep darkness" (Isa 9:2; Matt 4:15–16; Luke 1:79). We have been, and will continue to be, in that valley of the shadow of death so long as we live in bodies of matter that die, namely during the Atlantean and the three Evolutionary Epochs that follow it, of which we are in the first. Isaiah recognized that this human condition would continue "until the Lord moves men far away," or in other words until humanity leaves the world of matter as John's Apocalypse describes. Yet, the loss of vision is not uniform among all of humanity, for there have always been some individualities who, in their incarnations, have been initiated into higher levels of spiritual perception. Certainly the individualities in Lazarus/John and Paul were among those, and I judge that Rudolf Steiner demonstrated immense powers of seeing, hearing and understanding in the spiritual realm. John's Revelation itself suggests that the more advanced souls will come to this state progressively before those who are more entrenched in worldly materiality.

The seven seals and their opening, described in Revelation 5:1 through 8:1, are addressed in *ASJ*, lecture four and the part of lecture eight prior to its discussion of the seven trumpets. The period of the seven "Churches," the seven Cultural Ages of the fifth Evolutionary Epoch, called the Post-Atlantean, will be followed by the period of the seven "Seals" and their opening, in the sixth Evolutionary Epoch (*BB*, in the Chart **I-1** Grand Schematic; the present Post-Atlantean Epoch to end at approximately the year 7894 CE).

---

announcements as the spiritual realm was being closed to the prophets of Israel (see *BB* citing: Isa 29:9–14; Mic 3:5–7; Jer 5:13,30–31; 14:14; 23; 29:8–9; Lam 2:9,14; Ezek 13; 22:28; Zeph 3:4).

"The One Who is Worthy" and the End of Deception

We are told that the only one who is worthy to open these seals is the Christ, the Lamb who was slain (Rev 5:6–14):

> Let us imagine... that the soul has heard the call that from age to age the Christ-principle has uttered... in the messages to the Churches. Through seven ages has been laid into it what these ages can give. Let us imagine how the soul waits, how it waits on. It is sealed seven times. Each cultural age has added its seal. Within you is sealed what the Indians wrote in your soul; within you is also imprinted what the Persians, the Egyptians, Greeks and Romans have written in your soul, and what our own cultural age inscribes in it. The seals will be unloosed; that is, the things written there will be outwardly revealed after the great War of All against All. And the principle, the power, which brings it about that the true fruits of our cultural ages shall be made manifest in the countenance, is to be found in Christ Jesus.[3]

Earlier in the lecture, Steiner spoke of the change of countenance between the fifth and sixth Evolutionary Epochs, that is, in the first epoch after the great War of All against All:

> The souls who hear the voice which calls them to progress will survive the great period of destruction—the War of All against All—and appear in new bodies which will be quite different from those of the present day. For it is very shortsighted if one thinks, for instance, of the Atlantean bodies of men as being like the present bodies. In the courses of thousands of years the external physiognomy of men changes and after the great War of All against All man will have quite a different form. Today he is so formed that in a certain sense he can conceal the good and evil in his nature. Human physiognomy already betrays a good deal, it is true, and one who understands the subject will be able to read much from the features. But it is still possible today for a scoundrel to smile most graciously with the most innocent mien and be taken for an honest man; the reverse is also possible; the good impulses in the soul may remain unrecognized. It is possible for all that exists in the soul as cleverness and stupidity, as beauty and ugliness, to hide itself behind the general physiognomy

---

3   *ASJ*, lect. 4; 84–85 (CW 104).

possessed by this or that race. This will no longer be the case in the epoch following the great War of All against All. Upon the forehead and in the whole physiognomy it will be written whether the person is good or evil. He will show in his face what is contained in his inmost soul, indeed his whole body will be an image of what lives in his soul. How a man has developed in himself, whether he has exercised good or evil impulses, will be written on his forehead. After the great War of All against All there will be two kinds of human being. Those who had previously tried to follow the call to the spiritual life, who cultivated the spiritualizing and ennobling of their inner spiritual life, will show this inward life on their faces and express it in their gestures, in the movements of their hands. And those who have turned away from the spiritual life, as represented for us by the community of Laodicea, who were lukewarm, neither warm nor cold, will pass into the following epoch as those who retard human evolution who preserve the backward forces of evolution. They will show the evil passions, urges and instincts hostile to the spiritual in an ugly, unintelligent, evil-looking countenance. In their gestures and hand-movements, in everything they do, they will present an outer image of the ugliness in their soul. Just as mankind has separated into races and cultural communities, in the future it will divide into two great streams, the good and the evil. And what is in their souls will be outwardly manifest, they will no longer be able to hide what they have done with their souls.

The Defining Age of an Epoch

As previously stated, Steiner discusses the sixth Evolutionary Epoch—which the Apocalypse symbolizes with the seven seals and their opening—in both lectures four and eight of his June 1908 Nuremberg cycle. There is some overlap, or inter-penetration, of content that we must try to weave into one coherent account. Both lectures speak, for instance, of the particular age within each of the Atlantean and Post-Atlantean epochs that carries the highest and best of that epoch over as the salient, or principal, stream into its succeeding epoch. That highest age of Atlantis was the fifth; that of our Post-Atlantean is to be the sixth, the one of brotherly love known by the "Church" appropriately called Philadelphia. In each case, the ages, or age, that follow the most noble and highest, are "of very little importance" (lect. 8, 138). And in each case, those who carry the principal stream forward represent only a small part of those in that age. The others, including those of the more decadent ages that follow, survive, but they do so as a culture that has not advanced, in which there is "no living, burgeoning force" (lect. 8, 139).

As an illustration of this latter point on the last two races in Atlantis, Steiner says:

> You may still see stragglers of these old overripe races today, especially in the Chinese people. This Chinese people is characterized by the fact that it did not identify itself with what manifested in the fifth race ... It was when the etheric body entered into the physical body that man received the first germs which enabled him to say "I."[4] They missed the opportunity of that period; they did, however, develop the high civilization which is known today but which is not capable of development.... The sixth and seventh races of Atlantis allowed themselves to become hardened and therefore became stationary. As we have said, the Chinese civilization is a remnant of that. The old Chinese possessed a wonderful Atlantean heritage, but they could not progress beyond this zenith. Nothing remains uninfluenced from outside. You may examine ancient Chinese literature; it has been influenced from every direction, but its fundamental tendency bears the Atlantean character. This self-completeness, this capacity of making discoveries and going no further, never taking them beyond a certain stage—all this proceeds from the character of Atlantis.[5]

In the earlier lecture four, Steiner took note of the disturbing aspect of this race (or culture) carryover. His explanation in chapter 6 that no individual destiny is bound to the destiny of its race is here applicable. As he said there, it is important to "distinguish between race-development and soul-development, for no soul is condemned to remain in one particular race. The race may fall behind; the community of people may remain backward, but the souls progress beyond the individual races."[6]

---

4   Steiner, *The Influence of Spiritual Beings Upon Man*, AP (1961), lect. 4 (Berlin, February 29, 1908), 67–71, esp. the schematic on 71; *BB*, 402 and Chart **I-35** are based upon the 1961 edition; the 2014 Collected Works volume (CW 102) translated and published by RSP varies the schematics, while the textual content is substantively the same, CW 102, *Good and Evil Spirits and their Influence on Humanity*, RSP, 54–57.

5   *ASJ*, lect. 8; 139–140.

6   *ASJ*, lect. 4; 77.

It is important to bear this in mind when we consider individual Chinese today. A given individual may well be quite different from the "old Chinese" in Steiner's characterization above, whom he described as "stragglers." I think we cannot put that label on all Chinese today, possibly only a few, if any, for Steiner spoke these words well over a century ago, and much has occurred in the interval since then. Moreover, I do not construe his remarks as having been applicable to all Chinese at the time he made this observation, for the Chinese culture was even then very old and could hardly carry forward the Atlantean character in all those that incarnated into that culture over the centuries.

He relates in this lecture cycle what he has said in other of his works regarding the migrations from Atlantis:

> We must at least understand how this Atlantean civilization passed over into our own... The greater part of the Atlantean population was not sufficiently mature to develop further, it was incapable of coming over into our times. A smaller part, living in a region near to present-day Ireland, developed to the highest flowering of the civilization of Atlantis and then journeyed toward the East. We must understand that this was only the principal stream. There were always peoples who migrated from the West to the East, and all the later peoples of Europe, of Northern and Central Europe, proceeded from that stream which went from the West to the East. That most advanced part of the Atlantean population was under the guidance of a great leader of mankind and eventually settled down as a very small tribe of chosen individuals in Central Asia.[7] From this point the colonists migrated to the various regions of culture mentioned, to ancient India, to Persia, Egypt, Greece, etc.[8]

The Four Horsemen and the "Four Living Creatures"

We shall return to a mystery surrounding the migration of the principal stream, that of Manu (Noah). But let us first consider the seven seals and their opening (Rev 6:1–8:1). Each of the first four seals describes a horse and its rider (Rev 6:2–8).[9] Why this imagery?

---

7   The "great leader of mankind" was Noah, of the biblical tradition (Gen 6–10), known in other traditions as Manu.

8   *ASJ*, lect. 4; 76–77; see also lect. 8; 138–139.

9   Immediately this conjures up in our minds the ominous sounding "Four Horsemen of the Apocalypse." A Notre Dame University legend, spawned

One comes to comprehend it based upon the foundational fact that the human being (HB) was the first of the earth's creatures to come into being, to be created, but that creation was in, and long remained in, the spiritual world. The first chapter of Revelation deals with the HB in the ultimate sense. But in order to lay the proper foundation it is imperative to understand that while HB came first in the spiritual realm, it came into the material realm of earth last, all of the animal kingdom having descended first as it was expelled gradually and progressively from the HB which was evolving further in the spiritual realm.[10] Properly understood, Genesis 2:19 tells us that the Yahweh-Eloha brought each descending animal species to HB to name it as it fell away from HB into earthly material embodiment.[11]

We shall get to the horse, but first we need to recognize again the four "living creatures" (Rev 4:6b–7), in their stated order: lion (Leo), ox (Taurus), face of a man (Aquarius), and eagle (Scorpio), the four corners of the zodiac, or animal circle in the heavens. They are not only the four corners, but joined by their diagonals, they form a cross, and they are listed in the order of their appearance as the sun moves through the twelve zodiacal animal signs (see *BB*, Chart **I-19**, pp. 572–573). These four animal natures were successively the group-soul of HB during the first four ages of Atlantis. As each such animal species descended into earthly materiality, it left a remnant of its characteristic in the HB group-soul of that respective age. This is well described by Steiner:

> Animals are nothing more than beings that entered into a hardened, dense condition too early. What the human being carries in the astral

---

by Knute Rockne's student publicity aide, George Strickler, from a Grantland Rice write-up, appropriates this foursome image to describe the 1922 Notre Dame backfield after it beat Army 13–7 on October 18, 1924. However, a more powerful football image of the four horsemen, from my perspective, is the backfield of the Army football team that walloped Notre Dame 59—0 (its worst defeat ever) in 1944 and 48–0 in 1945. The three members of the Army backfield who played both of such years were Doc Blanchard, Glenn Davis, and Arnold Tucker. I believe Tom McWilliams filled the fourth slot in 1945, but I'm oblivious on who was the fourth member in 1944.

10   *BB*, "Overview," 17, 21; *DQWIM*, "Evolution," 9–14. *SLJ*, 9, 118; *TSRYR*, "Relevant Substance of the Ancient Mysteries," 183; *ASJ*, lect. 4; 80–82; *RPA*, Part 2, lect. 8 (Oslo [(Christiana], May 17, 1909), 113–114 (CW 104a).

11   *DQWIM*, "Creation and Apocalypse," 51.

body today in terms of desires and passions has come to expression in the physical body of the various animals.[12]

Each such remnant is one of the "living creatures" in Revelation 4:6b–7.

But why the horse in these first four Atlantean ages? And, a bit later, why only four?

As to the first question, Steiner says, "To what do we owe the fact that we have become intelligent? What animal form have we put forth from ourselves in order to become intelligent?–Curious and grotesque as it may appear, it is nevertheless true to say that if there were not around us the animals which belong to the horse nature, man would never have been able to acquire intelligence."[13] He goes on to give legendary examples of this relationship of the horse to man and the love between the two, then summarizing, "The horse species is not employed in legend without reason. Man has grown out of a form which once contained within it what is now embodied in the horse; and[,] in the form of the centaur[,] art still represented man as connected with this animal in order to remind him of the stage of development out of which he had grown, from which he had struggled free in order to become the present human being."[14]

As this applies, however, to the Epoch of the opening of the seals, after the great War of All against All," this gift from the horse is enhanced. Continuing, he explains:

What thus took place in bygone times in order to lead to present mankind will be repeated at a higher stage in the future.... Those who become clairvoyant at the boundary between the astral and the devachanic planes can see how man continually purifies and develops what he owes to the separation from the horse nature. He will accomplish the spiritualizing of intelligence.... The fruits of what was able to develop in humanity in consequence of the separation of the horse nature will be manifested.

That each horse had a rider tells us that HBs will become "victors over their lower nature through what they will have made of their souls. They will master their lower natures just as a rider masters a horse."[15]

---

12 *RPA*, Part 2, lect. 8 (Oslo, May 17, 1909), 113.

13 *ASJ*, lect. 4; 82.

14 *ASJ*, 83.

15 *RPA*, Part 2, lect. 9 (Oslo, May 18, 1909), 116.

We come, then, to the second question posed earlier, why only four horses and riders?

We must look ahead to *ASJ* lecture 9. That lecture gives an explanation of the meaning of the "seven heads and ten horns" of the beast that first appears in Revelation 13:1. That jumps ahead for now, but we borrow part of that discussion that is relevant here:

> Now you will remember that we spoke of the seven ages of the Atlantean evolution. These seven ages comprise the first four and the last three. In the first four man was completely group-soul. Then in the fifth age the first impulse for the ego-soul originated. Therefore we have four stages of development in Atlantis during which man first progresses as group-soul, and each of the first four Atlantean races corresponds to one of the typical animal forms—lion, eagle, calf or bull, and man. This passes over into the human stage in the fifth age. These typical forms are then lost.[16]

It is the Christ, the Lamb, who opens each of the seals, but on the first four it is the remnant of the four animals in HB's sentient group-soul that are the "living creatures" that speak out successively, each with a "voice of thunder," saying "Come"—whereupon, in each case, John sees a horse of a certain color (in order; white, red, black, and pale) carrying a rider with a designated mission.

We must take what appeared to John with the opening of these first four seals to represent what was stored in the heavenly book, the karma of HB no less, from each of the first four Cultural Ages of the Post-Atlantean Epoch, namely, the Ancient Indian, Persian, Chaldo-Egyptian, and Greco-Roman. Each of us lived in each of these Cultural Ages. Each lived more than once in each age since providence provided in each age at least one incarnation as male and one as female. In each age we each "took up what could be taken up." Then with reference to our experiences in each earlier age, "Although you have forgotten them, you will remember them again later," as the seals are removed in the sixth Great Epoch.[17]

The four horsemen of the Apocalypse are a symbolistic presentation of the first four ages of the Atlantean Epoch, moving through the

---

16   *ASJ*, lect. 9 (Nuremberg, June 26, 1908), 163.

17   *ASJ*, lect. 4; 84.

four animal natures, the zodiacal animals Leo (Lion), Taurus (Ox, or Bull), Face of a Man (Aquarius, or Water-Bearer), and Eagle (Scorpio, or Eagle/Scorpion), being, as mentioned earlier, the four reflected in the ancient sphinx and being ninety-degrees apart in the 360-degree zodiac. That posture suggests that they are the "four corners of the earth" or "four winds" (Rev 7:1; cf 9:14; Ezek 7:2; 37:9; Dan 7:2).

During this period, HB was in the early stages of gaining its upright stance and domed skull to permit its intelligence, and the last animal nature to sacrifice itself to make human intelligence possible, as we have seen, was the horse. So the setting for each of the first four seals has to do with this increasing intelligence as it moves through these "four living creatures" (Rev 4:6 and frequently thereafter). The intelligence derived from the horse's sacrifice is reflected as a horse as it gathers what each of the four progressions provides.

Consider then what each seal represents. The *first seal* (that of the "white horse") reflects what developed or played out in the first Post-Atlantean Cultural Age (Ancient India). That Age involved two clear characteristics, namely, the "whiteness" of purity indicated by hatred of the sensual signified by the Nicolaitans. By virtue of what the spirit had against the age, namely, wanting to look backward instead of for-ward, the spirit encouraged the adoption of a "conquering" mode— conquering the world of matter (Rev 2:4 and 7). The opening of the seal in Rev 6:2 indicates that man of that age did, in fact, progress on into the next age and thus "went out conquering."

The *second seal* (that of the "red horse") reflects the developments of the second Post-Atlantean Cultural Age (Ancient Persia). The most notable feature of Ancient Persia is the spiritual leadership of the ancient Zarathustra, who saw the Great Aura (Ahura Mazda; liter-ally, *Zarathustra*), in the sun sphere, and urged his followers to use that great being to spiritualize matter. But Zarathustra also saw the enemy of the spirit, Ahriman, and man moved into a time of primi-tive conflict in the world of matter, and the spilling of blood. But blood was involved in another way, namely, in the group-soul nature, where blood relationship was the guiding principle of human evolu-tion, hence, the evolutionary dominance of the color red.

The *third seal* (that of the "black horse") reveals what happened in the third Post-Atlantean Cultural Age (the Chaldo-Egyptian). This is the age when the application to commerce (balance scales), the grain situation of the Joseph saga, and the ever increasing involvement in the world of matter, including the study of weights and measures and the starry sky and its effect upon earthly life were taking place. But what probably made its color black was most profoundly indicated by the fact that the ability to see into the spiritual realm was quickly fading. Nothing is so suggestive of this as the fact that as the Age came to an end, it brought with it the "end of prophecy." Isaiah's vision in this is best reflected in what is sometimes spoken of as his "call," when man could no longer see, hear or understand, a theme which rings loudly through the prophets that were seeing their imminent demise. Humanity was pitched into spiritual blackness for very long ages to come. See Isaiah 6.

The *fourth seal* (that of the "pale horse"). The Greek word for the color is *khlōros* (χλωρός). The word is the root of "chlorophyll" and "chlorine." It "can mean either green/greenish-yellow or pale/pallid."[18] The fact that it represents the fourth Cultural Age, the Age of the Christ on earth, and the significance of his death by crucifixion, is aptly related to the significance of Death, and the fact that he came during our long journey through "the valley of the shadow of death," to reverse the course of our descent—all supports the concept of death. But the Greek word used, implying both pale (the pallor of a corpse), in effect white, and also green, takes us back to the meaning of jasper discussed in the preceding chapter. That precious stone involves both dazzling white and green, and brings us again to the powerful relationship between these two colors indicated by Steiner's drawing set out in *BB*, Chart **I-83**.

The reader will find other informed expressions of the meaning of the symbols in John's vision of the four horses and their riders.[19]

crucifixion and "First Fruits"

We saw earlier that the searing power of the Christ spirit that indwelt the bodies of Jesus of Nazareth for three years effectively

---

18 See https://en.wikipedia.org/wiki/Four_Horsemen_of_the_Apocalypse, n. 24, citing Liddell and Scott.

19 For Steiner's commentary, see *RPA*, Part 2, lect. 9 (Oslo, May 18, 1909), 116–118; Emil Bock, *The Apocalypse of Saint John* (Edinburgh: Floris Books, 1957), 56–61; Charles Kovacs, *The Apocalypse in Rudolf Steiner's Lecture Series* (Edinburgh: Floris Books, 2013), 39–43.

crucified his body of matter. John's Gospel indicates that Jesus "went out, bearing his own cross" (19:17), but the Synoptic Gospels suggest his weakened condition soon required another, Simon of Cyrene, to carry it for him (Mark 15:21; Matt 27:32; Luke 23:26). His formal crucifixion on the cross was necessary as a visible confirmation of the death of the body. Paul speaks of the risen Christ as "the *first fruits* of those who have fallen asleep" (1 Cor 15:20), but John calls those who attain to the 144,000 the "*first fruits* for God and the Lamb" (Rev 14:4).

The significance of Death, and especially the death of the material body of Jesus of Nazareth in the fourth Cultural Age, is followed by those "slain for the word of God" as the seal of our own fifth Cultural Age is removed to indicate the few who are given the white robe. The power to kill the body of matter links us to the crucifixion of our material bodies through progressive suffering and sacrifice over the ages, for of such is the realm of the 144,000. That only a small portion of humanity will attain to that realm during our current Age is suggested in the letter to the angel of the church in Sardis (3:1–6), as confirmed upon the opening of the seal of our age during the sixth Evolutionary Epoch (6:9–11).

Before we attend to the opening of the sixth seal, let us contemplate the relationship between the fifth age of Atlantis and the sixth age of our Post-Atlantean Epoch. We have seen that the principal stream from the fourth Epoch, Atlantis, to our Post-Atlantean Epoch came from the fifth Atlantean age and that the principal stream from our Post-Atlantean Epoch will come from our sixth Cultural Age, called Philadelphia. Let us consider when it is, in relation to these Epochs, that their principal stream is carried over to the next Epoch. Is it at the end of the age from which the stream comes, the fifth in Atlantis and the sixth in the Post-Atlantean, or is it at the end of the Epoch of which the defining, principal stream was a part—in other words, was it, or was it to be, after the seventh age in each case when the Epoch closes?

It seems clear that those who constitute the defining stream that carries the highest fruits of an Epoch over to the next Epoch are the human individualities, or spirits, that have attained to the full satisfaction of the goal of that Epoch, which has nothing to do with whether that individuality is incarnated at the end of the Epoch—or at the time that its stream is carried over to the next. Thus, whether living or dead at the time, in an earthly sense, is of no consequence.

Let us consider the Atlantean stream from its fifth age. One Steiner passage quoted earlier might be taken to suggest that the Noah group left Atlantis during, or at the end, of the fifth age of Atlantis: "We must at least understand how this Atlantean civilization passed over into our own.... A smaller part, living in a region near to present-day Ireland, developed to the highest flowering of the civilization of Atlantis and then journeyed toward the East. We must understand that this was only the principal stream. There were always peoples who migrated from the West to the East."[20] Does this mean that this principal Atlantean stream made its epochal voyage, or migration, over to Ireland and beyond before the final flooding submergence of Atlantis at the end of its seventh age? Some might take it so, but I think that is not the case. What Steiner said in Oslo the next year (1909) suggests otherwise in regard to the mystery centers of Atlantis:

> During those times...there were mystery centers that were especially concerned with the various planets in our solar system and the spiritual powers standing behind them. For this reason there were Mars, Venus, Sun, Jupiter, Mercury, Saturn and Moon oracles. However, the greatest and loftiest was the ancient sun oracle. The initiates of this sun oracle could survey all the other oracles and watch over them. The great sun initiate of the sun oracle stood at the top; *he saw prophetically the water catastrophe of Atlantis. Therefore, he had the task of seeing to it that the culture was guided through and beyond the catastrophe....* [emphasis mine].
>
> It is a law of spiritual economy that what has once been achieved for humankind is not lost. If we were to survey the various oracles we would find everywhere what is achieved through occult training: the etheric body is transformed and organized through and through by the "I." The etheric body of ordinary people who have not undergone this transformation dissolves at death into the world ether. However, with the highest initiate something different happens. An etheric body transformed in this way is preserved for the blessing and healing of humankind. The great sun initiate preserved

---

20 *ASJ*, lect. 4; 76–77.

the etheric bodies of the seven great Atlantean initiates as spiritual treasure and took them along to Asia. These were then imprinted into seven of the very best individuals so that they grew up endowed with the etheric bodies of the greatest initiates of ancient Atlantis.[21]

The Ark of the Covenant

The italicized portion suggests to me that the departure was not till the end of the Atlantean Epoch, when the great flood and final submergence occurred. Similarly, we will see that even those who have gained the white garments earlier, will not move into the seventh great Epoch until after the seventh seal is opened, and the seventh Epoch begins with the blowing of the trumpets. Common sense tells us, and Steiner has confirmed, that no HB, no matter how highly initiated and possessed of spiritual vision, can advance into the future ages of humanity's earthly journey beyond the rest of humanity.

Noah is said to have had three sons, Shem, Ham, and Japheth (Gen 6:10). Some readers may recall my consistent leaning to the view that these represented the last three ages of Atlantis, Shem the 5th, Ham the 6th, and Japheth the 7th and last before the final submergence.[22]

The dimensions of Noah's ark, 300 by 50 by 30 cubits (Gen 6:15) are those of the mineral-physical body of the human being as it came over from the Atlantean to the Post-Atlantean Epoch, and it is this body that was the original "ark of the covenant" (Gen 9:8–10).[23] And the animals that Noah brought into the ark were not animals as we think of them in our mineral-physical words, but are the remnants of all those animals that by then were in the astral bodies of those who

---

21 *RPA*, Part 2, lect. 2 (Oslo, May 10, 1909), 73–75.

22 *BB*, "Three Bodies," 471; that the etheric body of Shem continued through the last two ages of Atlantis, including in Noah's sons Ham and Japheth, Noah almost certainly having been a reincarnation in the last such age of the great leader of the Sun Mysteries during the 5th Atlantean age—to appreciate this likelihood, see Steiner, *The Principle of Spiritual Economy*, AP (1986), lect. 2 (Berlin, Feb 15, 1909), 15–18; lect. 3 (Munich, Mar 7, 1909), 44–46; lect. 9 (Oslo, May 16, 1909), 117–118 (CW 109); *SLJ*, "Melchizedek," 151–153; Andrew Wellburn, *The Book With Fourteen Seals*, RSP (1991), chap. 11, 150–155.

23 *BB*, 21; *TSRYR*, 194, citing Steiner, *Occult Signs and Symbols* (OSS), AP (1972), lects. 1 and 2 (Stuttgart, Sept 13-14, 1907), 14, 15–21 (CW 101).

came over from Atlantis to our own Epoch.[24] Philo expressed this as well (emphasis mine):

> We cannot therefore raise any question as to why it was ordained that all the different species of animals should be collected in the ark which was made at the time of the great deluge, while more were brought into the Paradise. *For the ark was an emblem of the body, which of necessity therefore contained all the most tameable and ferocious evils of the passions and vices.*[25]

The Crucified and the 144,000

Let us first clarify the spiritual status of the 144,000 as distinguished from the rest of humanity. It is Revelation's preeminent group. Is *144,000* number or symbol—or both? Except for one possibility, it seems clearly, as we will show, to be symbolical; that is, it does not mean that the elite group will comprise that number. Rather will that group be all those who by the end of the Sixth Evolutionary Epoch, the Epoch of the opening of the seals, will be able to *ascend to a spiritual state.* We begin to get some idea even in our own Cultural Age that only a very small and spiritually noble portion of humanity will be in that group. We are told in Rev 3:4 that *only a few in our Age* will not have "soiled their garments; and they shall walk with me in white, for they are worthy."

In his *ASJ* lectures, Steiner spends a great deal of lecture time discussing each of the Cultural Ages up through our own Fifth (the "Church" at Sardis). And even though it is clear that the Age of Philadelphia that follows our own is the one from which the "ripest fruit" of the Post-Atlantean Age (the "Churches") will be carried over into the Sixth Evolutionary Epoch (the "Seals"), he devotes only one paragraph to each of the two Ages that follow our own.[26] That the group from within the Age of Philadelphia that will carry over our Epoch's highest culture into the Sixth Evolutionary Epoch will be composed largely from within those "few" from our own Fifth Cultural Age seems to be an inescapable conclusion.

---

24 *BB*, 21, 241, 333, 667; *SLJ,* 61, 177.

25 *The Works of Philo*, Complete and Unabridged, New Updated Ed. (trans. C. D. Yonge), Peabody, MA, Hendrickson (1993), 177.

26 *ASJ*, 73–74.

We do now get the full picture of those who have not "soiled their garments" in our own Cultural Age, the "European", or "Sardis." What we do in our Age is revealed upon the opening of the fifth seal in the Sixth Evolutionary Epoch. Already in our Age great demands are made upon those who would attain to the 144,000. Of our Fifth Cultural Age, we learn, upon the opening of the fifth seal, the nature of those demands (emphasis mine):

> ⁹ When he opened the fifth seal, *I saw under the altar the souls of those who had been slain for the word of God and for the witness they had borne*; ¹⁰ they cried out with a loud voice "O Sovereign Lord, holy and true, how long before thou wilt judge and avenge our blood on those who dwell upon the earth?" ¹¹ Then they were each given a white robe and told to rest a little longer, until the number of their fellow servants and their brethren should be complete, who were to be *killed as they themselves had been.*

In lectures four and eight of *ASJ*, Steiner addresses the Epoch of the opening of the seals, and its relationship to its respective corresponding Ages of our Post-Atlantean Epoch. The two excerpts immediately below extract small but pertinent portions of those lectures quoted in chapter 6. From lecture 4:

> We have seen how we ourselves, in the spiritual movement to which we belong, should consider the words of the so-called fifth message as a summons to action, to work.... And we have seen how through this spiritual movement the next age is prepared which is represented by the community of Philadelphia, the age when among all those who have understood the word of the summons there is to be that brotherly love over the whole earth which is described in the Gospel of John....
>
> The present cycle is preparing indirectly for the next one, so that we may say our age of culture will gradually pass over into one of brotherly love, when a comparatively small part of mankind will have understood the spiritual life and will have prepared the spirit and attitude of brotherly love. *That culture will then again divide off a smaller portion of human beings who will survive the event that will have such a destructive effect upon our cycle, namely the War of All against All.* In this universal destructive element there will be everywhere individuals who lift themselves above the rest

of warring humanity, individuals who have understood the spiritual life and who will form the foundation for a new and different epoch, the epoch of the sixth period.[27]

And in the eighth lecture:

> The sixth cultural age will be the foundation for the new cultures which will arise after the great War of All against All.... On the other hand, the seventh age of culture will be characterized by the lukewarm [Rev 3:15–16]. This seventh age will continue into the new epoch, just as the sixth and seventh races of the Atlantean epoch continued in our epoch as races hardened and stiffened. After the War of All against All, there will be two streams in mankind: on the one hand the stream of Philadelphia will survive with the principle of progress, of inner freedom, of brotherly love, a small band drawn from every tribe and nation; and on the other hand the great mass of all those who will be lukewarm, the remains of those who are now becoming lukewarm, the stream of Laodicea. After the great War of All against All, gradually the evil stream will be led over to good by the good race, by the good stream. This will be one of the principal tasks after the great War of All against All; to rescue what can be rescued from those who after the great War will only have the impulse to fight one another and allow the ego to express itself in the most external egoism.

The *fewness* of those represented by the symbol 144,000, the *smallness* of the group, is a salient constant among its aspects. Consistent with its description in Rev 3:4 it is set in contrast above from "the great mass."

It is in the corresponding Fifth Age of the Sixth Epoch that, upon the very opening of what was sealed from our current Fifth Cultural Age, the first wave of those *slain* for the Word and for the witness given are recognized (6:9) and then "told to rest a little longer, until the number of their fellow servants and the brethren should be complete, *who were to be killed as they themselves had been* (6:11). Then upon the opening of the sixth seal horrific images

---

27   *ASJ*, lect. 4; 75–76.

are given. They are a prophetic recognition of what is to occur in the Seventh Epoch.[28]

What must it mean to be *slain* or *killed* within the meaning of these verses? The language conjures up for us the image of violent death, precipitous in the scope of time. At this stage of human evolution, it seems doubtful that such an event would fully satisfy what is encompassed with these terms. We may get an inkling of it in Steiner's description below of the meaning of the 144,000. Our highest example must be the life and sacrifice of Jesus of Nazareth, and then the Christ's brief three year bit of eternity in the mineral-physical body, as Jesus Christ. We've seen that his death on the cross was something of a sealing up of what was already totally spent, consumed, and extinguished by the power of the Christ Spirit incarnated within him. A literal description of what it means to be so *killed* is perhaps best described by second Isaiah in his suffering servant chapter.[29] Of necessity it will entail much pain, suffering, and sacrifice before the stature is attained—and that almost certainly over the course of many incarnations.

The seventh chapter of Revelation, where the term *144,000* first appears, describes two classes who will be given white robes, but it clearly distinguishes between the two classes. I suggest that the first group is the 144,000—those from our own Fifth Cultural Age who receive their white robes in the fifth age of the Sixth Epoch and are told to wait till their number is complete (6:9–11), to whom are added in the sixth age of the Sixth Epoch those from the Age of Philadelphia who are the complemental addendum completing the 144,000 status. The combined group will be those in such sixth age with the prophetic vision in Rev 6:12–17 of what lay ahead in the Epoch of the trumpets.

We may be assured that there are two such classes because Rev 7:14 identifies the second class as those who "have come out of the great tribulation," while the 144,000 have been sealed and thus saved from the ordeals that follow after the opening of the seventh seal and beginning of the Epoch of the trumpets (7:3).[30]

---

28 *ASJ*, lect. 4; 89.

29 Isa 53.

30 Saved from the ordeals, as in 9:4; two distinct groups, as in Rowland, NIB, vol. 12; 621.

We shall presently see in Steiner's explanation of the 144,000 what seems descriptive of the spiritual phenomenon by which this elite group is lifted out of the great tribulation that is to follow. It is in the paragraph of his explanation that starts with this sentence: "In the age represented by the seven seals something like a shower of meteorites will occur, caused by increasing materialism, and some human beings will ascend to a spiritual state."[31]

The Twelve Tribes of Israel

The composition of the 144,000 according to Rev 7:4–8 is twelve thousand from each of the twelve tribes of Israel.[32] The "twelve tribes" appear again 21:12 as the "sons of Israel," where each of the twelve gates of the holy city bears the name of one of the tribes. Steiner does not take this number up in his main lecture cycle on Revelation.[33] Only in his lecture in Oslo on May 21, 1909, does he deal with it a bit more extensively, and he there accepts John's composition of the 144,000 as being from the twelve tribes.[34]

This composition was, for a while, a hard pill for me to swallow. How are we to deal with it—being taken wholly from the twelve tribes of Israel?

Historically, as a delineated group with any continuing factual reality, they had become a fiction by the time of John's vision. The ten northern tribes, which became known as "Israel," were taken into captivity by the Assyrians in precisely the generational time frame that the Greco-Roman Cultural era began (when Isaiah's lips were seared by the Seraphim and he heard the voice of our descending Lord; Isa 6). The fall of Israel, the ten northern tribes, was completed within the span of twenty years, roughly 741 to 721 BCE, conquered by the succession of three Assyrian kings, Tiglath-Pileser III (744–727 BCE), Shalmaneser V (726–722 BCE), and Sargon II (721–705 BCE).[35]

---

31   *RPA*, lect. 12 (May 21, 1909); 132.

32   The tribe of Dan is not mentioned, for speculative reasons, and is replaced by Manasseh, a son of Joseph whose other son, Ephraim, is not mentioned.

33   *ASJ*, Nuremberg, June 17–30, 1908.

34   *RPA*, Part 2, lect. 12 (Oslo, May 21, 1909); 131–133, esp. 133.

35   A. Kirk Grayson, "Tiglath-Pileser III," ABD, vol. 6; 552; "Shalmaneser V," ABD, vol. 5; 1155; and "Mesopotamia, History of" (Assyria), ABD, vol. 4; 744–745.

Massive deportations of these northern tribes was imposed upon them; in short, they were dispersed and ceased to have a corporate existence or identity from that point forward. This was over eight hundred years prior to John's Apocalypse. Not only was this physical oblivion cast upon them, but over the course of that period of time the diffusion of them as a people occurred naturally through intermarriage and commingling in foreign societies. Individual Jews who might have existed in the earlier centuries were part of the march of humanity, through the reincarnation that all humanity has experienced from early Atlantean times. Souls move in and out of races, nationalities, and cultures, so that the twelve tribes, and most especially the northern ten of Israel, could not have any continuing validity as history moved on. Certainly that has become obvious in the millennia since then, and by the ascending of the 144,000 to which John's Apocalypse points, to occur many millennia from now, far more than from John to the present, the idea of twelve tribes as an existential unit is total fantasy.

Moreover, after he had completed his cycle(s) on John and the Apocalypse, and as he was beginning to get into the three Synoptic Gospels, Steiner said in a lecture in Stuttgart on November 14, 1909, that Christ Jesus was the fulfilment, "a fusion and at the same time a rebirth of all the former spiritual streams of humanity. In him the earlier streams are born anew, in an enhanced degree."[36] Later in the same lecture he points to Abraham as the one chosen out of all mankind to organize the world-phenomena by number and measure, when, immediately following the Melchizedek experience, Yahweh instructed him to look to heaven and number the stars (the twelvefold zodiac), for thus his descendants were to be.[37] The attributes of such a brain were to proceed through his people "for as long a time as it was their mission to carry it into humanity." That mission, of the Jewish people, the "Chosen People," was accomplished by the preparation of a body that was capable of hosting the Christ in earthly incarnation for a period of three (or three and a half) years (essentially 1,260

---

36 I have only a typescript copy of this lecture, provided by the Rudolf Steiner Library, bearing the title *The Gospels*, translator not indicated. The lecture will appear later in CW 117, the volume presumably to be named *The Deeper Secrets of the Development of Humanity in Light of the Gospels*.

37 Gen 15:5.

days). Paul recognized that this mission had been accomplished when he said, "a body thou hast prepared for me."[38]

But let us not so hastily dispose of these twelve tribes as the source from which the select group, called "the 144,000," will come. Those tribes take their fundamental character from the twelve stars in our zodiac, originally described "the word of the Lord" in Abram's "vision."[39] The descendants were to represent those twelve stars, the full spectrum of human character. Henceforth, references to the twelve tribes must, where appropriate, be understood to have a meaning applicable to all humanity as those governed by the laws of these twelve stars. Otherwise, the references to the twelve tribes can have, in reality, no meaning whatsoever—at least not as discrete ongoing entities.

We may thus take it that the 144,000 will comprise 12,000 from each zodiacal segment of humanity. Individual souls move not only from one culture or nationality to another through the course of their numerous incarnations, but also between zodiacal groups, for each human must, presumably, eventually experience incarnation(s) in every zodiacal group. Recall from the first paragraph of this section the sentence, "Except for one possibility, it seems clearly, as we will show, to be symbolical; that is, it does not mean that the elite group will comprise that number."

If we accept both John and Steiner on the 144,000 coming from the twelve tribes, the question then becomes, to comply with John's designation, is the identification of zodiacal attribute, on the one hand, to be determined from those within the ancient, and presumably original, tribe, or, on the other hand, only from those who might at any point during the existence of all the tribes have been part of such tribe? In the latter case the reference to the tribes would be diluted so greatly, and in so many ways, that the designation essentially loses all meaning.

It is possible, if not probable, that there are those individuals then living among those original tribes, being at that time a part of the Chosen People, who, as individualities, no matter how many incarnations outside of that tribe and dilution of Jewish heritage through constant

---

38 Heb 10:5–10, esp verses 5 and 10.
39 Gen 15:1.

ancestral intermarriage, are of such constant character throughout the ages that they will qualify for the 144,000. If that should be the reality, then the distinct possibility exists that the 144,000 might be not only a symbol, as in my description below, but also a specific number. If the biblical account is to be trusted on the matter, we read that the number of individuals, presumably aside from women and children, included in the twelve tribes exceeded 600,000.[40]

Immediately following his reference to the 144,000 being 12,000 from each of the twelve tribes, Steiner says the following:

> The writer of the Apocalypse knows the secrets of all evolution, and he tells them in a language generally little understood. He does this because human beings will be able to develop their consciousness soul precisely through the exertion of energy required to penetrate such riddles.[41]

I am extremely grateful for his timely gift of that insertion, because I have exerted more contemplative mental effort than I had anticipated would be necessary to comprehend Steiner's explanation of the 144,000. While I believe I now comprehend it, like Jacob at the Jabbok (Gen 33:24), I wrestled with it at great length, so far without breaking my leg. My understanding appears below in what is captioned "*Steiner's Explanation of the 144,000.*"

In his early *Christianity as Mystical Fact*, writing of the passage in Rev 7:4, Steiner said of the 144,000, "These are the ones who prepared the way for the Eternal before it took the form of Christianity, and who have been transformed by the impetus given through Christ."[42] If this expression is to be combined with his later and more extensive explanation below, it does seem to open the door to the original twelve tribes as the source from which the individualities later raised to the spiritually elite status envisioned by the 144,000 will come.

We then seem to have the following possibilities: The 144,000 shall be those who are slain for the word and for their witness,

---

40 Num 11:21; 26:51; Exod 12:37; 38:26.
41 *RPA*, 133.
42 *Christianity As Mystical Fact*, SB, CW 8, chap. 8; 93.

1. without regard to number, twelve tribes, or zodiacal allocation; or

2. with regard to one or more of number, twelve tribes, and zodiacal allocation.

My own position is to be open to each of the above as possibilities, but leaning strongly for now to the 144,000 being only symbol and not number. In that, I interpret the "until the number... should be complete" in 6:11 as saying to those who received the white robe in the age of the Fifth seal that others than those in their group will come in during the age of the Sixth seal. My focus is upon those who qualify under the two interpretations described below, that Steiner gives and what comes from my own spiritual search pertaining to the twelve and the golden mean or spiral of creation. I have high respect for Steiner's and feel that mine also has high meaning that is complementary to Steiner's. Both arrive, so to speak, at the same destination via alternate routes of reason. Each is strengthened in joinder with the other.

Steiner's explanation of the 144,000

Steiner does not take this number up in his main lecture cycle on Revelation.[43] Only in his lecture in Oslo on May 21, 1909, does he deal with it more extensively than in his early *Christianity as Mystical Fact*. Here is his explanation:[44]

> To begin with, the *human being consists of the four members*: physical body, etheric body, astral body, and the "I." However, if we wish to investigate Post-Atlantean evolution more precisely, we must also consider the ninefold aspect of the human being.... The "I" works to transform the astral body into manas or spirit-self, the etheric body into budhi [*sic*] or life-spirit, and the physical body, through breathing, into atma. In other words, the "I" transforms the astral body, the etheric body, and the physical body. But before this can happen consciously, it must have taken place through higher beings.
>
> Today the conscious transformation of these members occurs only in schools of initiation. For example, in the last third of the

---

43   *ASJ*, Nuremberg, June 17–30, 1908.

44   At the time of these lectures Steiner had not broken away from his position in the Theosophical Society in Germany, which he did in 1913. I have changed his references to "Theosophy" to Anthroposophy (in brackets).

Atlantean age the physical body was transformed to the point that it could be a bearer of an "I," but this occurred unconsciously. What was transformed in the astral body is called sentient soul, the etheric body transformed in this way is called the intellectual soul, and the physical body thus unconsciously transformed is the consciousness soul. Only when human beings have developed the consciousness soul can the spirit-self gradually—and at first, unconsciously—be woven into them.

In the cultural epochs of our earth evolution, manas is gradually being formed and slipped into the astral body. After it has been prepared in the last third of the Atlantean age, the consciousness soul must again be transformed by the Yahweh–Christ principle in the next cultural epoch.

In the ancient Indian age the etheric body was permeated by the "I," which by then had moved into the human being. In the ancient Persian age the astral body was permeated by the "I," in the Egyptian age the "I" permeated the sentient soul, in the Greco-Latin age the intellectual soul was permeated by the "I," in our culture, the "I" permeates the consciousness soul. In the age of "Philadelphia" the "I" will permeate the spirit-self, or manas. Then the human beings who, through [anthroposophical-]spiritual teachings, have made themselves capable of recognizing Christ will be in a position to see him in a new form of existence—in his delicate etheric body—for he will come again.[45]

The "I" will be educated through wisdom, through [Anthroposophy], so that it receives manas or spirit-self and will be able to recognize Christ again. [Anthroposophical] teachings have been given to humankind not in order to agitate for [Anthroposophy] but rather because they were necessary.

In the age represented by the seven seals something like a shower of meteorites will occur, caused by increasing materialism, and some human beings will ascend to a spiritual state. What the spiritualized human beings have acquired through their efforts in our Post-Atlantean age will completely permeate them within. When, in the age of the sixth seal, everything that

---

45 The future tense of this "coming again" was appropriate when he spoke. Soon after Steiner spoke these words in 1909, he introduced early in 1910 the matter of the reappearance of Christ (the "second coming"), the reappearance to occur in the earth's etheric realm in or about 1933 where he will be increasingly perceived by humanity over the centuries and millennia to follow.

the human being has in terms of sentient soul, intellectual soul, and consciousness soul has been worked into the other members, human beings will have achieved the ability to create an external imprint of their inner life in their gesture, features, in their whole life. Because they have worked on their development they will be able, in the fourth, fifth, and sixth ages in the epoch of the seals, to use these three soul forces—the sentient, intellectual, and consciousness souls—to permeate and work on themselves in order to take in manas.

When the human being has gone through a cycle fully so that nothing more remains to be done, this is characterized in occultism with a "0," or zero. Therefore, human beings will have permeated the three with four. For the next age, this permeation of the three with the four is expressed by multiplying three by four; they have gone through three cycles, that is, though three zeros. This is expressed thus: twelve with three zero's: 12,000. "Then I saw another angel ascend from the rising of the sun, with the seal of the living God, and he called with a loud voice to the four angels who had been given power to harm earth and sea, saying, 'Do not harm the earth or the sea or the trees, till we have sealed the servants of our God upon their foreheads.' And I heard the number of the sealed, one hundred and forty-four thousand sealed, out of every tribe of the sons of Israel, twelve thousand sealed out of the tribe of Judah, twelve thousand of the tribe of Reuben.... " (Rev. 7:2–5) Then the various groups of people who have matured will be united in the community of Philadelphia for mature brotherhood when every soul will feel for others. All those who have been separated out of the various groups can now be multiplied together because they will live within one another. Their life together will be such that they will not disturb one another, such that one soul will work into another soul in complete harmony. Twelve times 12,000 gives the number 144,000.

These are the people who will constitute human society in the age of the sixth seal.[46]

For the longest stretch of time and expenditure of effort I was unable to comprehend Steiner's explanation. I ran into numerous mental roadblocks. They seemed to all exist in my mind as one jumbled

---

46   *RPA*, Part 2, lect. 12 (Oslo, May 21, 1909), 131–133.

mass. Finally, I decided to work backward from the three cycles each of which produced a zero.

My conclusion is that Steiner is saying that the first cycle was completed during the Fourth Evolutionary Epoch, the Atlantean, when "to begin with HB consisted of four members," namely, the physical, etheric, and astral bodies and an "I" (Ego). In the last third of the Atlantean Epoch, higher spiritual forces transformed the physical body "to the point that it could be a bearer of an "I." "What was [there] transformed in the astral body is called the sentient soul, the etheric body transformed in this way is called the intellectual soul, and the physical body...transformed is the consciousness soul"; but these transformations were merely into a seminal state. All of this occurred unconsciously insofar as HB was concerned. *This is the first cycle.*

In our Post-Atlantean Evolutionary Epoch, the permeations or transformations continue to be accomplished unconsciously in HB, save in schools of initiation. The three permeations in our Epoch are of the etheric body in the ancient Indian Age, the astral body in the ancient Persian Age, and, collectively as one, the three soul forces (sentient, intellectual, and consciousness) in the three following Cultural Ages (Egyptian, Greco-Latin, and European). In the age of Philadelphia, the I will permeate the spirit-self, or manas, in which state those who have absorbed anthroposophical truths will be able to experience the second coming of Christ in the etheric realm. *This is the second cycle.*

In the Fourth, Fifth and Sixth Ages of the Sixth Evolutionary Epoch, the three soul forces will permeate and work on themselves to take in manas. The brevity of this description may perhaps be distinguished from the explanation in the first two cycles by the fact that all of that cycle is in the future. In any event, *this seems to be the third and final cycle*, in the production of the three zeros on the 144.

But how do we reconcile attaining the 144,000 during the Evolutionary Epochs while it seems clearly to be the 144,000 also at end of Earth evolution, a vast spiritual gulf separating those two stages? If we examine again *BB's* chart **I-1**, in chapter two, we see that the completion of our Evolutionary Epochs only moves us out of the Physical Condition of Form of the Mineral Kingdom of Life. There are three more Kingdoms to pass through before we reach the end of Earth Evolution and move into the holy city, or Jupiter Condition of Consciousness. To me this indicates that, just as we had to deal with the consciousness soul in each of the three cycles above, we have to recreate the 144,000 in each of the three following Conditions of Life, namely, the Plant, Animal, and Human Kingdoms. Steiner's 144,000 explanation only deals with the Mineral Condition of Life.

My own explanation of the 144,000, which follows below, seems to point to the successive returns to the twelve in solving the mystery of the 144,000. It could apply even beyond our Kingdoms into the three Conditions of Consciousness that follow the Earth Condition.

My Own Discovery of the Meaning of the 144,000

While perhaps merely a different way of expressing the same end result as above, my own investigation led me, some years ago, to a different way of expressing the meaning of this number. The explanation was first published, at length, in 2001 as part of the "Fire" essay in *DQWIM*.[47] In 2014, it was given again, in somewhat different perspective, in my autobiography.[48] Borrowing here portions of what was said there:

> Probably my most intense inner experience arose when I realized that I had intuited the meaning of the mysterious and problematical 144,000. It is the 144 that is important, the thousand was simply a term of magnification of importance, and perhaps was added because of the way the multiple of twelve seems to reverberate into even more distant stages of the long human journey, as suggested in what follows. The number 144,000 appears in an anticipatory way in Revelation 7:4, but it culminates in 14:1, 3 after the blowing of the "last trumpet," the seventh, in 11:15. Paul's letters were written before Lazarus/John's apocalyptic vision and account. Revelation's passages put flesh on the flashes of Paul's own intuition that seem, ever and again, in the letters to his churches, simply to emerge without elaboration, but are nevertheless sufficient to evidence the depth of his insight as it was more fully revealed in his "letter" to the Hebrews. Paul

---

47   *DQWIM*, 166–204, esp. 197–198.
48   *PWA*, 515–519.

speaks of the "last trumpet" in 1 Corinthians 15:52 when we shall "be changed" from perishable to imperishable, and again he speaks of this "trumpet" in 1 Thessalonians 4:16–17 when "we...shall...meet the Lord in the air," an appropriate way of suggesting a change in the nature of our existence after the sound of that last trumpet.

The significance of the last trumpet is described in the "Trumpet(s)" essay in *BB*. It is in the "Fire" essay in *DQWIM*, in the segment entitled "Fire, the Spiral, and the One Hundred Forty-Four Thousand," 166 to 204, and particularly in the sub-segment "The One Hundred Forty-Four Thousand," that we see that this number 144,000 is not a numerical limitation but a descriptive one. It is describing all those who will by then have reached the point, under the guidance of Christ as the Lord of Karma, when their physical (mineral or solid) and etheric (life) bodies have dissolved away through, in effect, a slow crucifixion of the lower bodies toward a Christ-like perfection over the ages, to the point where they are able to live in the astral world for the continuation of their long journey, including through ever higher realms in subsequent Conditions of Consciousness. The transition is at the point where earthly fire is transformed into matter-free spiritual fire—what Christ came to cast upon the earth (Luke 12:49). It happens immediately after the blowing of the last trumpet, when, as Revelation shows, we move from the sevens (letters, seals, and trumpets), into the twelves that take us through the end of Revelation and the Condition of Consciousness that follows the entirety of the Earth Condition of Consciousness—which in Anthroposophy is known as the Jupiter Condition. Steiner calls this the holy city of Revelation 21. Only those subjected to the "bowls of wrath" (Rev 16) remain in the realm of seven, those whose existence in future Conditions of Consciousness is in a lower, still to be perfected, realm, prior to the final union of all (Eph 1:9–10), unimaginably far into the evolving stages of consciousness. Only a small portion of humanity will be unable eventually to attain such union. A characteristic of these wretched souls is that their joy comes from inflicting great pain upon other creatures, such as vivisection and other torture, a practice that Steiner labeled as "black magic," in contrast to the "white magic" that helped raise other creatures.

But what was the path to my intuition of this meaning? Strangely enough, as seems the case with most of those events of destiny whose significance can only be seen in retrospect, it probably started with my investment activities [in the 1980s]. It was Robert Prechter's Elliott Wave theories that introduced me to the golden mean, or more precisely its famous Fibonacci ratio (1.618/1.00). That ratio is reflected not only in the creative spiral of our galaxies but manifests pervasively throughout the physical world's phenomena. I call it the spiral of creation. The number of creation is seven, as suggested in Proverbs 9:1. [Aside from the seven collateral bowls of wrath,] there are [three] series of seven in Revelation up through the seven trumpets. From there it moves into the realm of twelves all the way to the end of Revelation.

It was Prechter's expositions on the Fibonacci ratio where its progressive numbers are charted on a Cartesian graph into the creative spiral that instilled its significance in me for the rest of my life. Thus, the first step in the road to intuition started with one of life's practical observations of phenomena.

But what was it that brought the connection of this spiral to the 144,000? It was the intuition that I should check out whether there was a relationship of seven, the significant creative biblical number seven, to the number twelve that was the square root of 144. In the first book of the Bible, there are seven creative periods, "days," in Genesis and there are twelve zodiacal stars implicit in Yahweh's instruction to Abraham in Genesis 15:5 played out collaterally in the twelve sons of Abraham's son Ishmael, but then directly and primarily in the twelve sons of Abraham's grandson Jacob, for it was "through Isaac [that Abraham's] descendants [were to be] named" (Gen 21:12). Christ later called "twelve" disciples, and after the [three or] four realms of seven in Lazarus/

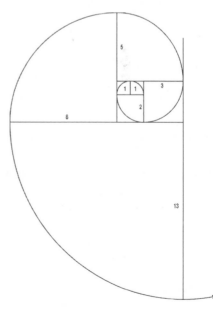

John's apocalyptic vision, the pathway forward becomes twelve-fold to the end, where we experience in many ways the number 144. Out of the twelvefold zodiacal realm of our galaxy, descent became subject to the creative laws of seven, but even in the depths of the valley the twelves appeared and then again as we journey from the material world upward in the far reaches of Revelation.

I began then to enter the Fibonacci numbers as follows:[49]

1.	1			=	1
2.	0	+	1	=	1
3.	1	+	1	=	2
4.	1	+	2	=	3
5.	2	+	3	=	5
6.	3	+	5	=	8
7.	5	+	8	=	13
8.	8	+	13	=	21
9.	13	+	21	=	34
10.	21	+	34	=	55
11.	34	+	55	=	89
12.	55	+	89	=	144

Voila! The spiral downward from the spiritual realm into the materialization of our galaxy and then our own Earth and Solar Mass would be the same spiral in reverse (the picture of the zodiacal Cancer of intertwining spirals [creating the crab image], a sign signifying transition). An exciting sequel to the 144 (expressed in thousands) that characterizes the passage out of the mineral and etheric Earth into the Jupiter Condition is that the intersection of the twelve multiple and the Fibonacci series reoccurs only on each subsequent twelfth Fibonacci number—this would seem to indicate passage upward through the subsequent major Conditions of Consciousness until complete union of all.

---

49 These, with their description, can also be found at *DQWIM*, 62, in the Apocalypse portion of the "Creation and Apocalypse" essay.

The first three subsequent intersections of the twelve multiple and the Fibonacci series (at 24, 36 and 48) are shown as follows:

13. 89 + 144= 233 233/12= 19.4167

14. 144 + 233= 377 377/12= 31.4167

15. 233 + 377= 610 610/12= 50.8333

16. 377 + 610= 987 987/12= 82.2500

17. 610 + 987= 1,597 1,597/12= 133.0833

18. 987 + 1,597= 2,584 2,584/12= 215.3333

19. 1,597 + 2,584= 4,181 4,181/12= 348.4167

20. 2584 + 4,181= 6,765 6,765/12= 563.7500

21. 4,181 + 6,765= 10,946 10,946/12= 912.1667

22. 6,765 + 10,946= 17,711 17,711/12= 1,475.9167

23. 10,946 + 17,711= 28,657 28,657/12= 2,388.0833

24. 17,711 + 28,657= 46,368 46,368/12= 3,864.0000

25. 28,657 + 46,368 = 75,025 75,025/12 = 6,252.0833

26. 46,368 + 75,025 = 121,393 121,393/12 = 10,116.0833

27. 75,025 + 121,393 = 196,418 196,418/12 = 16,368.1667

28. 121,393 + 196,418 = 317,811 317,811/12 = 26,484.2500

29. 196,418 + 317,811 = 514,229 514,119/12 = 42,843.2500

30. 317,811 + 514,229 = 832,040 832,040/12 = 69,336.6667

31. 514,229 + 832,040 = 1,346,269 1,346,269/12 = 112,189.0833

32. 832,040 + 1,346,269 = 2,178,309 2,178,309/12 = 181,525.7500

33. 1,346,269 + 2,178,309 = 3,524,578 3,524,578/12 = 293,714.8333

34. 2,178,309 + 3,524,578 = 5,702,887 5,702,887/12 = 475,240.5833

35. 3,524,578 + 5,702,887 = 9,227,465 9,227,465/12 = 768,955,4167

36. 5,702,887 + 9,227,465 = 14,930,352 14,930,352/12 = 1,244,196.0000

37. 9,227,465 + 14,930,352 = 24,157,817
$$24{,}157{,}817/12 = 2{,}013{,}151.4167$$

38. 14,930,352 + 24,157,817 = 39,088,169
$$39{,}088{,}169/12 = 3{,}257{,}347.2167$$

39. 24,157,817 + 39,088,169 = 63,245,986
$$63{,}245{,}986/12 = 5{,}270{,}498.8333$$

40. 39,088,169 + 63,245,986 = 102,334,155
$$102{,}334{,}155/12 = 8{,}527{,}846.2500$$

41. 63,245,986 + 102,334,155 = 165,580,141
$$165{,}580{,}141/12 = 13{,}798{,}345.0833$$

42. 102,334,155 + 165,580,141 = 267,914,296
$$267{,}914{,}296/12 = 22{,}326{,}191.3333$$

43. 165,580,141 + 267,914,296 = 433,494,437
$$433{,}494{,}437/12 = 36{,}124{,}536.4166$$

44. 267,914,296 + 433,494,437 = 701,408,733
$$701{,}408{,}733/12 = 58{,}450{,}727.7500$$

45. 433,494,437 + 701,408,733 = 1,134,903,170
$$1{,}134{,}903{,}170/12 = 94{,}575{,}264.1666$$

46. 701,408,733 + 1,134,903,170 = 1,836,311,903
$$1{,}836{,}311{,}903/12 = 153{,}025{,}991.916$$

47. 1,134,903,170 + 1,836,311,903 = 2,971,215,073
$$2{,}971{,}215{,}073/12 = 247{,}601{,}256.083$$

48. 1,836,311,903 + 2,971,215,073 = 4,807,526.976
$$4{,}807{,}526.976/12 = 400{,}627{,}248.000$$

The Opening of the Sixth Seal

Having considered at length the meaning of "the number" adverted to as the white robe was given at the opening of the fifth seal to those whose bodies had by then been "crucified," we turn now to the opening of the sixth seal.

We have previously seen that the Sixth Cultural Age of our present Epoch is the one from which the fruits of our Epoch will be carried into the Sixth Evolutionary Epoch, that of the seven seals.

The vision that comes to John upon the opening of the sixth seal is through the spiritual eyes of those from our Sixth Cultural Age who will carry the fruits of our Epoch over to the next, just as the Noah event carried from the fifth age of Atlantis the fruits of that Epoch over to our own. We are told, "When he opened the sixth seal, I looked, and behold, there was a great earthquake; and the sun became black as sackcloth, the full moon became like blood...the stars...fell to the earth...every mountain and island was removed from its place." The powerful "hid in caves" seeking to hide "from the face of him who is seated on the throne, and from the wrath of the Lamb; for the great day of their wrath has come, and who can stand before it?" (6:12–17).

In its literal expression, this reads as though the promise to those of Philadelphia (Sixth Cultural Age) who have been faithful that they will be kept "from the hour of trial which is coming on the whole world" (3:10) may have been violated—but to so read it is to miss what we are being told as the seal is lifted. For what they see is a spiritual vision of what is to occur in the next, the seventh and last Epoch. In the course of the human journey, the sun gave us physical life and the moon slowed us down to the pace necessary for our development. Now, as the return journey begins, the process becomes spiritualized and those who have been faithful see the reverse of what happened in human physical development. The external sun and moon disappear and become in their vision like a human being, the sun becoming black as "sackcloth of hair" and the moon becoming like blood. Human hair is the physical remnant of the spiritual guidance that used to stream into the human being, akin to the horns on Michelangelo's Moses, and blood is the sacred home of the human "I Am." It is a vision of the spiritualizing of humankind. They are capable, at this stage, of prophetic vision.[50]

That the promise to the faithful from the Age of Philadelphia has not been violated is confirmed by what is then given us in Revelation 7. The angel "with the seal of the living God" ordered the "four angels standing at the four corners of the earth" to hold off any destruction on earth until the servants of God, the 144,000, have been sealed upon their foreheads. They are "clothed in...robes...made...white

---

50   *ASJ*, lect. 4; 88–89.

in the blood of the Lamb; the Lamb...will guide them to springs of living water; and God will wipe away every tear from their eyes" (7:13–17).

Abel and the 144,000

What we are now compelled to contemplate is the being of Abel in relation to the 144,000. I suggest that the "blood of Abel," spilled when he was killed by his brother Cain in Genesis 4, is the impelling spiritual force behind the power of human beings to attain the status of the 144,000. This balance of the spilling of blood between the beginnings of Genesis and the ending of Revelation is striking, and is a highly appropriate opening and closing for an account of the human journey through the mineral-physical realm. "Only three chapters precede the first appearance of *blood* in the Bible and only three follow its last, and it pervades the pages in between.... "[51]

For this writer, it is clear that neither Cain nor Abel were human beings, but represented divinely implanted impulses within, and restrictions on, every human being. In short, each represented an element powerfully embedded in every human being. As respects Cain, it has already been extensively and cogently treated in the "Cain" essay in *The Soul's Long Journey*.[52] We must now consider Abel to have been of like nature to Cain in this respect, namely, a human tendency or impulse, with restriction, but representing the polar opposite of his brother. Genesis 4 is an allegorical expression of these respective characteristics, deeply embedded in all of Adam's earthly descendants, who, as discussed in the Cain essay, all descended through Adam's son Seth, not Cain.[53]

---

51 *DQWIM*, 318 (the "Blood" essay).

52 *SLJ*, "Cain," 86–99.

53 Rudolf Steiner confirmed that "the story of Cain and Abel...is an allegory for very profound mysteries." *The Temple Legend* (*TL*), lect. 2 (Berlin, June 10, 1904), 19, RSP (1985) (CW 93). Something of the profundity can be found in both lectures 2 and 5 of *TL*. A bit of this content is found in the "Appendix to 'Three Bodies'" in *BB*, pp. 460–462. Steiner gave a further elaboration on this allegory in *The Effects of Spiritual Development* (ESD), lect. 8 (The Hague, March 27, 1913), RSP (1978) (CW 145). To venture into the complexities of these presentations would carry us too far afield to accomplish our present objective. What is given in the text, though extensively condensed, is, I believe, fairly derived from, and is either clearly implied or directly supported

The "Cain" essay concludes with the statement that the human restrictions implanted in all as the Cain element "will continue until we have attained to that level where we, as the 'burning bush,' no longer need to dwell in those bodies"—which is precisely the condition of the 144,000. But if such is the limitation of Cain, what is the tendency or impulse implanted in all human beings through the blood of Abel? It is the deeply implanted urge in every human being to return to the spiritual home from which it descended. The urge had to be quickened by the incarnated Christ Spirit, especially when the blood of Jesus Christ fell into the earth and infused life, of the type mentioned in John 1:4, into every creature.

The very name of these two brothers suggests the characteristic each embedded in every earthly descendant of Adam. Cain means "possession," and it was the tendency to possess the mineral body on Earth that was implanted in all as the Cain element of their being; the name Abel means breath, nothingness, or something transitory, suggesting the tendency not to descend into matter.[54] Scholars have not been able to establish a meaningful reason why the sacrifice of Abel was favorably regarded by Yahweh whereas that of Cain was not (Gen 4:3–5). But one can readily gather from Steiner's teachings that there was a powerful reason. It was not the desire of Yahweh that HBs actually descend into bodies of matter. During the Hyperborean (second) Evolutionary Epoch, before the sun separated from the solar mass that still contained the earth, the HB looked down from the spiritual realms and perceived spiritual beings surging up and down in the astral body while the sentient soul "made the HB feel bound to the body of the Earth."[55] In picture consciousness they had the realization "This is yours" (*OES* 201), and later in the same Epoch, after the sun had separated but before the moon had, "This is my form" (*OES* 207). It was the desire of Yahweh to "develop the mirror of human consciousness in such a way that the influence of the Sun spirits would have dominated all of human soul life" (*OES* 299), but these desires were

---

by, these more elaborate presentations.

54 Richard S. Hess, "Abel" in 1 ABD 9–10, at 10 (1992); *The JPS Torah commentary, Genesis*, vol. 1, Jewish Publication Society (1989), 32.

55 Compare Jacob's dream of the angels ascending and descending in Gen 28:12.

thwarted by the old Moon beings (luciferic spirits) so that HBs "became entangled in earthly matter to a greater degree than had been predestined for them" (*OES*, 230).[56]

In the light of this most basic written work of Steiner, it is not hard to see why the offering of Abel was favored and that of Cain was not.

Paul, the deeply intuitive author of Hebrews said of Abel, "By faith Abel offered to God a more acceptable sacrifice than Cain, through which he received approval as righteous, God bearing witness by accepting his gifts; *he died, but through his faith he is still speaking*" (emphasis mine).[57] Later, but well before John's Apocalypse, Paul speaks of "the city of the living God, the heavenly Jerusalem ... and of the first-born who are enrolled in heaven," words that anticipated John's 144,000 and his new Jerusalem (Heb 12:22–23). But going on he refers to "Jesus, the mediator of a new covenant, and to the sprinkled blood that speaks more graciously than the blood of Abel" (Heb 12:24). What Abel gave to each human soul was the disposition to return, but it took the blood of the Christ on earth to make that possible, thus speaking "more graciously than the blood of Abel."

In both the Gospels of Matthew and Luke, the so-called "Little Apocalypse" passages, Christ Jesus speaks of Abel's blood in a way suggesting its archetypal, but etheric, aspect of human blood.[58]

We must surely see that the male character of Cain led the descent of HBs into matter, while it will be the more spiritual female character of Abel that will lead HBs back into the spiritual realm. On this, however, we must remember that each HB embodies a physical body of either male or female, which is balanced by an etheric body of the opposite gender, while the astral body and higher aspects of each human being have no particular gender but are common to both.

The Opening of the Seventh Seal

"When the Lamb opened the seventh seal, there was silence in heaven for about half an hour" (8:1). It bespeaks an ominous foreboding of the shattering effect of the seven trumpets, representing the

---

56 Steiner, *An Outline of Esoteric Science* (*OES*), AP (CW 13).

57 Heb 11:4.

58 Matt 23:35; Luke 11:50–51.

seventh and final Evolutionary Epoch, when "we reach the boundary of our physical earth development."[59]

59   *ASJ*, lect. 8; 143.

9

THE BLOWING OF THE SEVEN TRUMPETS

It is always well to keep things in perspective when talking of the Evolutionary Epochs. The end of our present Post-Atlantean Epoch is still approximately six thousand years in the future, according to our present mode of measurement. The period of the trumpets, the seventh and last such period, is two full Evolutionary Epochs in our future evolution. Even though matter will remain in the Sixth Epoch and, at least to some extent, in the seventh, it seems unwise to extrapolate our present method of measuring our "ages" into Epochs, and perhaps modestly even into our Cultural Ages, beyond our own. Time can exist only in the realm of matter, and movement through matter is dramatically affected by the density of matter. Such density is not a constant.[1]

---

1   Readers are encouraged to ponder this, considering: Mark 13:20 and Matt 24:22 on the Lord's "shortening the days"; Steiner, *Cosmic Memory* (tr.. Karl E. Zimmer), San Francisco, Harper & Row (1981) (1959 English copyright by Rudolf Steiner Publications, orig. publ in German in 1904), ch. 13; 171 (quoted in *BB* 192) (CW 11); the "Fire" essay in *DQWIM*, elliptical charts of the Evolutionary Epochs and Cultural Ages, 177–178; *BB*, chart **I-19** at p. 451 depicting the dates of the Cultural Ages of the Post-Atlantean Evolutionary Epoch, based upon Robert Powell's *Hermetic Astrology I*, Kinsau, W. Germany, Hermetica Verlag (1987)—Powell infers a constant number of years in each age of the Atlantean and Post-Atlantean Evolutionary Epochs citing Steiner's *Ancient Myths, Their Meaning and Connection with Evolution*, N. Vancouver, BC, Steiner Book Centre (1979), lect. 7 (Dornach, Jan. 13, 1918), 112 (CW 180), where Steiner indicates that the "seventh [age] of the Lemurian [Epoch]...lies about 25,900 years before our epoch. It was about 25,000–26,000 years ago that this seventh [age] of the Lemurian [Epoch] came to an end on earth"—one has to wonder if such inference can be fully sustained in light of the prior matters cited in this footnote—matter was far less dense at the end of the Lemurian Epoch than in the Atlantean and Post-Atlantean Epochs, for according to Steiner, the greatest density was in the Post-Atlantean (see "Christ, the J-Curve and the Right Time" in the "Fire" essay in *DQWIM*, 175–181).

The Significance of the Blowing Trumpet

At the outset of the "Trumpets" essay in *BB*, it was pointed out that originally the blowing of the trumpet was to sound an alarm. That function can well be imagined in John's account of the Epoch of the trumpets, but that hardly addresses all that needs be said on the matter. Many of the numerous Old Testament trumpet passages cited probably have that as a primary function. But in many of the OT passages it would seem that a deeper meaning should be perceived. Notable is the account of the falling of the walls of Jericho and the conquest of Ai, which have been previously addressed.[2] Other OT trumpet passages lend themselves to an understanding related to the meaning as used in the NT.[3] But it is in the NT passages where the trumpet passages must be seen in a significant new way from the interpretation commonly and depressingly pressed upon them by those who think in terms of our present existential condition. I speak, particularly, in canonical order, of Matt 24:31; 1 Cor 15:52; 1 Thess 4:16; and Heb 12:19, which take on a very specific and far more appropriate meaning in the light of what John's Revelation should be seen as revealing about them. That meaning has relevance also on the passages of Christ's coming on the clouds, even where trumpets are not mentioned.[4]

The Harvest of our Seventh Age

We have seen that it is the sixth Cultural Age, that of Philadelphia, in our Post-Atlantean, or fifth, Evolutionary Epoch that will carry over to the sixth Evolutionary Epoch the fruits of our fifth. It may then seem strange that, on the opening of the sixth Seal in the sixth Epoch, the most frightful disasters are described (6:12–17). We saw, though, in the chapter on the Seals that the appearance of these disasters was not revealing what had been sealed in the former Age of Philadelphia but was rather "a vision of the spiritualizing of mankind," a "prophetic vision" of the seventh and last age of the Seals, made possible to those

---

2   See *DQWIM*, 202, indicating that archaeology does not support the literal account at either Jericho or Ai.

3   See, for instance, Isa 18:3; 27:13; Ezek 33:3–6; Hos 8:1; Joel 2:1; and Zech 9:14–15.

4   Mark 13:26; 14:62; Matt 24:30; 26:64.

in such sixth age because of their spiritual capabilities.[5] The vision
had to do with what was sealed in the seventh Cultural Age of our
Post-Atlantean Epoch.

I must confess to having struggled with the question of whether
this "prophetic vision" was of the seventh age of the sixth Evolutionary Epoch, on the one hand, or of the entirety of the seventh and last
Evolutionary Epoch that would conclude humanity's life in human
physical bodies composed of matter, on the other hand.[6]

Reading in lecture 4 from the 1908 Nuremberg cycle (*ASJ*) and
lectures 9 (its ending part) and 10 (its opening part) from the 1909
Oslo (Kristiania) cycle (*RPA*), it would appear that some of the "earth-
quakes and tremors" and even more devastating physical cataclysms
occurred on earth during the period of the opening of the sixth seal.
It seems clear that Steiner is indicating that these events were at least
prophetic visions in that age of what was to occur in the seventh and
last Great Epoch. Were they also prophetic of what would begin to happen in the seventh and last age of the sixth Great Epoch, as the last seal
is opened? It seems that it should make no difference. For one thing, in
view of how far in the future we are speaking we may be straining at
a gnat. Particularly is this so in view of the fact that Steiner has said,
"The so-called seventh age will be of very little importance ... [it will]
"contain no principle of progress."[7] While it speaks of the period after
the War of All against All, the context seems to be that of the last age
of our fifth Great Epoch, the Post-Atlantean (Laodicea). But in Revelation, nothing is said about what happens when the seal on that seventh
Cultural Age is opened, other than that there was "silence in heaven

---

5   That it was prophetic is also suggested by 7:3 where the angels with the powers
of destroying matter were told not to do so till the 144,000 had been sealed,
anticipating the stage described in Revelation 14.

6   To start with, the matter is complicated by the fact that, at least in our English
translations, Steiner did not always use the terms *age* and *epoch* in a way that
is literally consistent with the terminology in the Grand Schematic (*BB's* chart
I-1), nor are capital letters always used consistently on these terms. One can
almost always tell, however, by the context which is meant. In my writing I
have attempted to use the terms *Age* and *Epoch* in a way that is consistent with
how they are used in the Grand Schematic—regardless of whether the term is
capitalized or not. Thus, to me, *age* refers to one of the seven subdivisions of
an evolutionary epoch, as they are shown in that schematic, which came from
the Nuremberg lecture cycle on the Apocalypse.

7   *ASJ*, lect. 8; 138.

for about half an hour" (8:1), whereupon it immediately launches into the blowing of the seven trumpets. We note that the description of the cataclysmic events during the sixth age of the seals is described in Revelation chapter 6; that the angels with destructive power are told in Revelation chapter 7, "Do not harm the earth or the sea or the trees, till we have sealed" the 144,000 which does not happen till Revelation 14. In interpreting 6:12–17, I'm influenced by the sequence as John presents it so that I do not see major earthly cataclysms occurring in the sixth age of the seals. Those awful events, from our present physical standpoint, await the Epoch of the trumpets.

There are indications that those who have already qualified for the status of the 144,000 by the end of the sixth age of the seals (6:9–11) might have already fully given up their material bodies and risen into an astral state whence they merely look down upon the events on earth. But if so they are not freed from responsibility for effectively working from there to bring others into their realm before the last trumpet is blown. And the obligation may be imposed upon them to enter into, or at least hover over, some of the bodies of those still below to work their salvation. We shall shortly look more fully at this obligation.

The Mission of the Manicheans

Consider again the matter of evil, that is, of good and evil, as presented by Steiner in the long insert in chapter 6 from the eighth chapter of the Nuremberg (*ASJ*) lecture cycle. The insert dealt with our present Cultural Age, the "European" (Rev 3:1–6). In particular, see the extract's last two paragraphs explaining the paradox of the ultimately beneficent effect of evil in human evolution.

Immediately following those two paragraphs in the *ASJ* lecture, Steiner continued:

> Those who are being prepared in their souls by such teachings, so that in the future they will be able to accomplish this great task of education, are the pupils of the spiritual stream called the Manichean School. The Manichean teaching is generally misunderstood. When you hear anything or read something about it, you find merely phrases. You may read that the Manichees believed that from the very beginning of the world there have been two principles: good and evil. This is not so; the teaching of the Manichees

is what we have just explained. By the name "Manicheism" should be understood this teaching and its development in the future, and the pupils who are so led that they can accomplish such a task in future incarnations. *Manes* is that exalted individuality who is repeatedly incarnated on the earth, who is the guiding spirit of those whose task it is to transform evil. When we speak of great leaders of mankind we must also think of this individuality who has set himself this task.... [T]his wonderful and lofty Manichean principle will win more and more pupils the nearer we approach the understanding of spiritual life.[8]

Not until the year following his lecture cycles on the Apocalypse did Steiner reveal, in two steps, the source of the spiritual forces of Manes. First, he identified the youth of Nain, whom Christ raised from the dead (Luke 7:11–17), as one who would become "a great religious teacher in a later life...who would advance Christianity" at a time when the "feeling" for such matters had been implanted by Christ in human souls.[9] The necessity for a second step was apparent from Steiner's introductory statement, "In an exoteric lecture I cannot identify this individuality by name." But obviously, to those more closely affiliated, he later not only identified the youth as Mani, or Manes," but gave "some illuminating indications concerning [his] Karmic path."[10] Steiner did, however, in his exoteric lecture distinguish the kind of resuscitation applied to the youth of Nain from that of Lazarus. In the latter, "the new initiate is immediately able to understand spiritual laws and processes. A different type of initiation merely plants a seed in the soul of the candidate, who becomes an initiate only when the seed begins to develop in a subsequent incarnation. The young man of Nain underwent the latter type of initiation. His soul, transformed during the event of Palestine, was not yet conscious of ascending into higher worlds. The forces implanted in his soul germinated only in his next incarnation" (201).

---

8   *ASJ*, lect. 8; 142.

9   Steiner, *According to Luke*, AP (2001) (lect. 10, Basle, September 26, 1909), 200–201 (CW 114).

10   Emil Bock, *The Three Years*, London, Christian Community Press (1955; 4th reprint with index, 1987; orig publ. in German under the title *Die Drei Jahre* in 1948), 154–156.

Mani was born on April 14, 216 CE in Mesopotamia (of Iranian descent) and proclaimed himself " the apostle of light, the Paraclete incarnate, and the seal of the prophets who would bring the final revelation to the world." He also proclaimed "the final revelation, the true universal religion which would unite all people through his teaching."[11] Steiner appears to recognize the spiritual reality of those proclamations.

On the threshold of humanity's great divergence, Steiner presents the Manichean stream and its critical, salvific mission—in lecture eight in Nuremberg where he reprises the seals and, in keeping with his characterization of seventh ages, peremptorily dispatches it: "The seventh epoch will be the descended heavenly world, the expression of it. And then the earth will have reached the goal of its physical evolution."[12] One reading the scriptural text about the blowing of the first six trumpets might find it hard, in an earthly context, to describe the situation as a "descended heavenly world" (8:2–9:21). Doubtless Steiner derived his description from what occurred upon the blowing of the seventh and last trumpet (11:15–19), when "God's temple in heaven was opened" (11:19).

But while he summarily dispatched with any literal account of the blowing of the trumpets in the Nuremberg cycle (*ASJ*), he touches upon them in *RPA*, where he also briefly refers to the three woes, described also, in accord with the Grand Schematic (chapter 2), as "the last three physical states" (8:13; 9:12).[13] One notes that the three woes appear, successively, after the blowing of the last three trumpets, raising both the specter of the last three ages of Atlantis as they relate to the first beast that is to arise in John's vision. Notable in regard to the specter is the appearance, after the blowing of the fifth trumpet, in light of the four horsemen in 6:2–8, of "horses arrayed for battle . . . with faces like

---

11   Paul Allan Mirecki, "Manichaean's and Manichaeism," *ABD*, vol. 4 (1992) 502–511 at 503; see also Arthur Zajonc, "Manichaeism—Religion of Light," in *Catching the Light*, New York, Oxford University Press (1993), 47–52; Mani (Prophet) in https://en.wikipedia.org/wiki/Mani_(prophet). For Augustine's involvement with Manicheism; see W. H. C. Frend, *The Rise of Christianity*, Philadelphia, Fortress Press (1984), 662–663.

12   *ASJ*, lect. 8; 145.

13   *RPA*, lect. 10; 122.

human faces [with] tails like scorpions" for stinging and hurting men (9:7–10). Revelation 10 opens:

> ¹ Then I saw another mighty angel coming down from heaven, wrapped in a cloud, with a rainbow over his head, and his face was like the sun, and his legs like pillars of fire. ² He had a little scroll open in his hand. And he set his right foot on the sea, and his left foot on the land, ³ and called out with a loud voice....
>
> ⁵ And the angel whom I saw standing on sea and land lifted up his right hand to heaven ⁶ and swore by him who...created heaven..., the earth..., and the sea...that there should be no more delay, ⁷ but that in the days of the trumpet call to be sounded by the seventh angel, the mystery of God, as he announced to his servants the prophets, should be fulfilled.

Jachin and Boaz

John's vision of the angel with "legs like pillars of fire" (10:1) with right foot on the sea and left foot on the land (10:2) invokes ancient symbolism. To build a temple to the house of the Lord, King Solomon brought Hiram, a "widow's son" from Tyre (1 Kgs 7:13). Hiram "cast two pillars of bronze" (7:15) which he set up at the entrance to the temple, the pillar on the south he called Jachin and that on the north he called Boaz" (7:21).[14]

Steiner explains John's reference to these pillars. "Our Earth was preceded by what we call the Cosmos of Wisdom [Ancient Moon], and that was preceded by what we call the Cosmos of Strength [Ancient Sun].... The mission of our Earth is to add love." The first half of Earth evolution, representing the Sun forces, is called Mars, and the second half, representing the Moon forces, is called Mercury. The days of our week reflect this, being Sunday (Sun), Monday (Moon), Tuesday (Mars), and Wednesday (Mercury).[15] "Up to the middle of the fourth period we speak of the Mars forces, of the forces given by water, so to speak, and we speak of the Mercury forces in the later time when the solid earth gives the supporting forces." So this is what one who ascends into spiritual realms observes as the state of the earth "when

---

14 This scenario is also given in 2 Chr 3:15–17; Jeremiah tells of the destruction of the pillars by the Babylonians in 587 BCE (Jer 52:17, 20–23).

15 *Rosicrucianism Renewed*, SB (2007), CW 284; 81; see also *BB*, 14.

earthly substance dissolves into the spiritual."[16] The image can be observed from the fourth apocalyptic seal (see footnote) that the right foot (Jachin, the Mars water forces), being on the left side of the seal as it faces the observer, is in the sea, and the left foot, on the right side of the seal, is on the strength of solid rock.[17] In a lecture in Dornach on December 29, 1918, Steiner tells how Brunetto Latini, the teacher of Dante, describing his own initiation, experienced this Jachin and Boaz imagery as a passing through the Pillars of Hercules.[18]

Considering especially the relationship between Anthroposophy as given to us by Rudolf Steiner and the spiritual teachings of Christian Rosenkreutz in the 15th century, as set out early in the first chapter of this book, I cannot leave our consideration of these pillars without noting that Steiner viewed them as representing his relationship with Rosenkreutz. On the last page of text (113) of *Rudolf Steiner's Mission and Ita Wegman*, by Margarete and Erich Kirchner-Bockholt, speaking of seeking imagination, inspiration, and intuition through "the Sun within me," and considering the imminent reference to the "altar" in Revelation 11:1:

> Rudolf Steiner said that one should think of oneself in a white garment, walking toward the altar, Christian Rosenkreutz with a blue stole standing to the left, Rudolf Steiner himself with a red stole standing to the right. One must think of this altar in the spiritual world. On another occasion Rudolf Steiner said that in the spiritual world the figures wearing these stoles stand side by side.[19]

---

16   *ASJ*, lect. 8; 147–149. Steiner (p. 149) says that the concept of these two pillars was, at the time of his lecture, "symbolically represented in the congress hall in Munich" (see the picture of the Munich audience and seals at the end of CW 284). His seven apocalyptic seals, the two pillars being the fourth, are reproduced at the end of *ASJ*, and facsimile reproductions can be found in plates 4, 12, and 13 at the end of CW 284.

17   This placement is confirmed by Kenneth A. Mathews, as is the meaning of the two names (Jachin being "a setting right," and Boaz being "strength"), *ABD*, vol. 1; 765, "Boaz."

18   *How Can Mankind Find The Christ Again*, 2nd ed., AP (1984), lect. 6; 109–115 (CW 187).

19   Margarete and Erich Kirchner-Bockholt, *Rudolf Steiner's Mission and Ita Wegman*, RSP (1977), 113.

The appearance in this excerpt of the blue on the left and the red on the right is consistent with the portrayal of the two pillars in the fourth apocalyptic seal in plates 12 and 13 at the end of CW 284, noted in an earlier footnote. Of particular additional interest to me is the reference to the "other occasion" where Steiner spoke about his relationship with Rosenkreutz. I have a recollection of having read something else he said on the matter, which I thought was in connection with these Jachin and Boaz pillars, but I have been unable thus far to find that reference.

We might ask why the colors were red and blue. They represent the red, oxygenated, and the blue, deoxygenated, blood.[20] These different colors of blood represent, esoterically, the two trees that compose the circulatory system in the human body, reflecting the tree of knowledge, enabled by oxygen in the blood, and the tree of life, that is, death, from lack of oxygen, that leads to life; the two trees in Eden and the two pillars in the Jachin and Boaz legend.[21] In a lecture on May 18, 1907, on the seven Apocalyptic Seals in the Munich Congress Hall, he gives a shorter version as he explains the fourth seal.[22]

The Eating of the Scroll

Then the "voice from heaven" (10:4) spoke again:

[8] Then the voice which I had heard from heaven spoke to me again, saying, "Go, take the scroll which is open in the hand of the angel who is standing on the sea and on the land." [9] So I went to the angel and told him to give me the little scroll; and he said to me, "Take it and eat; it will be bitter to your stomach, but sweet as honey in your mouth." [10] And I took the little scroll from the hand of the angel and ate it; it was sweet as honey in my mouth, but when I had eaten it my stomach was made bitter.[23]

---

20 There is no "blue" blood. It is actually only a deeper red that appears blue due only to the effect of seeing it through the pigmentation of bodily material that separates the flowing venous blood from the eye of the beholder.

21 *RPA*, lect. 4 (Munich, May 15, 1907), 58–61.

22 This lecture, labeled *OSC* for *Occult Seals and Columns*, is one of the six sources of Steiner material on the Apocalypse that are listed on page 54 of *DQWIM* at the first of its essay "Creation and Apocalypse." My copy of the lecture is an unpublished English typescript made from copy provided to me by the Rudolf Steiner Library. Perhaps it will be included in CW 285; it is not in CW 284.

23 Again, OT imagery plays into John's vision; see Ezek 2:8–3:3.

In closing his lecture 8, Steiner speaks of "the arising in the seer when he directs his gaze to the point when the Earth passes from the physically material into the astrally spiritual, when the Earth mission is attained":

> While, therefore, the soul is able to ascend—the soul of the seer described by the Apocalyptist—into spiritual regions, in order to receive the Gospel of Love, and in spirit is able to feel the bliss sweet as honey, yet the seer lives in a present-day body, and in accordance with this he must say that the ascent produces in the present body the antithesis of that bliss in many respects. He expresses this by saying that although the little book is at first sweet as honey, it gives him severe pains in the belly when he has swallowed it. But this is only a small reflection of "being crucified in the body." The higher the spirit rises, the more difficult it is for it to dwell in the body, and this is the symbolical expression for these pains: "being crucified in the body."
>
> Thus we have briefly sketched what will happen in our Earth evolution, what lies in front of man in his Earthly evolution. We have arrived at the point when man is changed into an astral being; when the best parts of the Earth disappear as physical earth and pass over into the spiritual; when only something like an isolated portion will through the divine wrath fall into the abyss. And we shall see that even then the last stage, at which salvation would no longer be possible, has not yet been reached, although what is in the abyss is pictured by the most frightful symbols, by the seven-headed and ten horned beast and by the two-horned beast.

Measurement of the Temple of God

Chapter 10 closes with the voice from heaven saying "You must again prophesy... (10:11). Then, "given a measuring rod... I was told:

> Rise and measure the temple of God and the altar and those who worship there, but do not measure the court outside the temple; leave that out, for it is given over to the nations, and they will trample over the holy city for forty-two months. And I will grant my two witnesses power to prophesy for one thousand two hundred and sixty days, clothed in sackcloth. [24]

---

24 Rev 11:1–3. In his lecture to the priests in Dornach on Sept. 18, 1924 (lect. 14), 199 in *The Book of Revelation and the Work of the Priest*, RSP (1998) (CW

John is told to "measure the temple of God." Considering the tenor of this book, we can hardly imagine that the temple is anything other than something constructed and existing in the realm of spirit. The writer of this book, describing the recriminative question the Jews asked Jesus upon his driving the money-changers out of the temple, gives Jesus' response, "Destroy this temple and in three days I will raise it up" (John 2:19). But then John said, "But he spoke of the temple of his body" (2:21).[25]

John is thus told what to measure, but he is also told what *not* to measure, "the court outside the temple...for it is given over to the nations [to] trample over the holy city for forty-two months" during which he will grant his "two witnesses power to prophesy"—for 1,260 days, "clothed in sackcloth"—with special powers through the forces of nature (11:5–6). Ezekiel's vision, "preparatory to the restoration and rebuilding of the temple" (Ezek 40:3–42:20), clearly portrays an outer court to the temple; see also his beautiful allegory of the temple and the water flowing through it like a river (Ezek 47:1–12).[26]

---

346), Steiner said, "I had to do a considerable amount of research before I discovered that these 1,260 days are an actual 'printer's error'..." and that '2,160 days' is what the passage ought to say.... "

I think Steiner may have been wrong on this, for the 1,260 days appears in both 11:3 and 12:6, and in 11:2 the time period mentioned is "42 months," which appears again in 13:5. The 42-month period is a recurring motif, and notably it expresses in years (3½) what then appears as days in 11:9, the initiation period of the author of the Apocalypse (see also Dan 7:25; 12:7; Rev 12:14). Based upon a 30-day month, 42 months is 1,260 days. It is hard to believe that a single printer's error accounted for all these instances of consistent numerical usage. Steiner was a very sick man when he was giving this lecture series to the priests shortly before his illness forced him to give up lecturing. It was delivered in an informal style and the lectures were "reconstructed from notes taken by participants." He does not elaborate further on the nature of his "research." My suspicion is that if he found a printer's change, it was more likely a "printer's correction" than a "printer's error."

25 See also Mark 14:58; 15:29; Matt 26:61; 27:40; and Acts 61:14.

26 Martin Rist, Exegesis to "Revelation," *The Interpreter's Bible*, New York/ Nashville, Abingdon Press (1957), vol. 12; 443–444. Rist also calls attention to the a somewhat similar procedure for measuring the righteous, "In an interesting incident in I Enoch 61:1–5, angels with cords measure the righteous and the faithful so that they may never be destroyed before the Lord of Spirits" (444).

The Building of the Temple

Rudolf Steiner gives a patient review of the building process in lecture nine of the June 1908 Nuremberg cycle. The building of the temple has been, and remains, an extremely long process. The human being of today is fourfold, consisting of "the physical body... developed on Saturn, the etheric body on the Sun, the astral body on the Moon, and the ego [the "I" or "I Am"] on the Earth."[27] It is this ego that is the builder of the temple, but much as one would ascribe the building of a mature human being to have started in its infancy— much help from the spiritual world was required while the ego had only dim consciousness. Steiner patiently traces out what he had given earlier in 1908, between January 6 and June 11, in his eleven lecture cycle in Berlin.[28] The ego's penetration of, and work within, the three human bodies is the subject of chart **I-35** in *BB* as well as schematically in the essay "Naked" in *BB* at pages 402 to 403. Since the deed of Christ that we call the Mystery of Golgotha, the work on the astral body has been through the Christ-inspired ego, or "I Am," expressed by Paul essentially as, "Not I, but Christ in me" (Gal 2:20). The purification of the astral body to the state required to dissolve the mineral-physical body in the development of manas (spirit-self) is the building of the temple.

We may rightly ask ourselves, how can the physical body be dissolved if the etheric body, that builds and maintains the physical body, still functions? We know from our basic anthroposophical studies that the transformation of the astral body is the ego's main task during Earth evolution.[29] But we also know that the etheric body is not unaffected in the process of the perfection, through the Christ in us, of the astral body. To some extent the etheric body is also spiritually enhanced.[30] Seemingly, it has to be in order to loosen its grip on the physical to permit the latter's dissolution. What is thus accomplished, "ennobled," toward its buddhi state is not lost. It is the "I Am" and the

---

27 *ASJ*, lect. 9; 154. The "Ancient" that typically precedes these three planetary Conditions of Consciousness is omitted.

28 *Good and Evil Spirits and Their Influence on Humanity*, SB (2014), CW 102, formerly *The Influence of Spiritual Beings Upon Man*, AP (1961).

29 *ASJ*, lect. 12; 213.

30 *ASJ*, lect. 12; 214.

astral body it has purified, as well as "the ennobled etheric...which can live in the astralized earth," that constitute the holy city (11:2 and chapter 21), which Steiner identifies as the Jupiter Condition of Consciousness.[31] The "outer court" comprises the physical body and whatever part of the etheric body still maintains its hold on the physical—it is that part of the etheric body of HB that still clings to the physical that figures into the "second death" that will appear later. Speaking of the etheric body as part of the temple, Steiner says, "That alone which man has made does he keep."[32]

That the nations "will trample over the holy city for forty-two months" seems to indicate that even those who have built the temple, the holy city, will be subjected to this trampling for a period of time (forty-two months), perhaps a time shortened for their salvation (Mark 13:20; Matt 24:22). Certainly the "two witnesses" will be subject to such trampling.

The Two Witnesses

Who are the "two witnesses"? Steiner says, "In the Christian tradition, *Elias* [Elijah] and *Moses* are seen as the personal representatives of what we found in yesterday's lecture in the two pillars. In Christian esotericism Elias and Moses are looked upon as those who give the teachings of the two pillars."[33]

The Christian tradition flows from the appearance of Elijah and Moses to Peter, James, and John on the Mount of the Transfiguration of Christ. Steiner cites "Christian tradition," in the first sentence above. In the second sentence he correctly noted that the teachings of the two pillars come from these two major prophets, both of whom preceded the time of the writing prophets and historians.

Recall, from chapter 1, that Paul and Lazarus/John were deemed herein to be the "two witnesses" in Revelation. The Transfiguration occurred before Christ initiated either Lazarus/John or Paul. The initiation of Paul doubtless opened his eyes to his prior incarnation as Moses. And we've seen, from Steiner's deathbed declaration,

---

31   *ASJ*, lect. 9; 156; "Paul calls the etheric or life body, spiritual body, after the physical has dissolved and the etheric passes into the astral earth," 1 Cor. 15:37.

32   *ASJ*, lect. 9; 161.

33   ASJ, lect. 9; 161.

that upon the raising of Lazarus, the spirit of John the Baptist, the reincarnated Elijah, penetrated Lazarus down through the consciousness soul, thus indwelling him and further justifying his identification thereafter as John. That these two lay dead for 3½ days invokes the initiation of Lazarus motif as if to confirm what is here being suggested—for Christ's "cursing" of the fig tree was his indication that the 3½ day initiation was no longer to be the mode of enlightenment after the Mystery of Golgotha. Therefore, their rising after that period upon the bid by a voice from heaven to "Come up hither!"—which they did "in the sight of their foes... in a cloud" (11:12)—could not have produced new spiritual insight in the ancient "fig tree" method, though perhaps through the use of such symbolism it may have indicated elevation to the higher realm of consciousness needed in that higher level to which they were bidden by the heavenly voice. An earthquake then killed "seven thousand," doubtless a symbolic number, and the rest "gave glory to the God of heaven" (11:13).

We are told that this was the second woe, and that a third was soon to follow (11:14), the first having transpired after the blowing of the fifth trumpet when its angel was given the key to the bottomless pit and torturous conditions rose therefrom upon the earth (9:1–11). It was "the beast that ascend[ed] from the bottomless pit" that made war upon, and killed, the two witnesses. Apparently this beast is not specifically identified, though there is an ambiguous reference in 13:12 where the beast with two horns "exercises all the authority of the first beast." Three beasts are mentioned, the first (11:7—from the bottomless pit) and third (13:11) both arise out of the earth, while the second arises out of the sea (13:1). The reference in 13:12 to the first beast must refer, however, to the one in 13:1 that rose from the sea with the seven heads and the ten horns, for it is patterned after the dragon in Revelation 12 that has seven heads and ten horns, and also refers to its "mortal wound that was healed," an apparent reference to its loss in battling Michael, but upon being thrown down to earth, recovering enough to battle the offspring of the spiritually majestic woman in Revelation 12. The third woe must refer to either the first or both beasts described in Revelation 13.

The Blowing of the Last Trumpet

As the last trumpet is blown, "there were loud voices in heaven, saying 'The kingdom of the world has become the kingdom of our Lord and of his Christ'... And the twenty-four elders... fell on their faces and worshiped God." (11:15–16). It is important to note that there are still just twenty-four elders, indicating that we have not yet moved from the Mineral Condition of Life into the Plant Kingdom of Life, on which, see the Grand Schematic in chapter 2. When we make that move, there will then be twenty-five elders.

We then come to 11:19: "Then God's temple in heaven was opened, and the ark of his covenant was seen within his temple; and there were flashes of lightning, voices, peals of thunder, an earthquake, and heavy hail." The lightning and thunder suggests we are in the spiritual realm, but the earthquake and heavy hail suggest that there are still problems for those below.

The temple should be understood as the collective assembly of those who have attained the spiritual realm of the (non-numerical) 144,000. The *ark* of his covenant is the ark from the Noah emigration from Atlantis at the end of the last great ice age, approximately ten to twelve thousand years ago. It was never the dimensions of a physical ship, but a description of the dimensions or bodily proportions, in the ratio of 3 to 5 to 30 (Gen 6:15), of those brought over by Noah (Manu) on his historic emigration.[34] Those he brought over near where Ireland is today made their way to an area of Central Asia, probably near what is now Mount Ararat (Gen 8:4).[35] The ark of the covenant suggests something more than a wooden box or ship (Gen 6:18), especially since it is formalized by the rainbow, the first of only three that appear in the canon, the significance of which will be presented in a separate chapter to follow (Gen 9:13–17). That Noah's ark appears in this spiritual realm some eleven chapters before the end

---

34 Steiner, *Occult Signs and Symbols*, AP (1972), lect. 1; 14 (CW 101). See also *BB*, "Three Days' Journey", 322–323.

35 Many have sought, or found, artifacts on the mountain that were claimed as evidence of Noah's ark. No such ark as they are looking for ever existed, other than perhaps in symbolic enclosures representing the assumed physical ark. The latest expedition making that claim was probably in 2010, but carbon dating put its age then at 4,800 years, more recent by thousands of years from the migration of Noah from Atlantis.

of the canon, while the covenant relating to that ark was finalized in the 9th chapter of the first book of the canon, makes it abundantly clear that Steiner was right in saying what the original "ark" was. It appears now in the spirit at a time when the physical body has been given up, or "crucified," as an absolute necessity for its appearance in this spiritual realm—for no mineral-physical body has ever, or could ever, enter that realm (1 Cor 15:35–50).

The seventh trumpet has been blown, and while its consequences continue in what follows the appearance of the temple in heaven, we will move with those consequences into the next chapter.

The "Great Portent" of the Woman that Appeared in Heaven

The Woman Clothed with the Sun

[1] And a great portent appeared in heaven, a woman clothed with the sun, with the moon under her feet, and on her head a crown of twelve stars; [2] she was with child and she cried out in her pangs of birth, in anguish for delivery. [3] And another portent appeared in heaven; behold, a great red dragon, with *seven heads and ten horns*, and seven diadems upon his heads. [4] His tail swept down a third of the stars of heaven, and cast them to the earth. And the dragon stood before the woman who was about to bear a child, that he might devour her child when she brought it forth; [5] she brought forth a male child, one who is to rule all the nations with a *rod of iron*, but her child was caught up to God and to his throne, [6] and the woman fled into the wilderness, where she has a place prepared by God, in which to be nourished for one thousand two hundred and sixty days.

(Revelation 12:1–6, emphasis added)

In the part of *BB's* Chart **I-2** that gives the "7 Great Epochs" we see that the earth separated from the solar mass during the second (the Hyperborean) Epoch and the moon during the third (the Lemurian) Epoch. The chart portrays the "Return of Moon" just before the end of the seventh Epoch. As that Epoch ends and those called the 144,000 are seen to comprise the temple in heaven, we have the "return of the sun," which is not designated as such on the chart. What is happening is not that these realms returned to the Earth but that the mineral aspects of the earth were being dismantled, so to speak, and the spiritual, or etheric and astral, aspects of the earth were expanding outward first to the Moon Sphere and thence to the Sun Sphere. These spiritualizing events are implicit in the description of the woman.

At the outset, the question arises, does the birth process that is described refer to the earthly Incarnation of the Christ, or to a state, so described, of the human spirit, or to both? We shall return to this inquiry in due course.

The two italicized phrases in the six verses quoted above—the "seven heads and ten horns" and the "rod of iron"—are mystery language the understanding of which is critical to comprehending the longer passage.

The Seven Heads and Ten Horns

The beast with the seven heads and ten horns appears in Revelation chapters 12, 13 and 17. The beast appears to be the same one portrayed in Daniel 7, generally now believed to have been written in the latter years of the reign of the Seleucid king Antiochus IV Epiphanes (175–164 BCE), purporting to describe a vision of Daniel in the sixth pre-Christian century.[1]

The situation of the woman in 12:1 is an exalted one, lying presumably in the far distant future in terms of human evolution, when already the 144,000 are in the temple in heaven (11:19). Yet there seems to be a conflation of imagery scanning an immense period of time, extending even into a state of timelessness.

But to comprehend the future aspects it depicts, we must reach back into the Atlantean and Post-Atlantean Evolutionary Epochs. There the terms *head* and *horn* have specific meaning. The etheric body forms and maintains the physical body. Every physical organ in HB was formed by its etheric predecessor. In esotericism, the domain of the Apocalypse, an etheric organ is called a "head" and the physical organ that it forms is called a "horn."

Recall that in chapter 8, in the part captioned "The Four Horsemen and the 'Four Living Creatures,'" appearing in Revelation 6, we jumped ahead for a partial comment about this phrase. The comment there is hardly sufficient to understand the phrase in the context of these later chapters of Revelation. Preparatory to the presentation of

---

1   Daniel L. Smith-Christopher, *The Book of Daniel*, NIB, vol. 7 (1996), 26.

that commentary, it is well to recall the citation in chapter 8 of the references to how the "I" penetrated into the three bodies, particularly the outer astral body, starting in the middle of the Atlantean Epoch, more particularly in the fifth age of that Epoch.[2] In regard to that, bear in mind that the high initiate of the Sun Mysteries, who led the important migration from Atlantis into the Post-Atlantean Epoch, was Noah (Manu), and that he had three sons, Shem, Ham, and Japheth, and that the seven "persons" who "came over" with Noah in that expedition were his wife, his three sons, and their wives (Gen 6:18), the three sons almost certainly referring to the last three ages of Atlantis, and the animals being the remnants of all the earthly animals that were still in the human astral body (the wild beasts of Mark 12:13). The inclusion of the wives of all of the males shows the progressive division of the etheric and physical bodies into sexes, the reversal of which figures into the overcoming of the beast with the seven heads and ten horns.

Steiner gave aspects of this seven-headed and ten-horned beast over the course of three successive lectures (9, 10, and 11) in his June 1908 Nuremberg cycle (*ASJ*). To preserve the flavor of his explanation, an extract from each successive lecture is set out here:

From lecture 9:

Now you will remember that we spoke of the seven ages of the Atlantean evolution. These seven ages comprise the first four and the last three. In the first four man was completely group-soul. Then in the fifth age the first impulse for the ego-soul originated. Therefore we have four stages of development in Atlantis during which man first progresses as group-soul, and each of the first four Atlantean races corresponds to one of the typical animal forms—lion, eagle, calf or bull, and man. This passes over into the human stage in the fifth age. These typical forms are then lost. Now imagine that in the present epoch man permeates himself with the Christ-principle and thereby conquers his animal nature more and more; but if he does not permeate himself with the Christ-principle, he does not overcome the animal nature. The four typical heads, lion, eagle, bull and man remain, so to speak, as something which assumes its form again as soon as it has the opportunity, and in addition come three others, those of the last three races of the Atlantean epoch, when

---

2   Cited in a footnote of that chapter are the schematics at *BB*, 402 and Chart **I-35**.

man had already begun to be human. These three also remain if man does not work in his soul so that this animal nature disappears. How then will a man appear on the spiritualized earth who during our epoch has not taken into himself the Christ-principle? He will appear in materiality; he will reappear in the shapes from which he has come. He has had these animal forms and has passed through three others as well. He has left unused what could have overcome the animal nature. The animal nature springs forth again, in seven forms. As once in Atlantis there emerged the four heads, the animal-man, so out of the transformed earth, the astralized earth, seven such typical heads will again emerge, and the drama that took place at that time will be re-enacted. The germ of the spiritual man was there, but he could not yet develop an individual form; he developed the four animal heads. The embryo man of that epoch is also represented by the woman who brings forth man. The man of the future is also represented by the woman who gives birth to the spiritual man. But what has remained in the flesh is represented on the secondary earth by the animal with seven heads. Just as there were four heads in the period before man had the possibility of overcoming the animal nature, so those who have remained in the animal nature will appear as one entity, as the beast with the seven heads.

We have now to reflect upon all that we have heard; for this is something of which even the Apocalyptist says: Here is wisdom [13:18].—We shall only understand this wisdom, which the writer of the Apocalypse has put into the appearance of the seven-headed beast with ten horns, if we carefully ponder over what "horn" really is in relation to "head" in the language of the mysteries. We shall see that the beings who have kept these seven heads, because they have remained behind in evolution, have, in fact, acquired in the abyss a physical body which consists of ten hardened members of the physical body.[3]

From Lecture 10:

Now when man began to harden himself from the etheric into the physical, he developed four different parts of the body in accordance with his fourfold group-soul. And through the former

---

3   *ASJ*, lect. 9; 163–166 (CW 104).

group-soul consciousness, man had within him, at the beginning
of the fifth age of Atlantis, a conjunction of the earlier fourfoldness. He bears within him the four heads which are summed up in
his head which gradually arises. It is composed of the four group-
heads as it develops in the course of the fifth period. Man has four
parts of the physical body corresponding to the four heads. These
are the four "horns." So that you may imagine that because man
was etheric, he had four heads, four animal heads, only the last is
already man-animal, for that is what is meant. He was four-headed,
and each force-system corresponding to one of these heads formed
physical organs.

❦

He then evolves further toward the individual human being. This
begins in the neighborhood of the present Ireland. Man passes
through the last three ages in such a way that he possesses the germ
of the ego-being. He no longer develops an animal body outwardly,
but has risen to become human. He matures his human nature more
and more until he absorbs the Christ-principle. If we regard present-
day man, we see that he was not always as he appears today. In order
for him to become what he now is, he had to pass through four animal group-souls, he had to be incarnated in bodies corresponding to
the present lion form, the bull form, the eagle form and the human
form. He then rose higher and became more and more human, and
the form of the earlier group-soul disappeared. It is no longer there,
man has assumed human shape.

We must now understand an important event which then took
place when man assumed human form, for without this understanding one cannot comprehend the Apocalypse of John; it was an event
of the greatest importance. Up to this event when man passed into
human soul nature, something was totally hidden from his vision
which later was revealed. Man had a kind of dim, hazy consciousness. When he awoke in the morning he saw everything surrounded
by misty formations, so to speak; and when he went to sleep he
was in the spiritual world. This appeared to him in pictures; for
such is the nature of the spiritual world. I shall now describe something which took place before man passed over physically into the
human condition, before he passed from the group-soul nature to
full ego-consciousness.

What he lived through here upon earth consisted only of a number of experiences. He then went to sleep and during his sleep was in a dim consciousness in a spiritual world where he lived among gods and spirits, of which an echo remains in the myths and legends. There he experienced mighty pictures; for example, the picture in which he encountered two other beings who threw stones behind them, and out of these stones other beings like themselves grew out of the earth. These were experiences which man had throughout the fourth age of the Atlantean epoch. To express it plainly, we must say that the reproduction of man took place in sleeping-consciousness, not in waking-consciousness. When man was outside his physical body and in the spiritual world, he set in motion, as it were, while he was in this state of consciousness in which everything appeared to him in pictures, whatever had to take place for reproduction; the whole act of reproduction was veiled in a spiritual element and appeared to him in the picture of throwing stones behind him. The act of reproduction was enveloped in spiritual consciousness; it lay behind the day-consciousness. Man had no knowledge of sex. In the day-consciousness he did not see himself as existing in two sexes, his soul was untouched by any thought of sex. Not that it did not exist; it did exist, but it rested in the obscurity of a spiritual consciousness; during the day-consciousness man knew nothing of it.

With the acquisition of the first germ of ego-consciousness man first became aware of sex. That is the moment presented to us in the Bible when Adam and Eve become aware that there is such a thing as sex [Gen 3:7]. This important event took place at this stage in the earth's evolution. If with spiritual vision you look back to the time which preceded that time, you see only that part of man which is the instrument of the spirit. All the rest was invisible. Only the upper part of man could be seen. From the point of time we have mentioned, the whole man began to be seen. It is now comprehensible why men began to cover themselves up. Previously they saw nothing which required covering. In this way man gradually emerged into the external world.

If we regard the outer human form as the condensed part of the etheric, we have in the fourth Atlantean age the four horns in addition to the four group-soul heads. Now, however, in the last three ages of Atlantis something twofold begins to develop physically. At each stage where a group-soul head was to develop, a double physical, male and female, was formed. In the first four stages you find man formed with four heads, the condensed etheric with four horns. We now have three more heads which are invisible because the external human form absorbs them.[4] These three are only perceptible to clairvoyant vision, three etheric heads, the principal human heads, and in between them two others which are like shadows beside each, like double shadows. Thus when the Atlantean Flood burst, we have seven race or group-soul heads, of which the last three always appear in such a way that they have their physical part in a double form, as male and female. From this you see that at the end of the Atlantean epoch the entire group-soul nature of man—although the later portion remains invisible—has seven heads and ten horns. The horns of the first four heads are not separated into male and female, but only the last three.[5]

From Lecture 11:

Now from all that has been said you will be able to gather what the relation is between what we call "heads" and what we call "horns"; but in connection with this the question will still arise in your soul: Why is it that just certain organs which appear in the physical body are called "horns"? Why does one designate as horns the physical organs and their vestiges in the astral when the earth shall have become astral?—It can be easily understood that those who have not taken up the principle of Christ must fall back again into the condition in which man was before he could partake of the Christ-principle. Man was formerly a non-individual being with a group-soul; and we have seen that during the first four ages of the Atlantean epoch he was furnished with the group-souls which are correctly symbolized by the lion, bull, eagle and man-like heads, the last being conceived of as an animal-head. Thus we must imagine that when man reappears in the spiritualized earth and has failed to take in the Christ-principle during our epoch, he will then again appear in the old form, because he has contributed nothing toward the higher development of his previous group-soul

---

4   Every HB, whether male or female in physical body, has an etheric body that is of the opposite sex. That sexual body is thus "hidden" from normal vision, but it is there. Sex only exists in the physical and etheric bodies. The astral body, ego, and all higher aspects of the human being are asexual, though they both affect and are affected by the experiences in these lower bodies.

5   *ASJ*, lect. 10; 182–186 (CW 104).

nature; and not only in this form but with three heads more, which were added during the subsequent ages. Before the great Flood of Atlantis three further ages followed after the first four. In these three ages those who later received the Christ-principle also had in a certain way the possibility of taking up three further group-soul heads; but they have transformed them, they have raised the animal nature in man to a higher stage. They appear in a spiritual-ized form when the earth is spiritualized. The others, who have rejected the Christ-impulse, will appear with seven heads, because there were before the Flood seven ages during which the animal nature was developed. And because in the last three Atlantean ages bi-sexuality reigned in contradistinction to the first four, each head, so to speak, appears with two possibilities toward the animal nature, with male and female possibilities, so that in these three later ages each head appears with two horns; that is man with ten horns altogether.

Someone might now say: I quite understand that those who do not work upon themselves so as to strip off the form which they have and lift it up to the human, will reappear in the animal form; but I do not understand why horns are spoken of; it is quite com-prehensible when heads are spoken of, but why horns?—I will now explain why one not only speaks of horns, but must speak of them. The expression is not merely to be understood symbolically, it is reality. Those who fail to take up the Christ-principle into them-selves will actually appear in astral form also; but because they have so shaped their instincts that they have held fast, so to speak, to the animal group-soul, the corresponding instincts appear in the astral body which men will then have, in the form of horn-like protuber-ances. It is an actual form.[6]

The "Rod of Iron"

The phrase "rod of iron" appears in the canon only in the following four places (emphasis mine):

Psalms 2:7–9:
[7] I will tell of the decree of the Lord: He said to me, *"You are my son, today I have begotten you."* [8] Ask of me, and I will make the nations your heritage, and the ends of the earth your possession.

---

6   *ASJ*, lect. 11; 187–189 (CW 104).

[9] You shall break them with a *rod of iron*, and dash them in pieces like a potter's vessel.

Revelation 2:24–29:
[24] But to the rest of you in Thyatira, who do not hold this teaching [of Jezebel], who have not learned what some call the deep things of Satan, to you I say, I do not lay upon you any other burden; [25] only hold fast what you have, until I come. [26] He who conquers and who keeps my works until the end, I will give him power over the nations, [27] and he shall rule them with a *rod of iron*, as when earthen pots are broken in pieces, even as I myself have received power from my Father; [28] and I will give him *the morning star.* [29] He who has an ear, let him hear what the Spirit says to the churches.

Revelation 12:1–6 (this entire passage is quoted at the beginning of this chapter 10; only verses 4b–6 are reproduced again below):
[4b] And the dragon stood before the woman who was about to bear a child, that he might devour her child when she brought it forth; [5] she brought forth a male child, one who is to rule all the nations with a *rod of iron*, but her child was caught up to God and to his throne, [6] and the woman fled into the wilderness, where she has a place prepared by God, in which to be nourished for one thousand two hundred and sixty days.

Revelation 19:11–16:
[11] Then I saw heaven opened, and behold, a white horse! He who sat upon it is called Faithful and True, and in righteousness he judges and makes war. [12] His eyes are like a flame of fire, and on his head are many diadems; and he has a name inscribed which no one knows but himself. [13] He is clad in a robe dipped in blood, and the name by which he is called is The Word of God. [14] And the armies of heaven, arrayed in fine linen, white and pure, followed him on white horses. [15] From his mouth issues a sharp sword with which to smite the nations, and he will rule them with a *rod of iron*; he will tread the wine press of the fury of the wrath of God the Almighty. [16] On his robe and on his thigh he has a name inscribed, King of kings and Lord of lords.

To understand the phrase "rod of iron," we must start with the "iron." For that, see chart **I-27** in *BB*, at pages 593–595. From it we see that as the seven bodies of our classical solar system separated out of their vastly expansive nebular mass, what came to be Mars had to pass through what was then the Earth-Moon. Obviously, if we look at the orbits of these planets, realizing that at that early stage they were each still nebular, it is obvious that one could still pass through another. The Mars portion of the mass was nearer the Sun and had to pass back through the larger orbit of what was to become the Earth-Moon. In doing so, it left "behind what later developed into iron (a necessary component of human blood)" and of all other warm-blooded creatures.

The days of our week (see *BB* chart **I-8**) recognize that earth evolution is divided by the Christ Event, the part that preceded it being called Mars, the part following Mercury. While less visible than the brighter Venus, Mercury is also called the "morning star" (and "evening star"), so the Cultural Age of the Christ event is expressed in the letter to that Age (identified as the church of Thyatira)—and to those who conquer will be given the Christ (2:28).[7] And those who so conquer "shall rule...with a rod of iron" (2:27).

The place of iron, so essential to warm blood in earthly creatures, in our discussion of the ultimate power of the *rod of iron*, is perhaps best shown in the "Blood" essay in *DQWIM*. Over 40 percent of the "Blood" essay is devoted to Steiner's *Occult Physiology*.[8] That book comprises the eight lectures given in Prague, March 20 to 28, 1911. Its lecture 4 (Mar. 23), entitled "Man's Inner Cosmic System," is the one under which the discussion excerpted below (with minor editing changes) is found:

> When we come to discuss the relationship (mentioned in lecture 2) that esotericism from old has developed between the seven planetary bodies and the human being's organs, certain points should be made.
>
> In these lectures (save for lecture 8), the outer planetary forces (Saturn, Jupiter and Mars) are seen as embedded in the spleen, liver and gallbladder—see **I-86**.[9] But in **I-21** they are seen as embedded in the crown of the head (the pineal, Saturn), forehead (pituitary, Jupiter) and larynx (Mars). It should be noted that in

---

7   See the discussion of Mercury as the morning star in chapter 6, in the section captioned **Greco Roman**,

8   Steiner, *An Occult Physiology*, 3rd ed., RSP (1983) (CW 128).

9   Chart references in this excerpt are to those found in both *BB* and *DQWIM*.

I-21 we are dealing with the direction of spiritualization called the "lotus flowers" (progressive organs—evolution) whereas in **I-86** we are dealing with the earthly organs of flesh (retrogressive organs). In *An Occult Physiology*, lect. 8, especially at p. 187, Steiner tends to equate the lower retrogressive embodiments of the planetary forces with their counterparts in the development of the higher progressive lotus flowers. According to this, Mars relates to the lower gallbladder and the higher larynx, Jupiter to the lower liver and the higher forehead (or pituitary gland), and Saturn the lower spleen and to the higher crown of the head (or pineal gland).

Steiner here most particularly illustrates the transformation of the Mars forces. The iron elements of the Mars forces relate to the aggressive gall, but also to the larynx, which will become  the reproductive organ of the future. In *The Apocalypse of St. John* (*ASJ*, lect. 11; 189), Steiner graphically portrays the thrust of air from the lungs up through and beyond the larynx, taking the form, whether so intended or not (he does not expressly say so), of the male phallus (but in anatomy the phallus represents both the penis and the clitoris, so that it could symbolize that time when the sexes reunite and spontaneously generate of themselves[10]):

This relationship of the larynx and the rod of iron is dealt with in *DQWIM*, as follows:

> This thrust of air represents the time when the reproduction by the human being will be by its "word" in the *image* of its creator (cf. John 1:3; Gen 1:26–27). The mouth is thus truly a "sharp sword" (Isa 49:2; Rev 1:16; 2:12 and 19:15). The relationship of the iron of Mars to the larynx should help us to perceive a far deeper meaning to the rulership by the redeemed with a "rod of iron"—see Rev 2:27; 12:5 and 19:15.
>
> Not only so, but here again is the illustration of another duality, the activity of the three outer planetary forces (Saturn, Jupiter

---

10 In *Egyptian Myths and Mysteries*, SB (1971), lect. 6 (Leipzig, September 8, 1908); 67 (CW 106), Steiner shows how the lungs (relating to air) are female (Isis) while the larynx (relating to iron) is male (Osiris), who, together produced Horus, the future human being. Every person has both, symbolic of the day when they will create through the new word.

and Mars; **I-86**) in the lower human organism being transformed into the higher human organs (**I-21**, Figure 13). This is what must happen in the transformation of the human being's three bodies into its three higher spiritual states (**I-9**)—the evolutionary events telescoped so magnificently into the single sentence parable of the three loaves in Matthew 13:33. This is the transformation of the three bodies into the festal garments required at the wedding of the bride/bridegroom (see Matt 22:1-14 and Rev 16:15 and 21,2, as well as the essay "Naked" in *The Burning Bush*).

In something of the same way, Mercury, which in **I-21** represents the navel or solar plexus region, is shown by Steiner in **I-86** as also representing the lung region. He tells us that the metal mercury (quicksilver) has not yet fully attained to its ultimate state. One might so surmise, it being a metal yet in the liquid state. One can see in this immature state the hint of a future relationship between the lungs and the larynx in human reproduction. There is something highly polar about the density of mercury as a metal and the levity of what comes forth as air from the lungs. The planetary forces of Mercury in the human body actually reflect their heavenly position in that these bodily forces (solar plexus and lungs) encircle the heart more closely, both below and above, than any other. This makes the juxtaposition of the "rod of iron" (Mars/larynx) and the "morning star" (Mercury/lungs) in Rev 2:27–28 immensely stirring to the soul, for the "morning star" Mercury represents the last half of Earth evolution,[11] and the last half of Earth evolution commenced with the Mystery of Golgotha and the dropping of Christ's blood into the Earth. It was with that event that the higher "I Am" could begin to transform the lower Mercury/Mars forces into their higher manna state. Does this not also make Christ's dying refusal of "gall" on the cross (Matt 27:34) highly significant? For he was there initiating what would permit the lower Mars forces to be transformed into the higher.[12]

---

11 See the earlier discussion in this chapter about the days of the week, especially Tuesday and Wednesday (Mars and Mercury). It is important to note that this "morning star" appears in the message to the angel of the fourth church, the fourth Post-Atlantean Cultural Age, the middle one, the Greco-Roman, during which Christ's blood was shed.

12 *DQWIM*, 361–362. Several other references to the larynx or to the rod of iron exist in *DQWIM*: those are at pages 34 n. 23, 161 n. 35, and 390 (2 references to both); those to only the larynx are at pages 181, 277 (5), 278 (2), 326, and 360 (5).

We may ask ourselves where it is to be in our evolutionary journey that this power of reproduction by the larynx will appear. It is not an imminent but is rather still a distant prospect, and its development will not be abrupt, but gradual in relation to the healing process of the three bodies, respectively (first astral, then etheric, then physical), and then to the reproduction, the bringing "forth beings similar to man."[13] Its early stage will begin approximately three thousand years from now, in the middle of the sixth Cultural Age (Philadelphia) and extend till the Earth and Moon are again one, near the end of the seventh and last Evolutionary Epoch, when the mineral-physical Condition of Life is nearing completion.[14]

The moon separated from the earth during the Lemurian Epoch. The division of HB into male and female occurred during that transition and at the beginning of the Atlantean Epoch. As we have seen, consciousness of the reproductive act did not exist during the group-soul of the first four ages. The reproductive cycle of the female is moon related. Reproduction by sexual union, which began with the separation of the moon from the earth, will end with the rejoinder of earth and moon. Women will progressively become barren as this time is approached, and in the signs of end times given in the Little Apocalypse passages of Matthew and Luke, we find the revelation that it will not be good for women who are with child at that time—presumably because they are not sufficiently spiritually advanced to move into the astral realm.[15] Sexuality exists only in the physical and etheric realms,

---

13 Sergei O. Prokofieff, *Eternal Individuality*, TL (1992); German ed. *Ewige Individualitat*, Dornach, Switzerland, Verlag am Goetheanum [1987]), 190, citing Steiner lect. (Vienna, November 5, 1907) (CW 98). Such lecture is not yet published in English. This brief quote was taken from a sentence translated for me by Paul V. O'Leary, as follows: "In the future the larynx will not only bring forth words, but it will one day become the creative organ, the organ of reproduction that will bring forth beings similar to man." In regard to this November 5 lecture, Prokofieff observes "that the heightened interest displayed in our time toward the sphere of physical relationships between the sexes is the strongest manifestation of the forces that are *opposed* to the future mysteries of the Divine Sophia. Interests of such a kind are consciously supported and disseminated by those occult circles in the West which have set themselves the task of preventing the sixth cultural epoch from happening at all" (Prokofieff, *Eternal Individuality,* 356 n. 562).

14 *Eternal Individuality*, 192–196.

15 Matt 24:19; Luke 23:29.

and the "ennobled etheric body," discussed earlier, that moves into the astral realm will have ceased to bear a sexual nature.

The Woman Clothed With the Sun

We return to Revelation 12:1–6 and its "woman clothed with the sun." We now ask ourselves, as before, the identity of the mother and child; does it describe the Christ Event, or is it the human being at the point where the Earth and Sun again become one? Or is it both?

These questions reprise our discussion of *one like a son of man* (1:13). Here, as there, we must see dual application, having moved, however, from a "son" holding seven stars to a mother crowned with twelve. In both cases we have a two-edged sword issuing from the mouth of the child (the "rod of iron" joined with the two-edged sword in 19:15). The face of the son in 1:16, "was like the sun shining in full strength," while the mother in 12:1 was "clothed with the sun."

Highly to be commended is Emil Bock's treatment of this passage.[16] The "woman" is the divine eternal feminine, embodied in the Marys of the canonical nativity accounts. "Out of the 'eternal feminine' of the Cosmos, the male principle, the cosmic ego [the "I" or "I Am"], is to be born"; hence she delivers a "male child" (12:5).[17] While the male child is "caught up to God and to his throne" (12:5) before the woman's flight into the "wilderness, where she has a place prepared by God, in which to be nourished for one thousand two hundred and sixty days" (12:6), it is hard not to see that time period of three and a half years being the same as the period of the Christ's presence in the body of Jesus.[18] Those acquainted with Steiner's exposition of the nativity account in Luke's Gospel will recognize that the mother of that Nathan Jesus child, the truest representative of the Divine Sophia, died shortly after the birth of that child, and while it would be thirty

---

16 Emil Bock, *The Apocalypse*, London, Floris Books (1957; but first published in Stuttgart, Germany by Verlag Urachhaus Stuttgart in 1951), chap. 7, esp. 94–98.

17 Bock, *The Apocalypse*, 98.

18 See note on page 170. Scholars have also considered the possibility of Jesus having gone to Jerusalem more often than for the three Passover festivals mentioned in John's Gospel. His close friendship with Lazarus and his sisters seems hard to reconcile with his having been there only for those three festivals.

earthly years before the Christ would enter the bodies of that child at
the baptism, that very young earthly mother would have returned to
the spiritual realm, the "place prepared for her by God" (12:6). Woven
into the divine fabric of this transition, however, at the baptism of
Jesus in the Jordan the primeval soul of the Nathan Mary of Luke's
Gospel entered into the Mary of Matthew's Gospel transforming that
Solomon Mary's bodies so that she again became virginal, for those
in the spiritual realm continue to affect earthly events.[19] And it has
been plausibly suggested that the earthly Solomon Mary and her then
husband Joseph, fled into the Egyptian "wilderness," the earthly coun-
terpart of the place of protection to which the Nathan Mary "fled."[20]
Readers will recall Steiner's teaching that the young Nathan mother
and the elderly Solomon father had both died, and the two surviving
parents had wed, all prior to the twelve-year old incident in the temple
(Luke 2:41–51).

So what we have appearing is that this account of the woman
clothed with the sun was, in fact, being played out both historically
and prophetically so that it portrays both the Christ Event historically
and the human being prophetically—as above, so below.[21]

What shall we make of 12:4, the dragon's tail sweeping down to
earth "a third of the stars of heaven"? Do we have here a metaphor
with dual meaning? Immediately after the six verses that open chapter
12, we find a war in heaven between Michael and the dragon. Such
"battle" follows a spiritual archetype. In his lecture in Dornach on
October 14, 1917, Steiner elaborated upon the Michaelic battle of 1879,
a fulcral battle, so to speak, stemming from an "1841 event in the
world of the spirit" manifesting on earth in 1917. But in regard to these
Michaelic battles, Steiner there said:

> If you were to go back to very early times in evolution, you would
> find a battle similar to the one I have just described. As already men-
> tioned, these battles have recurred over and over again, but always
> on different issues. In the distant past, the crowd of ahrimanic spirits
> were also cast down from the spiritual worlds into the earthly realm
> when they had lost such a battle. You see, they would return to the

---

19   *BB*, 66; *IBJ*, 74.

20   Emil Bock, *The Apocalypse*, 98–99.

21   See "As Above, So Below" in *DQWIM*, 98–115.

attack again and again. After one of these battles, for example, the crowd of ahrimanic spirits populated the earth with the earthly life-forms which the medical profession now calls bacilli. Everything which has the power to act as a bacillus, everything in which bacilli are involved, is the result of crowds of ahrimanic spirits being cast down from heaven to earth at a time when the dragon had been overcome. In the same way the ahrimanic, mephistophelean way of thinking has spread since the late 1870s as the result of such a victory. Thus we are able to say that tubercular and bacillary diseases come from a similar source as the materialism which has taken hold of human minds.

We can also compare the occurrences of the last century with something else. We can point to something which you know already from [*An Outline of Esoteric Science*]: the withdrawal of the Moon from the sphere of Earth evolution. The Moon was once part of the Earth; it was cast out from the Earth. As a result, certain Moon influences took effect on Earth, and this, too, followed a victory won by Michael over the dragon. We are therefore also able to say that everything connected with certain effects relating to the phases of the Moon, and all impulses, which reach the Earth from the Moon, have their origin in a similar battle between Michael and the dragon.[22]

John's vision occurred in the fourth Cultural Age of our Post-Atlantean Epoch. We note that the context in which the dragon's tail swept "a third of the stars of heaven" casting them "to the earth" (12:4) was that of the "twelve stars" in our zodiacal circle (12:1). The last four Cultural Ages of our Evolutionary Epoch, preceding the War of All against All could thus be envisioned, since four represents a third of the twelve zodiacal "stars."[23]

Lecturing in Munich May 8, 1907 Steiner noted the passage "And a great sign appeared in heaven" (12:1) as meaning "we are dealing in the Apocalypse with signs representing the great phases of evolution of humanity." He pointed out that the Lemurian Epoch was destroyed by fire, the Atlantean by water, and our Post-Atlantean will be destroyed "in conflict between selfish, egoistic powers in the war of all against all," the line of evolution descending "deeper and deeper; [so that]

---

22 *The Fall of the Spirits of Darkness*, RSP (1993), lect. 9, 139–140 (CW 177).

23 *BB*, chart **I-2**, bottom of page 552 and **I-19**, page 573.

when it arrives at the bottom everyone will rage against everyone else. A small part of humankind will escape this, just as a small part escaped during the destruction of the Atlantean race. It is up to every individual to find a connection to the spiritual life in order to be one of those to go over into the sixth root race. Mighty revolutions stand before humankind; they are described in the Apocalypse."[24]

Let us now return to what Steiner said in his Nuremberg cycle (lect. 9, June 26, 1908) that focuses upon the human aspects of the woman in the sun passage, and then what he said to priests of the Christian Community gathered in Dornach on September 16, 1924 (lect. 12) that focuses more on the cosmic perspective—Steiner was even then a man who was ill, it being a mere twelve days before he rose, after an interval of at least two days, from his sick bed to give a shortened "Final Address" on September 28.

In the Nuremberg lecture, he said:

If we now turn our attention away from the earth itself and what is upon it, and consider it in connection with the whole space of heaven, we shall find we have arrived at a very important matter at the time of which we are now speaking. Earth and sun comprised one body. The earth developed out of the sun, and the moon split off. We have said that this had to take place to obtain the right speed of evolution. But now, when man has passed through these stages of development, after he has spiritualized himself, he is ready to unite again with the forces upon the sun, he can proceed at the same tempo as the sun. An important cosmic event now takes place; the earth reunites with the sun. While that of which we have spoken is taking place, the earth unites with the sun. We said that the sun-spirits descended to the earth at the event of Golgotha, that this Christ-principle will be the means of bringing evolution to the point we have described. The earth will then be ready to unite with the sun; and what was necessary in order that evolution should not proceed too quickly, namely the moon, will be overcome, for man will no longer need it. The forces of the moon will be overcome. At this stage man can unite with the sun; he will live in the spiritual-ized earth and at the same time be united with the force of the sun; and he will be the conqueror of the moon. This is seen in spirit vision as represented by the symbolical figure of the fifth occult

---

24 Steiner, *RPA,* SB (1993), 41 (CW 104a).

seal; the woman who bears the sun within her and has the moon beneath her feet. Thus we have arrived at the moment when man is spiritualized, when he reunites with the forces of the sun, when earth and sun form one body and the moon forces are overcome. (See the fifth occult seal picture.)

Now we must remember that only the most advanced beings, who have been impregnated by the principle of Christ, have passed through this development. They have reached thus far; but those who have hardened in matter have fallen away and formed, so to speak, a kind of secondary planet of hardened, flesh-like matter.[25]

The three-plus pages of Steiner's lecture nine that follow the above recap things we already know a bit about but puts them in the context of how they apply to "those who have hardened in matter and fallen away and formed" that "secondary planet." He reviews the process of how the seven heads and ten horns develop. Those who do not, during the Post-Atlantean Epoch become "impregnated with the Christ" will appear as the beast with the seven heads and ten horns. However, while the path doubtless becomes more onerous, the possibility of becoming so impregnated through the spiritual powers and those who have been so impregnated by the Christ appears to remain until the earth has rejoined the sun, in the astral realm, after the end of the seventh and last Evolutionary Epoch, that of the trumpets. Failing such impregnation they shall remain as the beast with the seven heads and the ten horns. Those in this category will thus have the "mark of the beast" that appears in Revelation 16:2; 19:20; and 20:4, and be subject to the dire results John's vision portrays for them.

While his Nuremberg lecture thus seems to approach the "woman" passage more from the standpoint of the individual HB, let us now see a bit different approach in the lecture to the priests sixteen years later and sixteen days before his abbreviated "last address" on September 28, 1924:

Before seeing the birth of Christ as a male being in the sun in the middle of the Atlantean period, the priests saw a female being in the sun. The important change that took place in the middle

---

25   *ASJ*, lect. 9; 162–163.

of the Atlantean period is that before the middle of that period the cosmic female was seen in the spiritual aura of the sun, "the woman clothed with the sun." Putting it this way corresponds exactly with what happened in the supra-earthly world, in the heavens: "The woman clothed with the sun giving birth to a male child." The apocalyptist rightly calls him a male child, and this is the same being who later went through the Mystery of Golgotha and who had earlier gone through other forms of existence. What took place during that Atlantean period was a kind of birth, which was actually a complicated kind of metamorphoses. One saw how the sun gave birth to what was male in it, to what was of the nature of a son. But what does this mean for the earth? In the middle of the Atlantean period there was of course quite a different feeling about what a sun existence is. Nowadays the sun is regarded as a conglomeration of craters and fiery masses; what today's physicists describe is an abomination. But in those times the initiates saw what I have just described. They really saw the woman clothed with the sun, with the dragon beneath her feet, and giving birth to a male child. Those who saw and understood such a thing said: For the heavens that is the birth of Christ, for us it is the birth of our "I." They said this although the "I" only entered into the human being much later.

Since that moment in the middle of Atlantis, evolution has meant that human beings have become ever more aware of their "I." They were of course not as aware of it as we are today, but in a more elementary way they became ever more aware of it when the priests of the Mysteries showed them: The sun kindles the "I" in the human being. Through the birth shown by the apocalypstist in that picture, the "I" was continuously kindled from the outside through the way the sun worked, right up to the fourth Post-Atlantean age when the "I" had finally fully entered the human being. The human being, it was felt, belonged to the sun. This was a feeling that entered deeply into human nature.[26]

Steiner continued this lecture with a rather amazing set of drawings on eight plates, portraying the developments described above, and more.

The late Sergei O. Prokofieff brings the "woman clothed with the sun" into a discussion about the very last part of a human being's

---

26 *The Book of Revelation and the Work of the Priest*, RSP (1998), 171–172 (CW 346).

journey between lives; he writes (italics, brackets, and internal footnotes are his; brackets in footnotes are mine):

> And when, finally, the forming of the new human etheric body has been completed, immediately before the astral body and ego have united with it (which in the majority of cases leads to the gradual extinguishing of the spirit-consciousness that is natural to the soul in the spiritual world between death and a new birth) something of the greatest importance takes place. For immediately before that moment when spirit-consciousness is fully extinguished, the human being is given a clairvoyant insight into the principal events of his future earthly life. Just as at the onset of death a kind of memory-tableau [of the past life] has stood before the human ego, so now there appears a preview of the life that is to come.... And what a man thus sees becomes the source of active forces which he must carry with him into his new life.[27] But this is not yet all. For at that moment when the spirit-consciousness lights up for the last time, the human soul is not only shown a perspective of its next earthly life but, like a radiant *blessing* on the part of the entire spiritual cosmos which the soul is now leaving behind in order that it may incarnate on the Earth, once again experiences in a mighty cosmic imagination—which is, so to speak, an *imaginative memory*—its whole spiritual path from the cosmic midnight hour[28] to the union with its newly formed etheric body in the Moon-sphere.[29]

Prokofieff then indicates (p. 182) that this "mighty cosmic imagination" is that of the Divine Sophia, the woman clothed with the sun, in Revelation 12. He there says, "This is the sublime imagination of the Divine Sophia, who is experienced by every man—albeit at various levels of consciousness—immediately before incarnation on the Earth as the source of the forces necessary for the fulfilment of the tasks that have been placed before him in the present earthly life."

---

27 Steiner, *An Outline of Esoteric Science,* the chapter entitled "Sleep and Death." [SOP's footnote is numbered 521. His reference is found in *OES*, SB (1997) at page 98.]

28 Rudolf Steiner uses this expression to refer to the highest point of the soul's ascent in the spiritual worlds between two incarnations. See his Fourth Mystery Play. [SOP's footnote is numbered 522.]

29 *Eternal Individuality,* 181.

The passage from *An Outline of Esoteric Science* that he cites in support of this final imagination, and the context in which it is given, does not support, in my judgment, all that Prokofieff then presents relating to the image of the woman in Revelation 12. And it is a bit confusing to say that the soul experiences, at that final moment of spiritual consciousness before incarnation, the "woman" but that the experience is at various levels of consciousness. A rock has a certain level of consciousness in the higher spiritual realm.

Out of deep respect for the profound insights that SOP has given to us all, I am not saying that such an experience does not exist for every incarnating human being. It is a beautiful thought. I am simply not recognizing specific support for it in what he has cited to support it, and it does seem to be stretching the passage from *An Outline of Esoteric Science* that he quotes to encompass such a magnificent spiritual imagination.

Let us not close this chapter with any negative thoughts about this powerful image of the woman clothed with the sun. It is buried deep within each of us, and it is one every human heart should hunger to experience.

CHAPTER 10 ENDNOTE

Note from Footnote 18

In his *Chronicle of the Living Christ*, SB (1996), 456, 459, Robert Powell dates the baptism of Jesus (the entry of the Christ) on September 23, 29 CE and the crucifixion on April 3, 33 CE, a period of only a shade over 1,260 days (cf. 12:6). While it relies upon the mediumistic visions of Anne Catherine Emmerich, Steiner apparently did recognize some of her visions as being remarkably accurate for a "somnambulist" (Powell, *Chronicle,* 17–18), but Steiner only made this confirmation after he had done his own independent spiritual investigation on the matter. Powell's citation recognizes that her visions were of the "mirror image" type—Steiner specifically rejected such visions as something he would rely upon, a principle that was not violated by his affirmation of her visions here. His rejection of any type of mediumistic disclosure, including mirror imaging, as a basis for spiritual knowledge, is made clear over and over in his ten lectures given in Dornach October 10–25, 1915 published as *The Occult Movement in the Nineteenth Century*, RSP (1973), see esp. lect. 10, p. 168 on "mirror images" (cf. 1 Cor 13:12 "see in a mirror dimly") (CW 254).

11

THE TWO BEASTS

The Dragon in Revelation 12

Two "portents" were described in the 12:1–6 passage. A portent is "something that foreshadows a coming event."[1]

The first portent was the Divine Sophia, acting from the sun sphere in her painful labor of bringing about the earthly birth of the descending Christ Spirit. The second portent was of the seven-headed and ten-horned dragon that would attempt to abort her delivery or consume her newborn infant. The delivery occurred at the baptism of Jesus when the Christ Spirit entered his three bodies and dwelt for the 1,260 days of his earthly ministry. The dragon's attempt to "devour her child" upon delivery (12:4) is described in Mark 1:12–13.[2] But the portents themselves were in the realm of the sun ("in heaven"; 12:1, 3).

The rest of Revelation 12 (vss 7–17) tells of the heavenly battle between the Archangel Michael and his angels against the dragon and his angels, in which Michael and his angels were victorious. They threw the dragon and his angels to the earth where he has made war to this day with all those who are followers of her child (12:17).

Chapter 12 ends with the dragon in an angry state standing "on the sand of the sea."

---

1   *Merriam Webster's Collegiate Dictionary*, 11th ed. (2004), 967.

2   Mark 1:13 identifies the tempter as "Satan"; Rev 12:9 describes the dragon as "that ancient serpent, who is called the Devil and Satan, the deceiver of the whole world."

The two beasts of chapter 13

Chapter 13 tells of two beasts: one with seven heads and ten horns, rising out of the sea, whose "portent" we have already considered, and one with two horns that rose out of the earth.

This appearance, at the end of a period of spiritual journey, instantly calls to mind the appearance of the two beasts in the book of Job, Behemoth (Job 40:15–24) and Leviathan (Job 41). Are the two beasts in Revelation the same as the two in Job? If I read him right on the matter, it seems that Emil Bock sees them as the same.[3] Bock sees confirmation of his conclusion in the 60th chapter of the book of Enoch, from which he quotes segments from verses 7 to 9 as follows:

> And on that day were two monsters parted, a female monster named Leviathan, to dwell in the abysses of the ocean over the fountains of the waters. But the male is named Behemoth, who occupied with his breast a vast wilderness named Dûidâin....[4] And I besought the other Angel that he should show me the might of those monsters, how they were parted on one day and cast, the one into the abysses of the sea, and the other on to the dry land of the wilderness.

Bock then states, "The twofold Beast appears also at the end of the Book of Job." This is a judgment call by Bock. I have expressed high admiration for Emil Bock and his works and writings, but on this I have a contrary conclusion. The original writings attributed by their author to the ancient Enoch were "composed between the 4th century BCE and the turn of the era.... The collection...is extant in its entirety only in...(ancient Ethiopic) translation of a Greek translation of Aramaic originals which are attested, nonetheless, by

---

3   Emil Bock, *The Apocalypse*, 103–104; Emil Bock, *Kings and Prophets*, London, Floris Books (1989; but first published in Stuttgart, Germany by Verlag Urachhaus Stuttgart in 1936), chap. 27, at 339. Bock shows some hesitancy in his conclusion though as he considers the meaning of Job 40:19 where it is said of Behemoth, "He is the first of the works (or ways) of God."

4   In *The Ethiopic Book of Enoch*, Oxford, Clarendon Press (1978), 143, the name of Bock's "Dûidâin" is called "Dendayn." There, the first part of the ellipsis in the quote reads, "on the east of the garden where the chosen and righteous dwell." Compare Gen 3:24, and consider the essay "Eden's Locus" in *SLJ*, 195–204.

manuscript fragments from the Qumran caves."[5] The book of Daniel was written in roughly the middle of this same stretch of time, a time when prophetic vision was dimming. *The Ethiopic Book of Enoch*, at 60:24–25 seems to confirm the evil nature of these "two monsters" and to indicate their eventual punishment by "the Lord of Spirits," a view fitting both Daniel 7 and the two beasts in Revelation.[6] But the book of Job seems to come from a much earlier source, imported into the Hebrew writings from non-Hebrew sources.[7] These two later books, Enoch and Daniel, were perhaps conflating the two beasts from Job with the two that were later to appear more appropriately in John's Apocalyptic vision.

My conclusion is that the two sets of beast were the polar opposites of each other. The set in Job, which describes the evolutionary human journey from beginning to end, is incredibly similar to that described by Steiner's works, being salvific, while that in Revelation is evil. Though in the immeasurably long human journey the presence of evil is necessary to bring out the greater ultimate good, as Steiner has said, the evolutionary goal of the two beasts in Revelation 13 is to draw humanity and creation into the abyss and ultimate destruction.

Job's two beasts represent the two "guardians of the threshold" in the human journey. This is brought out in the essay "Job" in *SLJ*, and the functions of those two guardians is described with powerful clarity in the last two chapters of Steiner's *How to Know Higher Worlds*.[8] The second of these guardians is described by Steiner as "a magnificent form of light" (202). While this is not consistent with the literal description of the Leviathan in Job 41, we note that it is God who presents these two beasts to Job. Of the first one, the Behemoth, it is said that "He is the first of the works (or ways) of God" (40:19) and that "the mountains [spiritual realms] yield food for him" (40:20) and that he lies under the lotus plants that shade him (40:21–22); compare Steiner's discussion of the "lotus flowers" in chapter 6 of *How to Know Higher Worlds*. The more daunting description of the Leviathan in

---

5   George W. E. Nickelsburg, *Enoch, First Book of,* New York, Doubleday, ABD, vol. 2; 568.

6   Oxford, Clarendon Press (1978), 148.

7   See the essay "Job" in *SLJ*, at page 99.

8   SB (1994), chapter 10 "The Guardian of the Threshold" and chapter 11 "The Great Guardian of the Threshold."

Job 41 is, in a metaphorical way, descriptive of the immensity of the threshold guardianship exercised at this stage in one's spiritual journey. Particularly is this suggested by its placement between what is said in the chapters immediately preceding chapter 41 and the fact that in what follows it in Job 42, to complete the book, is Job's complete submission to the Lord and his restoration to the high state he occupied at the outset, but elevated now by what he has gained in the long journey he has completed.

The First Beast

We have already considered how the seven heads and ten horns of the first beast were developed. Now we look for aspects of that beast added by chapter 13.

At the outset we note that the beasts described there have only a partial reflection of the four beasts, the "living creatures" that reflected the four "corners" of the zodiac, discussed in chapters 8 and 10. Instead of the lion, bull, eagle, and face of a man, we have only a single animal with characteristics of three animal species, the leopard's appearance, bear's feet, and lion's mouth. Daniel 7 lists four beasts, lion, eagle, bear, and leopard. The dragon in chapter 12 had diadems on its seven heads, while this first beast in chapter 13 has diadems on its ten horns. Some authors have suggested that here, as with the rest of Revelation, John was importing contemporary empirical-political power structures and circumstances, an explanation I have generally accepted only to the extent it gave contemporary cover to an expression of the deeper spiritual insight that Steiner has revealed, as in the case of the seven churches. However, I have no better suggestion in this instance than that John's vision projected the dragon image to those structures and circumstances, while still importing the nature of the beast as described by Steiner in our discussion in chapter 12.

An interesting idea does arise, however, from a possibly analogous comparison drawn by Emil Bock. The latter, in his *The Apocalypse* (102), says, "The transition from the picture of the Dragon in chapter 12 to the twofold Beast in chapter 13 is similar to the way the pictures of the fourfold heavenly Beasts in chapter 4 led to the picture of the Lamb in chapter 5." He had reference to the two-horned beast in chapter 13. But the suggestion seems even more apt with reference to the first beast, for, having an inherent fourfold animal residue in chapter 12, in chapter 13 it was indeed only one, hence the four became one hideous creature.

The "mortal wound" on one of the beast's seven heads (13:3) would seem to refer to the wound Michael and his angels inflicted on the dragon in heaven. "Mortal" is a death adjective, applicable to the dragon's life in the spiritual realm. In the process of adjusting to its situation on the earth, its wound was healed so that it could apply its full earthly powers against the followers of the Lamb.

By the time these two beasts appear, at the blowing of the last trumpet, only those who have the mark of the beast will be involved in buying or selling (13:16–17), for those able to rise into the astral realm will have left that activity behind.

The most mysteriously gripping part of chapter 13 is the number "six hundred and sixty-six [666]" (13:18), "This calls for wisdom: let him who has understanding reckon the number of the beast, for it is a human number, its number is six hundred and sixty-six." The first beast is an animalized human being, while the second beast is a fallen hierarchical being. To which does the 666 apply? Steiner makes it clear that it applies to each of them, though the two are different, at least at the beginning and up to a point.

Let us look at what "wisdom," according to Steiner, has to say about the meaning of "the number of the beast" in the case of each of them. For this purpose, in regard to the first beast, have *BB's* charts **I-1** and **I-2** available, particularly **I-1**.[9] Chart **I-1** was presented by Steiner in the tenth Nuremberg *ASJ* lecture. In the 11th lecture he tells how the 666 was derived and what it means in regard to the first beast. On such an important matter, it is better to hear his description through. It is given below:

---

9   For chart **I-2**, the source given is inaccurate. *The Temple Legend* is correct, but the chart is referred to in note 6 in lecture 10, on page 125, which refers to the chart that is found in *The Temple Legend* on page 385 and is apparently from Steiner's "Notes" associated with the lecture. *The Temple Legend* will be in CW 93, when published, perhaps clarifying this source. Lecture 10 was given in Berlin on December 23, 1904, three and a half years before the more schematic chart **I-1** was given in lecture 10 in Nuremberg on June 27, 1908. Each of them is of great value.

When evolution has progressed beyond the seventh epoch, beyond the epoch indicated by the sounding of the trumpets, the earth then spiritualizes itself and passes over first into the astral, then into the lower devachanic and finally into the higher devachanic condition. It returns again to the same conditions by condensing more and more from the finest spiritual; and the condition comes which is usually described in theosophical textbooks as the fifth round, which again will have 7 conditions of form, and in the middle will again pass through a development of what might be characterized as 7 successive race conditions.

Now let us, even if it be somewhat difficult, look a little more deeply into the coming conditions of our Earth evolution. Let us turn our gaze to a quite definite point in our future evolution, just as we have been considering the present point. Let us start with our present, namely the 172nd condition.[10] Prior to this 172nd condition the Earth had already completed three sub-conditions; the 172nd condition is the earth itself. Three have already been completed and it is now in the fourth of these conditions. We are at the moment considering only the conditions of form. We reckon that we are in the fourth condition of life or fourth round. Granted this is so, we say: In this fourth condition of life or round we have already passed through three conditions of form and are now in the fourth.—Now we ask further, how many of the sub-conditions have we passed through? The first, second, third and fourth. The last was the Atlantean epoch. This is now completed. We have passed through four conditions and are now in the fifth, the Post-Atlantean. Of this fifth epoch we have again passed through four sub-conditions, namely the ancient Indian, the ancient Persian, the Egyptian and the Greco-Latin, and are now in the fifth age. So that we can say: Before our immediate present stage of evolution we have completed 3, 4, 4 conditions. These 3, 4, 4 conditions which we have completed are

---

10 These "conditions" are Conditions of Form. In each of the three Conditions of Consciousness (Saturn, Sun, and Moon), we passed through seven Conditions of Life, each comprising seven Conditions of Form. Thus each Condition of Consciousness comprised 49 Conditions of Form. The three prior Conditions of Consciousness comprised a total of 147 Conditions of Form. Three Conditions of Life in the Earth Condition of Consciousness have preceded our own Mineral Kingdom, thus 21 more conditions. Three Conditions of Form preceded our own Physical Condition of Form in the Mineral Condition of Life. Thus $147 + 21 + 3 = 171$ conditions prior to our present one, which is the 172nd.

described in Apocalyptic language as the *number of evolution*. When, therefore, it is asked: What is the number of evolution, our evolution?—the answer is: 344 (spoken three, four, four). This is not read according to the system of ten, but according to the system of seven. 3 conditions (out of the seven) have been gone through, and 4 conditions (out of the next smaller seven) have been gone through, and 4 conditions (out of again the next smaller seven). That is what is really meant by 344. One must not simply read it off like other numbers, but it contains, written side by side, the number of conditions passed through.

Now let us think of the following: When the Earth is spiritualized and has developed to its next conditions, then more and more stages will have been gone through. And the time must come, when 6 conditions of the first kind, 6 of the second and 6 of the third will have been passed through. Just as we now have 344 as the number of evolution, in the future when 6 conditions of life, 6 fundamental races, and 6 sub-races have been gone through, the number 666 (six, six, six) will apply, read in the manner described, which is the method used by the writer of the Apocalypse. Thus a time will come when the number 666 is the number of evolution. This will only be in a very distant future, but this future is already being prepared at the present time. Three great main conditions have been completed and we are now living in the fourth. But when the time indicated by the seven seals has passed, when we have reached the great War of All against All, we shall have gone through 6 of the middle kind. When the first trumpet sounds we shall have passed through 6 such main races, and when the first six trumpets are over, we shall have experienced 66. Up to then mankind will have had the opportunity to prepare for the terrible time which will follow much later, when not only 66 but 666 will be reached.

All that lies in the future is already being prepared now. The time that will come after the War of All against All, the time when the seventh trumpet sounds, will see men who, through having excluded themselves from the Christ-principle, will have attained a high degree of evil, of the tendency to sink into the abyss. By then these men will have seen to it that when the point of time 666 comes they will be able to descend very deeply into evil, into the abyss. Men will have taken into themselves, already in the period after the great War of All against All, when the seventh trumpet sounds, the germs of this descent into the abyss in the far-distant future. It will, indeed, for a long time be possible for those who have taken these germs into themselves to turn round and be converted, to turn back in their development in order even then to receive the Christ-principle. But the first predisposition will have been formed, and those who retain this tendency will no longer be able—when that distant future has come which is indicated not by 466 but by 666—to change this tendency into good. They will succumb to the frightful fate of which we have still to speak.

Thus we see that with this number 6, whether it is single, double or treble, there is connected something bad for human evolution.[11]

The Second Beast

Clearly there are two beasts described in Revelation 13, the first being human, the second being an evil spirit that is not human. Revelation 13:17–18 says that the number of the beast's name is "a human number," so it can only apply to the first beast. Aside from Steiner, scholars have, in effect, reduced the two to one and assumed that the one number they derive covers both. They have not given an interpretation of the number 666, except by applying the ancient art of gematria,[12] "the practice of assigning numerical values to letters of the alphabet, a favorite practice not only of Jews but also of people in the Greco-Roman world."[13]

Witherington and countless others have concluded, based upon the sum of the numbers of the letters in the name Nero Caesar, written in Hebrew characters, that 666 refers to Nero. I have not attempted to come up with that, but so he says, and something like that must be so for it is neither a new nor infrequent conjecture.[14] He explains (177) that getting from a name to a number is easy, but that getting "from a number to a name is much more difficult and usually results in a wide number of conjectures, as the centuries-long speculation about Rev. 13:18 shows."

---

11   *ASJ*, lect. 11; 194–196.

12   Pronounced with hard *g*, long *a*, and middle syllable emphasized.

13   Ben Witherington, *Revelation*, Cambridge, U.K., Cambridge University Press (2003), 176.

14   Elaine Pagels, *Revelations*, New York, NY, Viking (2012), 33; Christopher C. Rowland, *The Book of Revelation*, in NIB, vol. 12; 659.

The first beast described by the number 666 is human. The second beast is not itself human.

It seems that Steiner is alone in giving, as above, a completely rational explanation of the number 666 as it applies to the human being—the first beast. It is not clear whether Steiner would have gone ahead and given his number of the second beast had scholars not used only the gematria approach themselves in giving one explanation. Notably, Emil Bock only gives the explanation that relates to what Steiner gave for the first beast, based upon the Grand Schematic (107), though he did later state, ambiguously so it seems, "The number of the Adversary—666—is, as we have seen, the sign of the ever-increasing *tempo* of life, which brings restlessness and discord into human souls" (177).

To my knowledge, Steiner never said that the number 666, as it applied to the second beast, was a human number; only that the beast, that is also described, in wisdom, by that number, would appear when humanity had reached the point in its evolutionary journey where it is described by that number.

In his April 22, 1907, lecture in Munich, Steiner said:

But the passage concerning the two-horned beast was a real cross for the commentators. They had heard a rumor concerning the way numbers are to be read but it was dripping with occultism. How does one read in numbers? Every letter also signifies a number; the esotericists wrote in numbers when they wanted to hide something. One had to replace each number with the correct letter; one had to be able to read the letters and then also know what the resulting word meant. Who then, is the beast whose number is 666? The commentators thought it must be something in the past. One wrote the letters in Hebrew—wrongly—in the place of the numbers. That resulted in "Nero." The horns were then related to the generals or the enemies of the Romans, for example, the Parthians. If one had written correctly with Hebrew letters (right to left) and then read correctly (also from right to left), the following would have resulted: 60, Samech, 6 Waw; 600 was written by esotericists as 200 + 400: 200 Resch + 400 Taw. Hence we get 666, which in Hebrew letters spells "Sorat." *Sorat* is also the corresponding word in Greek. Sorat has meant "Demon of the Sun" since ancient times. Every star has its good spirit—its intelligence—and its evil spirit—its demon. The adversary of the good powers of the sun is called Sorat. Christ was always the representative of the sun, namely, the intelligence of the Sun. Sorat is, then, the adversary of Christ Jesus.[15]

As noted, the name Sorat went back to ancient times. One searches for it in the ancient literature available and normally comes up empty. Steiner's perceptions go back into pre-historic, even primeval, times. Scholars did not apply their gematria principles to that name, Steiner did.

The Hebrew letters Tau, Resh, Vau, and Samech, which, supplying the vowels and reading from right to left (i.e., backward to us), spell Sorath in Hebrew. It is the sum of the numbers for these letters that totals 666, as follows:

400	200	6	60	=	666
ת	ר	ו	ס		
Tau	*Resh*	*Vau*	*Samech*		

Steiner says, "For Sorath, the Sun-Demon, there was this sign, noting that the bottom is shaped like a "Barb or Sting," which he describes as "a thick stroke bent back upon itself and terminating in two curved points" noting that "it has two horns like a lamb" (13:11), which is quite apparent.[16]

But Who Is This Sun Demon?

Is it Ahriman, or is it an even more powerful evil spirit? Let us first consider what was perceived by the ancient Zarathustra, the highest spiritual leader of the Ancient Persian Cultural Age, the second such Age in the Post-Atlantean Epoch.[17] According to *BB*'s chart **I-19**, on page 573, that second Age began about 5067 BCE, or about 7,250 years ago. Steiner's important lecture about Zarathustra was given in Berlin on January 19, 1911, and is the first of the lectures in Berlin featuring the six great historical spiritual leaders that constituted the

---

15 *RPA*, 19.

16 *ASJ*, 200.

17 References to this ancient Zarathustra appear often in *BB*; see 22–23, 36, 38–41, 43, 48, 55, 58–60, 68, 84–86, 92–93, 95, 105, 154, and 228.

"Turning Points in Spiritual History," as compiled originally by Marie Steiner.[18] In that lecture, Steiner stated, "Greek historians have stated over and over again that the period ascribed to Zarathustra should be put back very many years, possibly five to six thousand years before the Trojan War [the date of which has been placed at about 1200 BCE]," which Steiner essentially corroborated, though it would result in one or two thousand years earlier than indicated in chart **I-19**, while later in the lecture he says that Zarathustra "lived at least eight thousand years before the present era."[19]

For our purposes, the most notable fact about this ancient Zarathustra is that, in contrast to the Ancient Indian Culture, he urged his people to look outward upon the world, seeing spirit within it. In doing so, he perceived the Creator, the descending Christ, in the light of the sun, calling him Ahura Mazda (the "Great Aura), but he perceived, interlaced within the light, its opposition, the spirit of darkness which he called Angra Mainyu, whom he also called Ahriman.[20]

If we could stop with this, we could say that the Sun Demon is Ahriman. But it is not quite that simple. We know that it is the Elohim, within the Spiritual Hierarchies, also known as Exusiai or Authorities, that are in charge of the Earth Condition of Consciousness and the evolution that occurs therein.[21] In my work on *BB*, the first of my writings, in particular in its chart **I-32**, in citing *The Book of Revelation and the Work of the Priest* [REVP] in chart **I-32**, I misapprehended the status of Ahriman as having fallen from the ranks of the Archai. It is now my judgment that Lucifer fell from the ranks of the Angeloi, Ahriman from the ranks of the Archangeloi, and Satan from the ranks of the Archai (all listed in chart **I-6**), although the name Satan appears to be used also to refer to Ahriman prior to the latter

---

18   The current English version of this is *Turning Points in Spiritual History*, SB (2007). Because of my constant solicitation of the Press to put that title back into print, I was asked to write the introduction. My urgency in getting it back in print was that the most critically important lecture on Elijah available in English could be found only in that publication. The first four lectures among the six will appear in CW 60, and the last two will appear in CW 61.

19   *Turning Points*, 3 and 6, respectively as to the quotes.

20   *Turning Points*, 12–32.

21   *BB*, chart **I-16**.

parts of Revelation, and scripture often seems to use the terms *devil* and *Satan* almost interchangeably.[22]

We must go back to Steiner's lecture 5 in Munich on August 21, 1910, in the cycle of ten lectures there in the month of August that has been published under the book title *Genesis*.[23] It deals with the first three verses of Genesis (italics mine):

> [1] In the beginning God created the heavens and the earth. [2] The earth was without form and void, and *darkness* was upon the face of the deep; and the Spirit of God was moving over the face of the waters. [3] And God said, "Let there be *light*"; and there was *light*.

The Elohim are called "God" in these verses. The "without form and void" had to do with matter, the earth was void of any matter, but the spirits of the Elohim were active, the Elohim being the hierarchical rank governing the Earth Condition of Consciousness (chart **I-16**). At each stage of evolution there are beings that reach their goal for such stage and there are those who do not attain the goal and remain behind.

The definition of "darkness" that immediately pops into the common mind today is simply the absence of light. In the face of that common understanding, especially as it regards the darkness in verse 2 above, Steiner poses the question, "Was the darkness there of itself, or does spiritual Being lie behind this also?"[24]

We can see from **I-16** that the Elohim (Exusiai/Authorities) were in charge of earth evolution, that is of the Earth Condition of Consciousness. It was their sacrifice that brought about the Saturn Sphere.[25] To accomplish the mission of Saturn, they appointed as their "helpers" the seven Archai.[26] Saturn was to prepare for the next Condition of Consciousness, the Ancient Sun, which was to take place within the

---

22 In *BB*, chart **I-66**, at the top of page 644, I either misapprehend what Tomberg said about the rank from which each of the three, Lucifer, Ahriman, and Asura, fell, or else I can no longer agree with his assessment on that matter.

23 Steiner, *Genesis*, RSP (2002).

24 Ibid., 61.

25 The orbit of Saturn; see **I-27**, esp. at *BB* 595. The later-discovered "planets" of Uranus, Neptune, and Pluto were not within the creative cycles of the human being; 596.

26 Ibid., 68. The Archai are Steiner's "Spirits of Personality"; see **I-6**.

Jupiter Sphere.[27] Some of the Archai reached their goal for Saturn (attained human status) and thus became Archai as they moved into the Ancient Sun Condition of Consciousness.[28] However, those who did not attain the goal of Saturn, who did not attain their human status there, nevertheless moved on into the Sun Condition of Consciousness; but in doing so they remained Saturn beings during Ancient Sun. Stated differently, they were backward Archai, not able to emanate light during the Sun Condition.

In the earlier part of the lecture, Steiner had said:

How would one recognize, during the ancient Sun existence, beings who were still Saturn beings? By the fact that they had not reached the level of being of ancient Sun that was of the nature of light. But because these Saturn beings were nevertheless there, the Sun condition, which I have described as an interweaving of light, warmth and air, had darkness interspersed in the light. This darkness was the expression of the beings remaining at the Saturn stage just as much as the weaving light was the expression of those beings who had reached the Sun stage in a regular way. The outer aspect showed a manifestation of the interweaving of retarded Saturn beings with Sun beings who had progressed normally. From the inner aspect these beings moved in and out among one another, and outwardly they manifested as an interplay of light and darkness. Looking at the light we can call it a manifestation of the beings who had progressed to the Sun stage, and looking at the darkness we can call it the external manifestation of the beings who had remained behind at the Saturn stage.

Once we realize this we can expect to find that during the recapitulation of ancient Saturn and ancient Sun on planet earth the relationship between the advanced and the retarded beings will reappear. And because the retarded Saturn beings represent an earlier stage of evolution, so to speak they will be able, during the recapitulation, too, to appear sooner than the light. Thus, quite rightly, in the first verse of Genesis we are told that the darkness prevailed over the elemental masses. This is the recapitulation of the Saturn condition, but it was the retarded Saturn condition. The other one, the Sun condition, has to wait. It comes later on, at the point where

---

27   The orbit of Jupiter; again **I-27**.

28   "And thus became Archai," or Principalities/Spirits of Personality; see **I-15**.

the Bible says: 'Let there be light.' Thus we see in a most pertinent way that with regard to these recapitulations, too, Genesis gets it just right.[29]

Later, Steiner says, "When, from what has remained of ancient existence, they think out the two complexes of thoughts, it transpires that the darkness interwoven in it is the expression of the retarded beings."[30] Steiner comments upon the necessity of these backward beings, noting that while we characterize them as "evil" they are a necessary part of the evolution of the human being: "We should not harbor feelings and ideas of such a kind as regards these tremendous realities of the universe. That would lead us completely astray. On the contrary we should remind ourselves that everything happens out of cosmic wisdom, and that whenever Beings remain behind at a particular stage of development, it means something.... They are in their proper place in their backwardness."

The interweaving of darkness within the light was something that the ancient Zarathustra perceived at the beginning of the Ancient Persian Cultural Age. He saw the Ahura Mazda, the Great Aura, the Christ Spirit, but he also saw Angra Mainyu, the darkness that he called Ahriman. The major essays on "Fire" and "Light" in *DQWIM* are followed by the separate essay on "Darkness" which, among other things, cites *OES* and the backward Archai as discussed above.[31]

Clearly then, for a very long time yet, identifying the second beast as Ahriman, the demon of the sun should be our greatest concern. The term "Satan" through most of our canon and most of Revelation will properly refer to Ahriman. But ere we reach the end of Revelation, we must recognize that ultimately the reference to Satan rises to the level of the fallen Archai. For that insight, we turn to Steiner's lectures to the priests in September, 1924, particularly lecture 11 (September 15). Three levels of deception and evil are involved as we move toward the end of the book of Revelation. It would seem that we should take them to be Lucifer,

---

29 Ibid., 60–61.

30 Ibid., 63.

31 *DQWIM*, 307–308. Many relevant references to darkness and the matters discussed above can be found in each of *BB* and *DQWIM* in its respective Index of Scriptures Cited, especially therein under Gen 1:2.

Ahriman, and the Asuras.[32] Steiner describes them as three successive downfalls: the first, of "corrupted human beings"; the second, those spirits who "take possession of the bodies of human beings," these spirits being called "the demonic Beast and his Prophet"; and the third, Satan, "an exalted being who, however, treads another path than those that can be trodden on the earth. The Beast and the False Prophet are powers who seduce human beings, who have the will to tempt humanity on to the wrong paths both morally and intellectually."[33] But on this being, the more ultimate of the three, as Steiner explained to the priests:

> The power, dear friends, whom we mean when we talk of the fall of Satan, this power has quite other plans. He not only wants to throw humanity off course but he also wants to do this to the earth as a whole. From the point of view of human beings and of the earth this power is a terrible adversary of God.
>
> But, you see, we can say hypothetically—for only in this way can we do so without falling into intellectual sin or more especially into spiritual sin—we can say the following. We can ask: If we do not look at this from the point of view of human, earthly evolution, if we consider it from other, higher viewpoints—what, then, is the position of this power of Satan over against other spirits in the cosmos?
>
> It is not surprising that Michael, whose standpoint differs from that of human beings, has quite a different view about Satan. Human beings remain in the abstract and think that Satan is an evil power. But Satan is also an exalted power, even though he is in error as regards the directions that are suitable for the earth. He is an exalted power. Michael, who has the degree of an archangel, does not have the rank of Satan, who has the degree of an Archai. Michael is 'only' an archangel. From Michael's point of view Satan is not a power to be despised but a power to be immensely feared, for Michael sees this power who belongs to the hierarchy of the Archai as being more exalted than himself. Michael, however, has chosen to go in the direction that is the same as that of earth evolution.[34]

---

32 See **I-22** in *BB* at 586–587.

33 *REVP*, lect. 11; 156–157.

34 Ibid., lect. 11; 157.

Jumping ahead, Steiner continues:

> We are here confronted with an adversary of Christ, one who wants
> not merely to corrupt single individuals, nor one who wants to cor-
> rupt a group of individuals, a human community, as do the Beast
> and the False Prophet. With Satan and his cohorts we are faced with
> endeavors to attack the earth in its context within the planetary sys-
> tem as a whole. That is the third downfall in the Book of Revelation.[35]

From Revelation 14 on, the vision as given by John becomes
almost chaotic and difficult to follow, the way we have trod up through
chapter 13 having been more systematic. In *REVP*, lecture 11, we shall
see that Steiner gives three different levels from which the evil powers
are disposed of by the forces of good. In regard to the third and final
level, he says:

> In the third stage it will be noticed that something about the laws of
> nature becomes inexplicable. It will be the greatest and most signifi-
> cant experience through which human beings will have to go in the
> future when they have to recognize that something inexplicable is
> going on in the laws of nature, that phenomena are occurring that do
> not fit in with the laws of nature. This will happen to a high degree,
> and it will not be merely a matter of miscalculating the position of
> a planet, so that it does not arrive at the position one has calculated.
> Satan will succeed in taking his initial steps toward bringing
> disorder into the planetary system.[36]

To put it in terms of modern metaphor, when a building has either
fully served its purpose or otherwise become unusable, the battering
rams or balls are brought in to destroy it so that it may be hauled away.
Spiritually, this is the work of the Asuras, fallen Archai.

The first of the three downfalls Steiner mentioned will be of "corrupted human beings"; the second of "the demonic Beast and his
Prophet"; and the third and last of Satan where that name applies to
the Asura, the fallen Archai. Speculating, the first seems to be related
to the fall of "Babylon" in 14:8 and 16:19—the second to the fall of

---

35   Ibid., lect. 11; 159–160.
36   *REVP*, 160.

Babylon in 18:2, 10, and 21—the third to the fall of the Asura Satan in chapter 20.

Mention was made of the increasingly chaotic nature of the Revelation starting in chapter 14. We must understand that we are peering, in these chapters, toward a very distant part of our journey, where even for John and Steiner the detail becomes less clear as it becomes essentially irrelevant to where we presently stand. In the next chapter we will look at some things worthy of comment within these chapters 14 through 20.

12

SEPARATING THE SHEEP FROM THE GOATS (MATT 25:31–46)

The Big Picture

The akashic record is there for the seer into periods that are past. It is different in the foretelling of future periods, which seems obvious, but as Steiner also indicates:

> Spiritual researchers are in a different position with regard to communications about the future than they are with regard to those about the past. We are not initially able to confront future events as impartially as we confront the past. What will happen in the future stirs up our feeling and willing, but we tolerate the past quite differently. Anyone who observes life will know that this is true even of our ordinary existence, but only those who are aware of certain things in the supersensible worlds can know what forms this tendency assumes and to what an enormous extent it increases with regard to life's hidden facts. This is the reason why knowledge of these things is kept within very specific limits.[1]

He traces developments that have led to the present.[2] Moving from there into the future, he continues:

> This is how evolution is proceeding from one age to the next. Supersensible cognition observes not only future changes involving the Earth alone, but also ones that occur in interaction with the neighboring heavenly bodies. There will come a time when both the Earth and humanity have made such progress in evolution that the forces and beings that had to separate from the Earth during Lemurian times to enable earthly beings

---

1   *OES*, chap. 6; 383.
2   Ibid., 383–392.

to continue to progress will be able to reunite with the Earth. At that time, the Moon will reconnect with the Earth. This will happen because sufficient numbers of human souls possess enough inner strength to make these Moon forces fruitful for further evolution. This will take place at a time when another development that has turned toward evil will be taking place alongside the high level of development reached by the appropriate number of human souls. Souls whose development has been delayed will have accumulated so much error, ugliness, and evil in their karma that they temporarily form a distinct union of evil and aberrant human beings who vehemently oppose the community of good human beings.[3]

Moving then to the responsibility of the good forces of humanity to work to redeem the evil portion, he continues:

In the course of its development, the good portion of humankind will learn to use the Moon forces to transform the evil part so that it can participate in further evolution as a distinct earthly kingdom. Through the work of the good part of humanity, the Earth, then reunited with the Moon, will become able to reunite with the Sun after a certain period of evolution, and also with the other planets. After an interim stage that resembles a sojourn in a higher world, the Earth will transform into the Jupiter state.[4]

It seems to be precisely this stage, when the transformation of evil becomes the essential work of the redeemed of humanity, that the Manicheans must surely constitute the vanguard. See again what was said in chapter 9 under "The Mission of the Manicheans." Note Steiner's statement there that "This wonderful and lofty Manichean principle will win more and more pupils the nearer we approach the understanding of spiritual life." The incremental aspect of this group's mission seems clearly implied. I suggest that it kicks in to some modest extent by our own Sixth Cultural Age, that called Philadelphia, enhancing during the Sixth Great Epoch, that of the seals, and leaping into high gear after the blowing of the last trumpet.

---

3   Ibid., 392–393.

4   Ibid., 393.

Thence it must continue so long as salvation remains a possibility.[5] As we have seen, this lasts through the Venus condition.

The Redemption of the Kingdoms

On this matter of the redemption of the kingdoms, not only are we concerned with the human. We are also charged to redeem the mineral, plant and animal. The two witnesses: Lazarus/John, indwelt by the eternal spirit of Adam/Elijah/John the Baptist; and Paul, the reincarnation, I believe, of Moses, through their combined spiritual vision, bring us to this recognition. We shall later look at the spiritual helper Lazarus/John needs here in the latter part of his Apocalypse to complete this important charge.

The two witnesses work here together. Paul's vision gave us the following two powerful insights on what lies ahead for humanity:

> **Romans 8:19–22:** [19] For the creation waits with eager longing for the revealing of the sons of God; [20] for the futility, not of its own will but by the will of him who subjected it in hope; [21] because the creation itself will be set free from its bondage to decay and obtain the glorious liberty of the children of God. [22]We know that the whole creation has been groaning in travail together until now.

> **Ephesians 1:9–10:** [9] For he has made known to us in all wisdom and insight the mystery of his will, according to his purpose which he set forth in Christ [10] as a plan for the fullness of time, to unite all things in him, things in heaven and things on earth.

---

5   That the Manichean mission will be fully engaged during the Sixth Great Epoch is clear from *The Temple Legend (TL)*, RSP (1985), lect. 6 "Manicheism" (November 11, 1904), 70–72 (CW 93). There the Great Epochs of *BB's* chart **I-1** are called "Root Races" in its **I-2**. Sometimes TL mistakenly calls them "Rounds," which are also called the "Kingdoms" or Conditions of Life in both charts. In *Foundations of Esotericism*, RSP (1983) (lect.13, Berlin, October 8, 1905), 94 (CW 93a), Steiner says (emphasis added): "Thus there existed for instance in the Middle Ages the sect of the Manicheans [fn omitted]. The secret of the Manicheans was that they realised that in the future there would be two groups of human beings, the good and the bad. *In the Fifth Round there will no longer be a mineral kingdom, but instead a kingdom of evil.* The Manicheans knew this. They therefore made it their task already then so to educate people that later they might become educators of the evil men. Again and again a deeper profundity is seen in the sect of the Manicheans."

Steiner's *OES* was first published in December 1909. In a lecture on August 12, 1908 in Stuttgart, he had said that through an increasingly spiritual love, "man will draw along with him the lower beings of the earth, will transform the whole earth." He takes this process through each of the lower three kingdoms.[6]

From my earliest days of reading Steiner, it seemed clear to me that we were charged with the redemption of the three lower kingdoms along with our own. Until my continued study in the preparation of this book, a clear picture of the progression of redemption of the lower kingdoms did not exist.

In reflecting back, I judge that my conclusion about the redemption of the lower three kingdoms was based upon the parabolic journey from the spiritual realm into materiality and back again to the spiritual realm. In its most basic format, my reasoning was that the redemption of the animal kingdom would be during the Jupiter Condition of Consciousness in the retracement of the Ancient Moon Condition of Consciousness, the redemption of the astral realm and the animal nature that emanated from it. The redemption of the plant kingdom would thus be in the Venus Condition of Consciousness, the retracement of the Ancient Sun, while the mineral kingdom would be in the Vulcan Condition of Consciousness relating to the mineral kingdom's ancestry on Ancient Saturn.

Let us look first at what Steiner wrote in the sixth chapter of his *Outline of Esoteric Science*, on "Cosmic and Human Evolution," being perhaps the passage from which I derived my early understanding:

> During the Jupiter stage, what is now called the mineral kingdom will not exist; mineral forces will have been transformed into plant forces. The lowest kingdom appearing during the Jupiter stage will be the plant kingdom, which will have a form entirely different from what it has now. Above that will be the animal kingdom which will have undergone a comparable transformation, followed by a human kingdom consisting of the descendants of the evil union that came about on Earth. Above these, there will be a higher human kingdom consisting of the descendants of the community of good human beings on Earth. A great deal of the work of this second human kingdom will consist of ennobling the fallen souls in the evil union

---

6   *Universe, Earth and Man*, RSP (1987), 113–117 (CW 105).

so that they will still be able to find their way back into the actual human kingdom.

At the Venus stage, the plant kingdom will also have disappeared, and the lowest kingdom will be the animal kingdom, transformed once more. Above that there will be three human kingdoms of different degrees of perfection. During the Venus stage, the Earth will remain united with the Sun; in contrast, as evolution proceeds on Jupiter, the Sun will once again break away from Jupiter and influence it from outside. Then a reunification of the Sun and Jupiter will take place, and the transformation into the Venus stage will gradually continue. During the Venus stage, a distinct cosmic body will break away, containing all the beings who have resisted evolution and constituting an "unredeemable moon," so to speak. It will move toward an evolution that is so different in character from anything we can experience on Earth that there are no words that can possibly express it. The part of humanity that has continued to evolve, however, will move on to the Vulcan phase of evolution in a fully spiritualized form of existence. Describing this state falls outside the scope of this book.[7]

If we follow this, it appears that during the Jupiter "stage" (condition) the mineral will step up to the plant level, the plant to the animal, and the animal to the human. Similar steps up would occur during the Venus and Vulcan conditions. This seems to support the sequence that I originally had in mind.

There is some potential for confusion at this point. For instance, the fact that at the Venus stage "the lowest kingdom will be the animal kingdom," taken alone, may seem to suggest that such kingdom, as it exists on Earth, is the last to be redeemed. But we need to remember that the animal kingdom on Venus was the mineral kingdom on Earth. The first statement Steiner made in the sequence of redemption above was, "During the Jupiter stage, what is now called the mineral kingdom will not exist; mineral forces will have been transformed into plant forces." These are then the lowest forces on Jupiter. And so the upward transition continues as we come to Venus and Vulcan.

To nail these concepts down firmly, the following tabulations from *BB* are helpful (from *BB* page 413):

---

7   *OES*, chap. 6, "Cosmic and Human Evolution Now and in the Future," 393–394.

HUMAN COMPONENT	ORIGIN
physical body	Ancient Saturn
etheric body	Ancient Sun
astral body	Ancient Moon
Ego (the "I")	Earth

Bearing in mind that in any earthly incarnation, the Ego is the "Soul" in the threefold (body-soul-spirit) human being, and that it is threefold in the ninefold human being: sentient soul—intellectual soul—consciousness (spiritual) soul (see *BB* chart **I-9**), during earth evolution the consciousness soul is the highest to be perfected (*BB* 413); from *BB* p. 414:

FUTURE HUMAN COMPONENT	IN WHICH MANIFESTED
manas, or Spirit-Self	Jupiter
buddhi, or Life-Spirit	Venus
atma, or Spirit-Man	Vulcan

From *BB* p. 416:

He [Steiner] compares the etheric body to the hour hand and the astral body to the minute hand of a clock,[8] but one can carry the simile further by equating the three bodies as:

second hand	=	astral body
minute hand	=	etheric body
hour hand	=	physical body

The redemption of the three lower kingdoms, along with the perfection of the human being, can perhaps best be illustrated through the diagrams of fission and fusion. Picture the structure of the fission side of these principles on *BB* chart **I-22**, p. 585. It pertains only to the four elements as reflected in the etheric realm. Below, we expand this to the kingdoms and the human elements. The fission portion would appear as follows:

---

8   Steiner, *The Lord's Prayer*, SB (1970), 15 (Berlin, January 28, 1907) (CW 96).

SATURN	SUN	MOON	EARTH
			Ego
		astral	
	etheric		
physical/human			
	animal		
		plant	
			mineral

Then the fusion portion would appear as follows:

EARTH	JUPITER	VENUS	VULCAN
Ego			
	astral/manas		
		etheric/buddhi	
			physical/atma
		animal	
	plant		
mineral			

As mentioned earlier, it was my understanding that the redemption of the three lower kingdoms would occur successively over the three Conditions of Consciousness *following* the Earth Condition. Certain things Steiner said seem to have the potential to confuse on this point, namely, on the one hand, if that understanding of mine was right or, on the other hand, if the entire redemptive process, including the lower three kingdoms, will occur *during* the Earth Condition of Consciousness. Other Steiner lectures may be deemed by some to bear on the question.

Let us now consider what he says, at least in regard to the human kingdom, in his Kristiania (Oslo) lecture of May 20, 1909:[9]

---

9   *RPA*, 128–129.

When the earth began its existence as "earth" it had to briefly repeat the Saturn, Sun, and Moon conditions once again. It went through recapitulations of those conditions before it became the present-day earth. Now, when actual earth conditions prevail, it must prophetically mirror the future embodiments of Jupiter, Venus, and Vulcan. In this way the earth goes through seven states during its actual earth condition. These states are usually called "rounds" [Kingdoms, or Conditions of Life, *BB* chart **I-2**]. During the prophetically mirrored Jupiter state, the earth will actually unite with the sun. On this Jupiter-Earth all the great cultural ages will appear again—with the seven intervals between them—but they will be far less sharply delineated. On this Jupiter-Earth, many beings still have the possibility of being saved, even the black magicians.

This will also be the case on the Venus-Earth, when we have a sixth planetary interval. Here also the beings that have remained behind will stubbornly struggle against help; but this Venus-Earth will at last be decisive.

Then, on the Vulcan-Earth, nothing more can be saved. On the Venus-Earth the last moment for salvation has come in the last sub-epoch. That is why the ancient cabalists formed the word *Sorat*, because the number 666 is contained within it. That is also the number of those human beings who, out of their own cunning free will, have become black magicians by placing spiritual forces in the service of their own egotism.

The first dragon is not a human being. It came out of the spiritual world. The second dragon is ascribed to animalistic nature but in a fundamental sense the Bible ascribes this number of the third group to human beings. So the number 666 is not a sign of the beast but a human number.

The Apocalypse is an outline of the whole of evolution. Venus-Earth is portrayed to clairvoyant sight in such a way that there is not much hope for those left behind. Human powers at that time will not be capable of very much. That is why everything appears so desolate and the worst vices will reign there in the most depraved ways. They must be expelled during the Venus state of the earth. On the Jupiter-Earth there are still many, many who will allow themselves to be saved and who will unite with the sun.

But during the Venus-Earth evil must be overcome and driven into the abyss; that is the "Fall of Babylon." (Rev.17–18) The people who have been saved can develop themselves further to a new sun state. What has been cleansed and purified will arise for the Vulcan–Earth.

Looking at the Grand Schematic (chapter 2 above), Jupiter-Earth is the Plant Kingdom (the fifth Condition of Life), Venus-Earth is the Animal Kingdom, and Vulcan-Earth is the Human Kingdom.

But he begins this passage in the *RPA* lecture by saying that these three earthly stages prophetically mirror the future embodiments of Jupiter, Venus, and Vulcan. Jupiter-Earth, Venus-Earth, and Vulcan-Earth are "prophetic mirrorings" of the three future Conditions of Consciousness (Jupiter, Venus, and Vulcan), and these mirrorings seem only to relate to their consequences for the human kingdom. They represent the plant, animal, and human Conditions of Life during the Earth Condition of Consciousness. Seemingly, in regard to the three lower kingdoms, it would seem that they are merely planting seeds that will find their perfection in the later Conditions of Consciousness. In this respect, however, we must bear in mind that all three of these kingdoms are part of the human being.

This being the case, we humans will not be fully restored to the spiritual realm until all of the lower kingdoms also have been. The journey is a very long one. The question, which I will only propose, not attempt to answer, is this: Will those human beings who have followed evil spiritual beings and who have gone finally into the abyss beyond redemption during Earth evolution, nevertheless be redeemed in the process of these higher three Conditions of Consciousness? Does the Pauline vision in Ephesians extend this far?

Often, as above, I have said that the long journey of humanity is one first of fission (the descending) and then one of fusion (the ascending).[10] What might suggest itself on this if we ponder the seven Conditions of Consciousness (*BB*, **I-1**) together with the parable of the ninety and nine—or, for that matter, other biblical passages?[11] If humanity, by these last Conditions of Consciousness has attained great spiritual power, might not it take on the character of the Lamb of God, not willing to let any ultimately perish? Steiner also has pointed

---

10 See *SLJ*, 5–6.

11 Matt 18:12–14; Luke 15:4–7.

to the necessity of evil as a part of creation, a part that prompts the greater good, suggesting that even it, in the end, will be redeemed.

This consideration is so incredibly far into the future that neither John's vision nor Steiner's lectures on it attempt to deal with it with any particularity beyond what is implied in the schematic introduced in *ASJ* lecture 10 (*BB* chart **I-1**). The Apocalypse ends with the holy city, the "new Jerusalem" (Rev 21–22), which Steiner identifies as the Jupiter Condition.[12]

When the goal of the Earth Condition of Consciousness has been reached and it is dissolved, those who have not been able to take in the Christ-being will be sloughed off into a form of material sphere, having suffered the "second death."[13] But the descent into the abyss that will eventually render them irredeemable is a slow one that extends to a period described as Venus, the last one before Vulcan. We must ask whether that Condition is the Venus Condition of Consciousness, or what Steiner later described as "Venus-Earth." That it is the Venus Condition of Consciousness seems to be what Steiner is saying in *ASJ*'s final lecture (lect. 12).[14]

Return to the "Smaller" Picture

The degree of difficulty in attempting any explanation of events with any particularity after we move beyond the seven Evolutionary Epochs, after the echoes of the last trumpet have died away, explodes upward geometrically. We saw Steiner recognizing this in regard to the fall of the Archai beast. We must accord to both Ahriman and the Archai two-horned beast something of the character of the "demon of the sun."

We note the phrase "lake of fire" which appears in 19:20 and 20:10, 14–15, and is probably also within that description as "the lake that burns with fire" in 21:8. Steiner envisioned that from the tangle of these last chapters, three falls were envisioned, one of human beings who had been deceived and had not yet taken in the Christ-being, the second and third being of evil spiritual beings. The first of these latter two are described as the demonic beast and his prophet (which I take

---

12   *ASJ*, 217.

13   Second death, Rev 20:6,14; 21:8.

14   Ibid., 217.

to be the Ahrimanic spirits), and the second of the latter two being the Asura, the backward Archai. Michael could deal with the Ahrimanic spirits, but only the Lamb could deal with the Archaic Asuric spirit, the ultimate demon of the sun.

The evil spirits are thrown into the lake of fire. Are the human beings who have not taken in the Christ-being included among these? We note in 19:20 it appears that only the beast and his prophet were thrown in, while the rest were slain by the sword of him who is described in 19:11–16. But that sword has a saving side to it, and the period during which souls could still gain a form of salvation extends far into the future. The Asuric sun demon is most likely the one described in chapter 20, and its lake-of-fire experience seems to come much later in the schematic process.

My conception is that the "lake of fire" is the sun, or sun sphere, in the astral realm (or higher; consider chart **I-33**); recall Christ's "I came to cast fire upon the earth."[15] Those human beings who have been able to rise to that level so as to be able to "live" there without physical or life bodies should not be adversely affected by the heat of that higher world. To rise to that level means that the earthly astral body and sentient soul have been transformed to the consciousness (spiritual) soul level.[16] The evil spirits have made the world of matter their domain. They cannot live in these higher realms.

John's "Helper"

As noted in the closing paragraphs of chapter 11, up through Revelation 13 and its beasts, Steiner's lectures systematically opened doors to a significant comprehension of what John's Apocalypse reveals. These doors had never before been opened to such an extent, and for so many, in the history of Christendom. The foundation that he laid up to that point, had many points of contact with the rest of Revelation, though not in such a systematic way as in the chapters that preceded. The chaotic nature of the following chapters, particularly 14 through 20, was commented upon by Steiner in his lecture to the priests some sixteen years after his 1908 lecture cycles of *RPA* (Kristiania [Oslo])

---

15 Luke 12:49; see also the "Fire" essay in *DQWIM*.

16 *BB*, chart **I-9**.

and *ASJ* (Nuremberg), and only days before his terminal health condition forced the end of his lecturing in September 1924.

Let us consider again what could have made it possible for Steiner to so confidently, and plausibly, provide for us such a meaningful explanation of John's Apocalypse, a book that, from the first, has baffled Christians, and their scholars, seeking to understand this otherwise puzzling vision. Much has already been said about Steiner's relationship with Christian Rosenkreutz, the reincarnated Lazarus/John, and how what Rosenkreutz taught became the content of Anthroposophy. Then there are the two witnesses represented by the Jachin and Boaz explanation of the mighty angel in Revelation 10:1–8.

It behooves us now to contemplate an even deeper aspect of the relationship between Steiner and Rosenkreutz, or more accurately between the Aristotle/Rudolf Steiner spirit and the Lazarus–John–Christian Rosenkreutz spirit.[17] The late Sergei O. Prokofieff (January 16, 1954–July 26, 2014) suggested it to us in his booklet *The Mystery of John the Baptist and John the Evangelist at the Turning Point of Time*.[18] He leads us through the relevant Steiner lectures to the conclusion that three human spirit-beings, all discarnate at the time of the Mystery of Golgotha, bestowed upon Lazarus/John, during his temple-sleep initiation, the three "cosmic bodily members of the Christ: John the Baptist, His Spirit-Self; Zarathustra, His Life-Spirit in the surroundings of the Earth [the Moon sphere]; and Aristotle, His Spirit-Man on the Sun [in the Sun sphere]."[19]

The Archangel Michael is the one charged with bringing, from his place in the Sun sphere, the divine cosmic intelligence into human beings. The regencies of the seven archangels extend over a period of about 2,127 years, each regency lasting about 354 years.[20] The last regency of the Archangel Michael before the Mystery of Golgotha extended from 602 to 248 BCE, a period that encompassed the spread

---

17 *BB*, "Pillars on the Journey," 343–344.

18 London, Temple Lodge (2005), first published in German by Verlag am Goetheanum, Dornach, Switzerland, under the title *Das Geheimnis der zwei Johannes-Gestalten* (2004); it is based upon his Whitson conference lecture of June 7, 2003 in Dornach.

19 Ibid., 31.

20 See *BB*, Chart **I-19** at page 575 (noting comment 1 in the Preface to the Revised Edition).

of Greek culture under the leadership of Aristotle and Alexander. The first Michael regency since the Turning Point of Time started in 1879.

Prokofieff directed our attention to two Steiner lectures that form the basis for understanding the relationship between Steiner and Lazarus/John, both lectures being in the summer of 1924 within the last ten weeks before his Final Address on September 27. Both were in his Karmic Relationships series, the first being on July 19 and the second on August 27.[21] In the August lecture, Steiner said that "Alexander and Aristotle had witnessed the Mystery of Golgotha *from the Sun*" (86). In the July lecture (148), Steiner said:

> By means of Aristotelianism, earthly Intelligence emerged as though from the shell of the Cosmic Intelligence. And from what came to be known as Aristotelian Logic there arose that intellectual framework on which the thinking of all subsequent centuries was based; it conditioned human intelligence....
>
> Michael had relinquished his dominion for the time being to [his succeeding archangel], and in the realm of the Sun, together with those human souls who were to be his servants, Michael witnessed the departure of Christ from the Sun.
>
> This, too, is something of which we must be mindful.—Those human souls who are connected with the Anthroposophical Movement may say to themselves: We were united with Michael in the realm of the Sun....
>
> A great and mighty impulse went forth from that moment in cosmic history when these souls witnessed the departure of Christ from the Sun. They saw clearly: the Cosmic Intelligence is passing over gradually from the Cosmos to the Earth! And Michael, together with those around him saw that all the Intelligence once streaming through the Cosmos was now sinking down, stage by stage, upon the Earth.

Moving then to the August lecture (78):

> And as a man who dies leaves his physical body behind on the earth and his etheric body which is laid aside after three days is visible to the seer, so Christ left behind Him in the Sun that which in my

---

21   *Karmic Relationships*, vol. 6, 2nd ed., RSP (1989), lect. 8 (Arnhem, July 19, 1924) (CW 240); and vol. 8, RSP (1975) (CW 240), lect. 6 (London, August 27, 1924).

book *Theosophy* is called "Spirit-Man," the seventh member of the human being [in the sevenfold HB, or the 9th in the ninefold HB: see *BB* Chart **I-9**].

Christ died to the Sun. He died cosmically, from the Sun to the earth. He came down to the earth. From the moment of Golgotha onward His Life-Spirit was to be seen around the earth.... After this cosmic Death, Christ left His Spirit-Man on the Sun, and around the earth [in the Moon Sphere], His Life-Spirit.

We know from what has been said before that the spirit of John the Baptist entered into the being of Lazarus/John.

From all of this, Prokofieff suggests, plausibly, that three powerful individualities in human evolution, that of John the Baptist, Zarathustra, and Aristotle were spiritually involved in the initiation of Lazarus/John in the four higher elements of his being (Ego, Spirit-Self, Life-Spirit, and Spirit-Man; see **I-9**). The lower two, Ego and Spirit-Self, came through John the Baptist; Life-Spirit through Zarathustra in the Moon Sphere—the Solomon Jesus child, who became Jesus of Nazareth, and then after his sacrifice at baptism and the crucifixion of his bodies, he became the guiding human spirit called Master Jesus; and finally Spirit-Man through Aristotle from the Sun Sphere.

Virtually without exception, I suppose, those versed in Anthroposophy come to realize that the individuality of Aristotle reincarnated again in the nineteenth century as Rudolf Steiner.[22]

For those who recognize, or sense, the reliability of what is given above, it should not be hard to accept the authoritative nature of the things Steiner says in his interpretation of John's vision.

Inexpressibility of Distant Vision

In the first verse of John's Apocalypse (1:1), the reader is slammed with the statement, as almost universally translated thus far, that the things John sees are to happen soon, or words to that effect. The same thing is repeated, in some context, seven more times, including four times in the last chapter.[23] The normal meaning of such widely

---

22 See *BB*, "Pillars on the Journey," 543–544, item 4. The Kirchner-Bockholt book (RSMW) became available to the public soon after *BB* was published, the restriction to members of the Society having been removed.

23 See Rev 2:16; 3:11; 11:14; 22:6, 7, 12, 20.

prevalent translation has caused some degree of discredit for the Apocalypse, since in the normal way we interpret things, the time for "soon" to have occurred was many centuries ago. Perhaps for many, this discrediting was a relief from the demands of understanding the strange content of the text. For many, it opened the door to the prevalent practice of interpreting the visions as being applicable to the then contemporary political and power structures as well as the circumstances then facing Lazarus/John and his fellow Christian believers.

Steiner's lectures on the Apocalypse give us a dramatically different interpretation, one that looks backward and forward over enormous stretches of timelessness and time—a journey from the spiritual realm to materiality and the return therefrom to the spiritual. When we reflect upon the vastness of the journey portrayed in our charts I-1 and I-2, we begin to see that even if the "soon" were accepted as a proper interpretation, all that John really covers in any meaningful way happens "soon" in the context of the entire journey. As we shall see, either John was unable to see clearly much beyond the seven Evolutionary Epochs, or recognized the inexpressibleness of such a distant vision. Steiner pretty well recognizes this of the Apocalypse, though he does say that the new Jerusalem, or the holy city, is the Jupiter Condition of Consciousness.[24]

We've considered the difference between spiritual perception of the past from the akashic record and the projection of spiritual vision into the future. Even on the past, Steiner has indicated how difficult it is to put in meaningful language any description of the first two Conditions of Consciousness, the Moon Condition being somewhat closer in concept to the Earth Condition.[25] He has also indicated the difficulty of expressing meaningfully the first three Conditions of Life of the Earth Condition of Consciousness, those described as "Elementary Kingdoms," that we had already passed through before the

---

24 *ASJ*, 217, where he speaks of "Jupiter consciousness." It seems likely he is not here limiting the reference to what he has called the "prophetically mirrored" Jupiter, meaning the Animal Kingdom Condition of Life of the Earth Condition of Consciousness, which he called "Jupiter-Earth"; see *RPA* 128, discussed earlier in this chapter. Rev 21 speaks of a "new earth," the "first earth" having passed away, suggesting the Jupiter Condition of Consciousness.

25 *OES*, chap. 4, "Cosmic Evolution and the Human Being," 129–130.

Mineral Kingdom.[26] Beyond the mineral kingdom, human comprehension does not yet exist. "What can man comprehend today? That is the point. He can today understand only the Mineral Kingdom. As soon as he comes to the Plant Kingdom he no longer understands it." The Animal and Human Kingdoms are even more remote from present human understanding.[27]

John's Apocalypse was written two thousand years ago, yet we are only one cultural age beyond his time. There are two more such ages in our Post-Atlantean Evolutionary Epoch. Then there are seven ages in each of the two succeeding Evolutionary Epochs, the Sixth and the Seventh. So, to complete the Evolutionary Epochs of the Mineral-Physical Condition of Form, there are 16 more ages comparable to our own, though not necessarily of similar length in time as we know it. There are three more Conditions of Form in the Mineral Kingdom after the end of the Evolutionary Epochs. Each such Condition of Form comprises 7 x 7, or 49 units spiritually equivalent to each of our cultural ages, thus 3 x 49 = 147. This brings us to 163 (16 + 147) cultural age equivalents to complete our Mineral Kingdom Condition of Life—all before we can begin to move into understanding of the Plant Kingdom. Each of the last three Kingdoms of Life (Plant, Animal, and Human) comprises 7 x 7 x 7, or 343 units comparable to a cultural age in evolutionary significance. The three remaining Kingdoms of life comprise 1,029 units (3 x 343).

Adding the 163 to the 1,029 means we have 1,192 such units to pass through before reaching the Jupiter Condition of Consciousness. Our vision blurs in the early portion of this vast stretch. In that cosmic context, it is easy to see how the word *soon,* could be most appropriate. Attempting to give, even if he were able, a description beyond the limits of comprehension would have been pointless. The important thing was to get humanity to the point of the 144,000 by the end of the Evolutionary Epochs.

Steiner did not spend much time in describing the sufferings involved in the seven "bowls of wrath." He was able to say that John's descriptions beyond the account of the beasts did not have the same

---

26 *ASJ,* 171–172.
27 *ASJ,* 173.

structural nature as what had preceded that point. He summarized chapters 14 through 20 as the three successive falls mentioned earlier. Some things in these chapters seem worthy of comment.

The Forehead (14:1)

The mark that is given to the 144,000 is upon the "forehead" in 14:1.[28] Normally, one should see a deep meaning in the scriptural use of forehead. For instance, the stone from David's sling hit the Philistine giant in the forehead.[29] The Greek and Roman legend of the Cyclops involved an "eye" or sense organ in this area, the condition of the human being into the Lemurian Epoch.[30] The forehead area, near the eyes, is the locus of the pituitary gland, esoterically called the two-petaled lotus flower. Steiner speaks of this in *How to Know Higher Worlds*:

> Out of the image of our lower personality, the true form of the spiritual I becomes visible. From this spiritual I, the threads are then spun out to other, higher spiritual realities.
>
> This is the moment to use the two-petalled lotus flower in the region of the eyes. Once this lotus flower begins to move, we are in a position to establish a connection between our higher I and higher spiritual beings. This is because the currents or streams emanating from this lotus flower move toward higher realities in such a way that we can be fully conscious of their movements. Indeed, just as light makes physical objects visible to our eyes, so these streams make the spiritual beings of the higher worlds visible to us.[31]

Attention is also drawn to *BB's* chart **I-21**, especially Figure 13 on page 582 showing the bodily location of the two-petaled lotus flower. Of particular interest is its relationship to the planet Jupiter. Somewhat related is chart **I-86**.

---

28 The "mark of the beast" is also on the forehead (13:16), and it is on the forehead of "Babylon the great, mother of harlots" (17:5).

29 1 Sam 17:49.

30 Steiner, *Good and Evil Spirits and Their Influence on Humanity*, SB (2014), CW 102, lect. 5 (Berlin, March 16, 1908), 60–61; *Cosmic Memory*, San Francisco, Harper & Row (1959), 122–123 (CW 11).

31 Steiner, *How to Know Higher Worlds*, AP (1994), chap. 8, "Some Effects of Initiation," 145 (CW 10).

A Sea of Glass (15:2)

Revelation 15:2 gives us a reprise of 4:6, both with its "sea of glass." In chapter 7 above, we saw where Steiner describes that first appearance as "the bursting forth, the budding forth of the mineral kingdom in its primary form." That the first appearance was in the presence of the twenty-four elders, the twenty-fourth having just attained that level upon the transition from the Mineral Kingdom's Astral to its Physical Condition of Form. In this 15:2 reprise, we are at the end of the Mineral Kingdom's Physical Condition of Form moving into the first of seven stages of its More Perfect Astral Condition of Form. The reverse of the "bursting forth" in 4:6 is occurring, we are laying aside the Mineral, having passed through all of its seven Evolutionary Epochs, completing the twenty-fifth Condition of Form, which means there are now twenty-five elders, as we will recall momentarily. The parabolic journey of humanity is thus confirmed as we pass, on our upward journey of fusion, the point where we passed on our downward journey of fission in 4:6. We do note that in 4:5 the fire element was present in the seven torches "before the throne," but it was not mingled with the glassy sea— while in the 15:2 reprise the fire element was "mingled" within the glassy sea, a descent of the fire element that seems descriptive of the direction of evolutionary travel.

The Temple Entry Deferred (15:8)

The temple appears meaningfully in John's Gospel, especially as it applied to the "bodies" of Christ, where the mineral-physical body was to be elevated to the higher, perfected bodily levels. The temple appears again as we move through Revelation, specifically in 3:12; 7:15; 11:1, 2, 19; 14:15, 17; 15:5–6, 8; and 16:1, 17. The term appears twice again, both in 21:22, but there the term appears to indicate that there is no temple in the holy city, its temple being the "the Lord God the Almighty and the Lamb."

Of particular interest to us before we consider 15:8, is the opening of the temple in 11:19, and particularly the seeing of "the ark of the covenant" within it. We saw, in the section "The Ark of the Covenant" in chapter 8, that Steiner said that it was the mineral-physical body of HB as it came over with Noah from Atlantis, and that it still housed all of the animal remnants within it, the wild animals of the astral body. But those wild animals in the astral body have been tamed and redeemed to the point that its master soul is worthy to enter into that temple. Its sighting there is still, however, anticipatory, for as we now come to 15:8, the seven trumpets having been blown, and the 144,000 having been recognized, we are now told that still "no one could enter the temple until the seven plagues of the seven angels were ended." We are reminded, at this point, of the second guardian of the threshold, the Leviathan of Job 41, who advises those who are otherwise worthy to enter higher devachan that they cannot enter it so long as any of their brethren remain to be redeemed. Here the Manicheans, and those of similar mission, must exert their best efforts to convert the evil element while there is still opportunity to do so. That period of opportunity will not expire until after the seven bowls of wrath have been poured out, as they are in Revelation 16.

The Great River Euphrates (16:12)

16:12—The sixth angel poured his bowl on the great river Euphrates, and its water was dried up, to prepare the way for the kings from the east.

The great River Euphrates

Based upon its Greek roots, the word *euphrates* literally means "good mind." Because of its importance on this verse, importing the following (footnote included) from the "Fire" essay in *DQWIM* (121) is illuminating:

> The etheric body in human beings has drawn progressively more and more into the confines of the physical body. It is this evolutionary process that over the ages has caused us to lose our conscious presence with the spiritual world (what the Bible sometimes calls God's "hiding his face"). At the same time it has brought brain thinking more and more into being.[32]

Its water was dried up

---

32   See note, page 220.

"The etheric body is in a state of constant fluid motion, and its symbol is Water (cf **I-22**, where the fourfold human being would be equated to the four elements as follows: Physical Body = Earth; Etheric Body = Water; Astral Body = Air; and Ego = Fire)."[33] Notice that all four elements appear in Rev 16 as the bowls of wrath are poured out: the *earth* in 16:2; *water* in 16:3–7; *fire* in 16:8; and *air* in 16:17. "Its water was dried up" means the etheric body is given up, leaving only the astral body and Ego.

To prepare the way for the kings from the east

"From the east" means from a more spiritual realm. This is extensively discussed in the "Eden's Locus" essay in *SLJ*.[34]

"It is finished" (John 19:30)—"It is done" (Rev 16:17)

The seventh angel had just blown its trumpet, "and a loud voice came out of the temple, from the throne, saying 'It is done!'" (Rev 16:17). It is hard not to hear this as a normal sequel to the cry from the cross, "It is finished," words heard by the one who stood beneath the cross, and then reported in his Gospel (John 19:30). One can only wonder if this witnessing and apprehending disciple may have silently uttered it upon his imminent death in Ephesus more than seven decades after the crucifixion. His Gospel and his Apocalypse had only in the latter portion of that time frame taken form. Both divinely echoing expressions had still to be deeply lodged in his spiritual consciousness.

The Tripartite Babylon (16:19)

"The great city was split into three parts..." This division seems consistent with Steiner's telling us that there were three falls—that is, three groups that fell.[35] Noting, with reference to these last chapters, presumably 14 through 18 or 19, he says, "something about the laws of nature becomes inexplicable," and again, "something inexplicable is going on in the laws of nature, that phenomena are occurring that do not fit in with the laws of nature."

"The great harlot who is seated upon many waters" (17:1, 15)

33   *BB*, 225; see also the essay "The Four Elements" in *DQWIM*.
34   See *SLJ*, 197–202.
35   *REVP*, lect. 11; 160.

We saw in our discussion of the great river Euphrates that the term *water* is an esoteric term for the etheric world. It hits us first in Gen 1:2. It is also related to the Moon. While the Ancient Moon was the time when our astral bodies were forming, from the standpoint of the four elements, Fire, Air, Water, Earth, the Moon was related to the fluid element. We need here but to observe that the earth and moon have already rejoined and the joinder with the sun (the lake of fire) is close at hand. The time of the final 666, as Steiner explained it earlier herein, with its "second death" (20:6, 14; 21:8), is approaching.

The seven kings (17:9–10)

[9] This calls for a mind with wisdom: the seven heads are seven mountains on which the woman is seated; [10] they are also seven kings, five of whom have fallen, one is, the other has not yet come, and when he comes he must remain only a little while."

Earlier in this chapter 12, in the segment captioned "The Redemption of the Kingdoms," we saw that the last three Conditions of Life, called "Kingdoms" (Plant, Animal, and Human), "prophetically mirror" the last three Conditions of Consciousness, Jupiter, Venus, and Vulcan.[36] Shortly thereafter, in reference to this passage on the seven kings, we read:

In the age when the sixth seal is broken the "people of twelve" will appear. The salvation of the "great whore of Babylon" will also occur in the sixth age.[37] In this sixth age the earth will have repeated the Saturn, Sun and Moon stages as well as the earth condition itself and Jupiter-Earth. On Venus-Earth the earth will finally have the five rounds behind it. Then the sixth state will have come. Nevertheless, the Vulcan state for the chosen will not be present yet. For this reason we read ["And there are seven kings: five are fallen, and one is, and the other is not yet come"] "...five are fallen..." and the remnant that has maintained itself: "...one is..." and the seventh: "the other has not

---

36 *RPA,* lect. 11 (in Kristiania, now Oslo), 128.

37 If the word *salvation* was a correct transcription and subsequent translation of what Steiner said, of which I am more than a little dubious, I do not comprehend his meaning.

yet come" (Rev. 17:10). We see how we again find the messages of the writer of the Apocalypse in Theosophy.[38]

In this paragraph, Steiner identifies the kings, and thus their "kingdoms," as Conditions of Life, within the context of chart **I-1**. Though we will note internal inconsistencies, what the passage is saying is that we are in the sixth Condition of Life (the Animal Kingdom) of the Earth Condition of Consciousness.

There are two obvious inconsistencies. First, we will not yet have completed the "earth condition." What I think is meant with "earth condition" is the Mineral Kingdom of the Earth Condition of Consciousness, not the Earth Condition itself, for it says we have completed "five rounds" and are in the "sixth," which would be the Animal Kingdom of Life.

The second inconsistency, or inaccuracy, is in the introductory reference to "when the sixth seal is broken." Unless "broken" has a different, though not explained, meaning from "opened," the statement cannot be accurate, for at this point humanity is far beyond the seven ages of the Sixth Evolutionary Epoch when the "seals" were opened. Since the cycle (book) that contains this paragraph is entitled *Reading the Pictures of the Apocalypse*, the "pictures" being Steiner's seven paintings of the respective seals, perhaps the term *sixth seal* was used simply to indicate it had the character of sixth ages. Generally there is a common thread of character running through each similar age in a sevenfold system of progression.

John himself, however, unless a scribal error intervened, seems to have failed to put things in proper sequential order in regard to the matter of the "elders." We have seen the meaning of the twenty-four elders. But by the sixth Condition of Life (the Animal Kingdom), as the passage above notes, "the earth will finally have the five rounds behind it." Yet later in the book, specifically in 19:4, it still speaks of "twenty-four elders"; with five "rounds" or "Conditions of Life" behind by then, the number of elders would be twenty-five.

But what is clear is that by 17:10, we are in the penultimate Condition of Life of the Earth Condition of Consciousness, and that

---

38 *RPA*, lect. 12; 134 [though Steiner spoke only from his own spiritual insight, he was still speaking as head of the German section of Theosophy, not yet having gone his separate way with what he then called "Anthroposophy"].

the last Condition of Life, the Human, "must remain only a little while," being thus reminiscent of what we have seen about the last stage of any septenary within the evolutionary journey portrayed by chart **I-1**.

The thousand year reign with Christ (20:1–10)

[1] Then I saw an angel coming down from heaven, holding in his hand the key of the bottomless pit and a great chain. [2] And he seized the dragon, that ancient serpent, who is the Devil and Satan, and bound him for a thousand years, [3] and threw him into the pit, and shut it and sealed it over him, that he should deceive the nations no more, till the thousand years were ended. After that he must be loosed for a while.

[4] Then I saw thrones, and seated on them were those to whom judgment was committed. Also I saw the souls of those who had been beheaded for their testimony to Jesus and for the word of God, and who had not worshiped the beast or its image and had not received its mark on their foreheads or their hands. They came to life, and reigned with Christ a thousand years. [5] The rest of the dead did not come to life until the thousand years were ended. This is the first resurrection. [6] Blessed and holy is he who shares in the first resurrection! Over such the second death has no power, but they shall be priests of God and of Christ, and they shall reign with him a thousand years.

[7] And when the thousand years are ended, Satan will be loosed from his prison [8] and will come out to deceive the nations which are at the four corners of the earth, that is, Gog and Magog, to gather them for battle; their number is like the sand of the sea. [9] And they marched up over the broad earth and surrounded the camp of the saints and the beloved city; but fire came down from heaven and consumed them, [10] and the devil who had deceived them was thrown into the lake of fire and sulphur where the beast and the false prophet were, and they will be tormented day and night for ever and ever.

To begin this book, we compared Churchill's characterization of Russia—"a riddle, wrapped in a mystery, inside an enigma"—to the book of Revelation. Perhaps the adage, "Fools rush in where angels fear to trod" and the maxim, "It is better to remain silent and be thought a fool than to speak (or write) and remove all doubt," should be pondered by any would-be interpreter.

Especially would these sayings seem applicable to this thousand year reign passage. I find little more than acknowledgment of the existence of these verses and their "thousand year" period in Steiner's works. The absence of meaningful elaboration by him on the subject could suggest that it was simply too far into our distant journey to be worthy of significant or separate investigation or presentation—coupled with the realization that we have three more "kingdoms," Conditions of Life, to pass through after completing the Mineral Kingdom. On this he said, "What can man comprehend today?...He can today understand only the mineral kingdom."[39]

Steiner's most direct reference to the "thousand years" is probably the following, in his lecture in Berlin of August 14, 1917:

> Thus it was inevitable that from early on, in the development of Christianity, faith was emphasized rather than knowledge. Christians were not to expect knowledge concerning the Mystery of Golgotha but experience it inwardly through faith.... Our intellect is the arena where the impulse of Christ fights the impulse of Ahriman. Man's evolution, his purely external evolution on earth, will take its course and Ahriman will not be as fettered as he is now. The "Thousand Years" will elapse and man will need a different force, he must have something over and above faith with which to establish the Christ impulse in his earthly consciousness.[40]

Yet, it is not entirely clear that Steiner was here referring to that stage in human evolution, at 666, when the "second death" is imminent, rather than to a more contemporary setting. The most extensive discussion on the thousand years by any anthroposophist is probably that of Emil Bock in his *The Apocalypse*, where he devotes four pages of text to it.[41] At one point he says, "In the spiritual sphere the 'Millennium' is to be found at any time, even when the power of Satan is

---

39 *ASJ*, lect. 10; 173.

40 Steiner, *The Karma of Materialism* (1985), lect. 3; 49 (CW 176).

41 Emil Bock, *The Apocalypse*, Edinburgh, Floris Books (1957), chap. 11; 174–177.

released on Earth. 'The Reign of a Thousand Years is always among us,' says Novalis" (177).

Steiner indirectly referenced the thousand years in his *Karmic Relationships* series, where he said of Amos Comenius, "It is often said, superficially, that Comenius believed in the Kingdom of a Thousand Years. That is a trivial way of putting it. The truth is that Comenius believed in definite epochs in the evolution of humanity; he believed that historical evolution is organised from the spiritual world."[42]

Finally, three times Steiner refers to "Gog and Magog" in his lecture of September 15, 1924 in Dornach to the priests of the Christian Community. In the first reference, he defines the two: "A time will come when the satanic power will have made great efforts to win over humanity's powers of intelligence and when this satanic power will have grown so great that it will approach all the groups that have formed; so the situation will really arise in which Satan's power will work into all the four corners of the world. These groups—smaller ones: Gog, and larger ones: Magog—will be exposed to temptation and seduction by the satanic power."[43]

Further gloss on the meaning of Gog and Magog can be inferred by considering Ezekiel 38 and 39.[44] As with the "four living creatures" of Rev 4:6–8 and thereafter throughout, being the same referred to in Ezekiel 1:5, 10, the prophet's imagery is used by John with his Gog and Magog.

Before moving to a more substantive approach to this thousand year passage, attention is called to Andrew Welburn's book, *The Book With Fourteen Seals* (*BFS*), where it talks about the sixth century BCE reincarnation of the ancient Zarathustra as Zaratas (Zarathas or Zoroaster) in Babylonia. There he became the teacher of the captive Jews, almost certainly including such prophets as Ezekiel. Welburn's book is a commentary on the *Apocalypse of Adam* (*ApocAd*), a Sethian writing that was part of the Nag Hammadi discoveries in the 1940s.

---

42 Steiner, *Karmic Relationships*, vol. 6, 2nd ed., RSP (lect. 2, Berne, April 16, 1924), 41 (CW 240); see also Comenius discussion in lect. 5, Stuttgart, April 9, 1924, 95–96 (CW 240).

43 *REVP*, lect. 18; 253–254.

44 Gog is mentioned in Ezek 38:2–3, 14, 16, 18, 21 and 39:1, 11, and Magog is mentioned in 38:2 and 39:6.

Fourteen "Kingdoms" were described in *ApocAd*, with the first being of the one we call the ancient Zarathustra and the eighth being this Zaratas.[45]

Included in his discussion of this Zaratas, Welburn says:

> Linear time unrolls, taught Zaratas, through twelve aeons, corresponding to the twelve signs of the zodiac, each one indicating a phase in the cosmic struggle. That struggle comes temporarily to a deadlock, or uneasy truce. But in the future the balance will shift decisively in favour of the Light. Mithra will come to banish the Darkness, and rule an age of millennial harmony before the end of the world as we know it, and the transition to the 'transfigured earth' (*frashkart*).[46]

It is striking that in this earlier incarnation of the Solomon Jesus child, this Zaratas spoke of such a thousand year period shortly before the end of the Earth Condition of Consciousness. It is Matthew's Gospel (4:16) that cites the "darkness," as in the "deep darkness" first prophetically described by First Isaiah (Isa 9:1–2). It was a phrase found in the writings of most of the prophets after him, including Ezekiel (32:8; 34:12). The Light and Darkness seen by the ancient Zarathustra, is with us through the Hebrew prophets, Matthew's Gospel, and into our present day, where it will remain till the final overthrow of Satan as seen by John and given in his twentieth chapter.[47]

It is worth noting that in his "Introduction, Commentary, and Reflections" on Revelation in *The New Interpreter's Bible*, Christopher

---

45   See *BB*, "Pillars on the Journey," 543, #3.

46   Andrew Welburn, *The Book With Fourteen Seals*, RSP (1991), chap. 7; 106. Welburn's book caught the interest of the four-centuries-old and conservative publishing house named "Brill," in Leiden, Netherlands, which offered to publish Welburn on the *ApocAD* provided he would don the straight jacket of the academy and abide by the rules of academic writing. The result was Welburn's *From a Virgin Womb/The Apocalypse of Adam and the Virgin Birth*, Leiden, Brill (2008). It rather thoroughly sterilized the coverage of the *ApocAd's* fourteen kingdoms, including the Eighth about Zarathas. Nevertheless, it gives an extensive discussion from the academic perspective, of many areas about Zarathustra and Zoroastrianism, and insights on Matthew's infant narrative that are helpful also to those with the broader view.

47   "Light" and "Darkness" are deep concepts, the subject of the essays under their respective names in *DQWIM*.

C. Rowland includes an "Excursus: The Millennium" in his coverage of Rev 20:1–15.[48]

It is not, in my view, accurate to say that Steiner gives us so little, as set out briefly above, on the millennium in Rev 20. He has told us that within the framework of the Earth Condition of Consciousness, the last chance for human beings to accept the Christ impulse and avoid the "second death" is in the Venus-Earth Condition of Life. On this, we seem to have a bit of a problem. If we follow the definition of the 666 as given in his *ASJ*, lecture 11, quoted at length in our chapter 11 above, the number 666 refers to a point late in the last Condition of Life (the Human Kingdom). The numbers in this system of seven only refer to stages that are past. Thus, in such eleventh lecture, on page 195 of *ASJ*, he says that our present number is 344. In regard to this, he states (194), "We are at the moment only considering conditions of form." The first digit, the three, refers to the three Conditions of Form preceding our present Physical Condition of Form; the second digit indicates that we have passed through the fourth Evolutionary Epoch, Atlantis and are in the Post-Atlantean Epoch; the third digit indicates that we have passed through the fourth Cultural Age, the Greco-Latin. On the next page of *ASJ* (195), he moves up to Conditions of Life, saying: "Just as we now have 344 as the number of evolution, in the future when 6 conditions of life, 6 fundamental races [Conditions of Form], and 6 sub-races [Evolutionary Epochs] have been gone through, the number 666 ... will apply."

What this means is that the 666 means that the first six Conditions of Form of the Seventh Condition of Life (the Human Kingdom), and the first six Epochs of the Seventh Condition of Life are past. We are only one Evolutionary Epoch from the end of the Earth Condition of Consciousness and moving into the Jupiter Condition. In other words, Venus-Earth lies six Conditions of Form behind us as we move into the last Condition of Form of the last Condition of Life of our Earth Condition of Consciousness.

How, then, can it be said that no salvation is possible beyond Venus-Earth? There are six Conditions of Life in Vulcan-Earth before the number 666 is accomplished, according to the method given in detail in the *ASJ* lecture. Yet, in *RPA*, lecture 11 in Kristiania, he says:

---

48 Christopher C. Rowland, *The Book of Revelation*, NIB, vol. 12 (1998), 708–713.

"Then on the Vulcan-Earth, nothing more can be saved. On the Venus-Earth the last moment for salvation has come in the last sub-epoch."

If forced to choose between these two, the later period of the 666 appeals more to me in relation to what John's vision says, as will momentarily be explained. In truth, there may not be a lot of difference between the two. Revelation 17:10, about the seven kings, indicates that at that point, which seems near the end, we are still in the sixth Condition of Life, the Animal, with only the Human Kingdom, the seventh, remaining. Of the seventh king, 17:10 says, "when he comes he must remain only a little while." It has been characteristic of seventh stages that nothing much of the good comes in them. Perhaps things are too far gone by seventh stages.[49] But the passing from one Epoch to another is a period when things in Earth take a rest before progressing to the next stage. This evolutionary period of rest between the last two Conditions of Life gives us an opportunity to give meaning to the thousand years when the Satan ("the dragon, that ancient Serpent, who is the Devil and Satan") was bound by a great chain and thrown in the pit, not to deceive the nations till the thousand years were ended.

Those who reigned with Christ for the "thousand years" (probably the rest period between the Conditions of Life) seem to be the 144,000, those who had been "slain for the word of God" (6:9–11), called "beheaded" in 20:4. They "came to life . . . in the first resurrection," and over them the "second death has no power."

The attack of Satan when loosed at the end of the thousand years is overwhelming. Steiner describes the furiousness of Satan's attack in that Vulcan-Earth, seventh and last, Condition of Life. We should not have been surprised to hear this in this last earthly period, for Steiner gave a preview of it in describing the far earlier stage at the sixth Evolutionary Epoch, that of the seals:

This sixth epoch will be radically different from ours. Great, tumultuous catastrophes will precede it, for the sixth epoch will be just as spiritual as ours is materialistic, but such a transformation can

---

49   Speaking of the seventh Cultural Age of our own Post-Atlantean Epoch, the Cultural Age following Philadelphia, and the age that will culminate with the War of All against All, Steiner said, "The so-called seventh age will be of very little importance," *RPA*, lect. 8; 138.

only occur through great, physical upheavals. Everything that will be formed in the course of the sixth epoch will call into existence the possibility of a seventh epoch which itself will form the end of these Post-Atlantean cultures and will know completely different conditions of life from our own. This seventh epoch will end with a revolution of the elements, similar to the one that brought an end to the Atlantean continent. The condition of the earth that will then appear will have a spirituality prepared through the last two Post-Atlantean epochs.[50]

But of the last Condition of Life, Steiner said:

> We are here confronted with an adversary of Christ, one who wants not merely to corrupt single individuals, nor one who wants to corrupt a group of individuals, a human community, as do the Beast and the False Prophet. With Satan and his cohorts we are faced with endeavours to attack the earth in its context within the planetary system as a whole.[51]

And in his lecture 18 to the priests on September 22, 1924, he spoke of Satan's work in the passages about Gog and Magog mentioned earlier.

That things break up quickly in Vulcan-Earth is suggested by the fact that nothing further is said after the Satanic attacks in 20:7–8 except that the evil forces "surrounded the camp of the saints and the beloved city," but as though the saints were protected by the powerful forces of good, the Satanic forces were thrown into the lake of fire (20:9–10).

We are then told that the book of life was opened and that all were judged by what they had done. Anyone whose name was not found in the book of life was thrown into the lake of fire in the "second death" (20:11–15).

What, then, happens to those who experienced the "second death"? Of these, upon the Jupiter Condition of Consciousness, Steiner tells us:

---

50 From a lecture in Paris on June 14, 1906, entitled "Cosmogony," added as an appendix at the end of *RPA*, at 141.

51 *REVP*, lect. 11; 159–160.

The new Jupiter will be accompanied by a satellite, composed of those who are excluded from the life in the spiritual, who have experienced the second death and are, therefore, unable to attain the Jupiter consciousness. Thus we have those men who have pressed forward to the Jupiter consciousness, who have attained manas; and those beings who have thrust away the forces which would have given them this consciousness. They are those who only upon Jupiter have attained to the ego-consciousness of the Earth, who exist there, so to speak, as man now exists on the earth with his four members. But such a man can develop himself only on the Earth, the Earth alone has the environment, the ground, the air, the clouds, the plants, the minerals which are necessary to man if he wishes to gain what may be gained within the four members. Jupiter will be quite differently formed, it will be a "new earth"; soil, air, water, and every being will be different. It will be impossible for beings who have only gained the Earth consciousness to live a normal life; they will be backward beings.

But now comes something that will once again comfort us. Even on this Jupiter there is still a last possibility, through the strong powers which the more advanced will have, to move those fallen beings to turn back and even to convert a number. Only with the Venus incarnation will come the last decision, the unalterable decision.[52]

But those who are "converted," accept the Christ impulse, only on Jupiter or Venus will be at progressively lower grades of humanity than those who attained to the Jupiter consciousness at the end of Earth evolution. For this, see again the two-paragraph insert, in the section above entitled "The Redemption of the Kingdoms," taken from *An Outline of Esoteric Science (OES)*. It speaks of two human kingdoms on Jupiter and three on Venus, and presumably, with the perfection at last of the Animal Kingdom by the end of Venus there would be four "human kingdoms of different degrees of perfection" on Vulcan.

Those who fail to attain redemption by the end of the Venus Condition will constitute "a distinct cosmic body...an 'unredeemable moon,' so to speak." It will be "so different in character from

---

52   *ASJ*, lect. 12; 217–218.

anything we can experience on Earth that there are no words that can possibly express it."[53]

Chapter Epilogue

All of Steiner's lectures on the Apocalypse occurred within the years 1904 through 1909, except his eighteen lectures to the priests in Dornach from September 5 through 22, 1924. He closed his sixteenth lecture to the priests, "I hope we shall be able to finish these considerations tomorrow or the day after." He gave his last two to the priests on those two days. He gave two lectures on the 23rd, and for all practical purposes his last full address on the 24th. He rose from his sick bed to give what amounted to a short farewell address, called "The Last Address," on September 28. He died on March 30, 1925, at sixty-four years of age.

Preliminarily, it is clear that for Steiner comets had cosmological significance. In his lecture sixteen to the priests, on September 20, 1924, he said:

> In 1933, dear friends, there would be a possibility for the earth and everything living on it to perish if there did not exist also that other wise arrangement that cannot be calculated. Once comets have taken on other forms calculations can no longer be accurate. What needs to be said in the sense meant by the apocalyptist is: Before the Etheric Christ can be comprehended by human beings in the right way, humanity must first cope with encountering the Beast who will rise up in 1933. This is what the apocalyptic language tells us. Here a view of the spirit unites with a view of nature. What is there in the cosmos becomes clear to us in its fundamental spiritual character.

Hitler's Third Reich came into full power in Germany in 1933, the same year that Christ's second coming commenced, in the etheric realm for all who had developed the spiritual capacity to perceive in that realm.[54] Polar opposites entered human evolution in 1933. The evil pole became obvious to all. For most, its opposite has yet to become

---

53   *OES*, 394.
54   See the essay "Second Coming" in *BB*.

observable, though most of us who see in Steiner an incomparable Seer accept its reality vicariously, until it is our own.

CHAPTER 12 ENDNOTE

Note from Footnote 32

Abraham is properly referred to in knowledgeable circles as the father of arithmetic. (The earlier works of pharaonic Egypt reveal astounding apprehension of numbers, but, as we see later herein, they were perceived not as numbers per se but rather as divine principles, and not through brain thinking so much as through revelation.) He fathered both Arab and Jew through his two sons, Ishmael and Isaac, through each of whom the number twelve appeared; Ishmael fathered twelve sons as did Isaac's son, Jacob. The basis for arithmetic and for the twelvefold nature of biblical revelation is established in Gen 15:5:

> And he brought him outside and said, "Look toward heaven, and number the stars, if you are able to number them." Then he said to him, "So shall your descendants be."

The "stars" here are what humans have looked overhead to see from ancient times, the twelve animals composing what we call the zodiac. Here God is telling Abraham both that his descendants will be influenced by these twelve heavenly forces from the beginning to the end of their journey and that he must learn to deal with the earthly phenomena of number. Immediately after this anointing of Abraham, God established his first covenant with him through the agency of fire (Gen 15:17-18), and then God tells him that everything between the river of Egypt (see "Egypt" in *The Burning Bush*, meaning the backward looking clairvoyance that had to be overcome) and "the great river, the river Euphrates," would be his—the entire gamut of insight.

In the western myth of Prometheus, the name "Prometheus" means "forethinker," while his brother, Epimetheus, means "backward looking," the same as Egypt, into the clairvoyance of even more ancient times when we dwelt consciously with spiritual beings. That Abraham was to bring humanity into the domain of looking forward is ordained here by the name of the river Euphrates, which means "good mind" (see the etymology of the cognate term "euphrasy" from the Greek *eu* [well] and *phren* [mind]). Notably, this river is the final one of the four rivers in Gen 2:10–14, and it is the river crossed by Jacob, the immediate father of the twelve tribes, at a critical juncture of his life (Gen 31:21). The ancestry of the fathers of this people had been "east" (a term related to the ancient clairvoyance) of that river (Josh 24:2). But this Prometheus was the one who stole fire from heaven and brought it down to Earth, and the myth tells what then had to happen to Prometheus before he could return (see *BB*, 241). It is a story of the evolution, both past and future, of humanity that Christendom still fails to comprehend. It is but another instance of things once known, then forgot, that must still be recovered in the transformation humanity is slowly undergoing.

13

Our Solar Companions

Today, spacecraft and high powered telescope permit us to penetrate deeply into outer space, far beyond the cocoon of our own galaxy. Billions of stars exist in more distant galaxies within the reach of our instruments. Curiosity compels our search for distant stars encircled by planets that might support life such as our own. We speculate that surely within the immense expanse of the universe there have to be numerous planets with live personalities such as ourselves.

Sadly, if successful in our search we would only find those who, like ourselves, walk in the valley of the shadow of death—evolving valleys where personalities live in bodies composed of matter that, like ours, have to die. Our instrumentation cannot seek the spiritual beings that exist on all heavenly bodies or in their respective spheres, beings which in many if not most instances will have risen higher than ourselves.

More noble, it seems, would be the lofty search for power to perceive in the supersensible realm, that we might behold the spiritual beings on all planets and within the domain of their respective succoring stars, including our own.

It is in the nature of that search that we now approach, in our study, the next higher Condition of Consciousness, that of Jupiter. We are at the threshold of the last two chapters of Revelation, chapters 21 and 22. Steiner has identified the "new heaven and new earth" and "the holy city, new Jerusalem" of Revelation 21 as the Jupiter Condition of Consciousness. The "City" is also present in Revelation 22, but we may ponder whether that final chapter also implies the succeeding Conditions of Consciousness.

We are told that in that city our sun and moon shall no longer exist, suggesting that all of the material bodies of our solar system will have come to an end. Before we move the focus of our contemplation upon that new city, it is appropriate to give thought to our solar companions, not only to our sun and moon but also to Saturn, Jupiter, Mars, Venus, and Mercury and their spiritual inhabitants.

In Anthroposophy, and in all my writings, the human journey has been portrayed as a parabola, first descending, bottoming (in the valley of the shadow of death), and then ascending. We are still in the bottoming process. The ascending portion will retrace, constructively, what occurred in the corresponding portion of the descent. Thus, Jupiter will retrace the Ancient Moon, Venus the Ancient Sun, and Vulcan the Ancient Saturn Conditions of Consciousness.

Before we can rightly move into contemplation of the Jupiter Condition of Consciousness that appears in the last chapters of John's Apocalypse, it behooves us to contemplate the solar setting we are leaving and the destiny of the beings created and developing on the other planets within that setting. In the journey toward Jupiter, how are we to regard our fellow solar beings, and how are we all dependent upon each other? As earthly beings we have seen that while the perfection of the Ego is essential for the Earth Condition of Consciousness to be the "planet" of Love, and hence fulfill its mission, work on the astral body is critical to that development. Earthly beings will not be able to properly enter the Jupiter Condition without perfecting their astral bodies to the point of being able to dwell in the astral realm without bodies of matter or ether, save as the latter has been sufficiently ennobled in the process of perfecting the astral body. It is primarily in the domain of the seven stars, our solar system, that the perfecting of the astral body must occur, as we shall see below.

For what this present chapter offers, the reader should start by reviewing the first parts of *BB's* chart **I-27** (*BB*, 593 through the top three paragraphs of 595). We see there not only the separating out of our various planets from the primeval solar nebula. We see also that there are evolving beings on all five of our neighboring planets and our moon. Those beings on Saturn, Jupiter and Moon stand at lower levels of evolution than we human beings associated with the

Earth, while the beings on Mars, Venus, and Mercury are at higher levels than we earthly humans. The term "beings" is used rather than "spiritual beings" since the spiritual hierarchies are not of our present concern, even though they, particularly their lower ranks, are involved in our solar system's planetary evolution.

Excerpt from An Outline of Esoteric Science (OES)

With that chart's review, it is now instructive to see the extract below from the first several pages of chapter 6 of Steiner's *OES*, 376–380:

This book (*OES*) has dealt with the Saturn, Sun, Moon, and Earth phases of evolution. Without observing the facts of previous evolutionary phases, we cannot understand the Earth phase of evolution in the sense of spiritual science, because in a certain respect the realities of the Moon, Sun, and Saturn phases are present in what confronts us now in the earthly world. The beings and things that were involved in the Moon phase continued to evolve, and everything that belongs to our present Earth came from them.

However, not everything that came from the Moon and has now become the Earth is perceptible to consciousness in the physical world of the senses. Part of what passed from the Moon to the Earth in the course of evolution only becomes evident at a certain level of supersensible consciousness. Having reached this level of cognition, we can perceive that our earthly world is connected to a supersensible world which contains the part of Moon existence that did not condense enough to be physically perceived by our senses. The supersensible world contains this aspect of the Moon as it is at present, not as it was during the ancient Moon phase of evolution. However, it is possible for supersensible consciousness to get a picture of conditions at that time.

When this supersensible consciousness concentrates on the perception that is possible at present, it becomes evident that this perception is gradually separating into two images all by itself. One image represents the form the Earth had during its Moon phase of evolution. But as the other image presents itself, we can recognize that it contains a form that is still in a seminal stage; only in the future will it become a reality in the way that the Earth is a reality now. On further observation, it becomes apparent that in a certain sense the results of what happens on Earth are constantly flowing into this future form, which therefore represents what our Earth is meant to become. The effects of earthly existence will unite with what happens in this other world, giving rise to the new cosmic being into which the Earth will eventually be transformed, just as the Moon was transformed into the Earth. We can call this future form the Jupiter stage.

If this Jupiter stage is observed by means of supersensible perception, it becomes evident that in the future certain processes will have to take place because certain beings and things are present in the supersensible part of the earthly world that came from the Moon. These beings and things will assume certain forms after various events have taken place within the physical, sense-perceptible Earth realm. This means that the Jupiter stage will contain something that has already been predetermined by the Moon phase of evolution, and it will also contain something new that is entering evolution as a whole only because of processes taking place on the Earth. This is why it is possible for supersensible consciousness to experience something of what will happen during the Jupiter stage.

The beings and facts that can be perceived within this field of consciousness do not have the character of sensory images; they do not even appear as delicate airy structures that might give rise to effects reminiscent of sense impressions. The impressions we receive from them are purely spiritual impressions of sound, light, and warmth that are not expressed through material embodiments of any sort. They can only be grasped by means of supersensible consciousness. It is possible to say that such beings have "bodies," but these bodies become apparent within the soul element, their present essential nature, like a sum of condensed memories that these beings carry in their soul nature. Within such beings, we can distinguish between what they are *now* experiencing and what they have already experienced and now remember. The latter is contained in them like a bodily element, which is experienced in the same way that earthly human beings experience their bodies.

At a higher level of supersensible cognition than that just described as necessary for perceiving the Moon and Jupiter, it is possible to perceive supersensible things and beings that are further evolved forms of what was already present during the Sun stage. At present, these figures have achieved such high levels of existence that they are not perceptible at all to consciousness that has only reached the level of being able to perceive Moon forms. This world's image also splits into two when we contemplate it inwardly. One image leads to knowledge of the past Sun stage, while the other presents a future form of the Earth. The Earth will assume this form when the effects of the Earth and Jupiter processes have flowed into the forms of this world. Spiritual science calls this the Venus stage. Similarly, a future stage of evolution that can be called the Vulcan stage, which has the same relationship to the Saturn stage as Venus to the Sun and Jupiter to the Moon, becomes evident to a still more highly developed supersensible consciousness. Therefore, in considering the past, present, and future of the Earth, we can speak of the Saturn, Sun, Moon, Earth, Jupiter, Venus, and Vulcan phases of evolution.

Several chapters in this book [OES] have described how the human world and human beings themselves move through the stages that have been given the names Saturn, Sun, Moon, Earth, Jupiter, Venus, and Vulcan. The relationship of human evolution to certain celestial bodies, which coexist with the Earth and have been given the names Saturn, Jupiter, Mars, and so on, was also indicated. Of course, these heavenly bodies are also undergoing evolutions of their own. At the present time, they have reached the stage where their physical aspects present themselves to our perception as the entities that physical astronomy knows as Saturn, Jupiter, Mars, and so on. In the sense of spiritual science, present-day Saturn is a reincarnation of ancient Saturn, so to speak, and came about because of the presence of certain beings prior to the Sun's separation from the Earth. These particular beings were unable to participate in this separation, because they had incorporated so many characteristics suited to Saturn existence that they were out of place on a cosmic body that concentrated primarily on developing Sun characteristics.

Present-day Jupiter, however, came about because of the presence of beings with characteristics that will only be able to develop during the future Jupiter stage of general evolution. A dwelling place was made where they could foreshadow this future evolution. Mars is a celestial body inhabited by beings who went through the Moon phase of evolution in a such [sic] way that they no longer had anything to gain from staying on

Earth. Mars is a reincarnation of old Moon on a higher level. Present-day Mercury is the dwelling of beings who are ahead of the Earth's evolution, because they have developed certain earthly characteristics in a higher form than is possible on Earth. In a similar way, present-day Venus prophetically anticipates the Venus stage of the future.

Perfecting the Astral
with Our Solar Companions

For the further consideration of what this chapter offers, the reader should review *BB's* chart **I-33**, particularly the parts captioned "Course of the Ego between Death and Rebirth" and "Pathway of the Ego's Course Through the Heavens" (*BB* 604–605).

Excerpts from Life Between Death and Rebirth (LBDR)[1]

LBDR is a book comprising sixteen lectures delivered in eleven different cities in the years 1912–1913.[2] All sixteen lectures being on essentially the same subject, there is considerable repetition in substance, but delivered in Steiner's usual freestyle they offer refreshingly modified expression. What follows is a selected sample.

Lecture 3, Hanover, November 18, 1912, LBDR 38–39

> This faculty to correct a member of our being, to rectify its errors in such a way as to further its development, we possess in respect of the ego.
>
> Man's consciousness does not, however, extend directly to his astral and etheric nature, and it extends far less to his physical nature. Although perpetual destruction of these members is taking place through the whole course of life, we do not know how to rectify it. Man has the power to repair the harm done to the ego, to adjust a moral defect or a defect of memory, but he has no power over what is continually being destroyed in his astral, etheric and physical bodies. These three bodies are being impaired all the time, and as we live on constant attacks are being made upon them. We work at the development of the ego, for if we did not do so during

---

1   Steiner, *Life Between Death and Rebirth*, SB (1968) (CW 140).

2   All lectures cited will appear in CW 140.

the whole of life between birth and death, no progress would be made. We cannot work as consciously at the development of our astral, etheric or physical body as we work at the development of our ego. Yet what is all the time being destroyed in those three bodies must be made good. In the time between death and a new birth we must again acquire in the right form—as astral body, etheric body and physical body—what we have destroyed. It must be possible during this time for what was previously destroyed to be repaired. This can only happen if something beyond our own power works upon us. It is quite obvious that if we do not possess magical powers it will not be possible for us to procure an astral body when we are dead. The astral body must be created for us out of the Great World, the Macrocosm.

We can now understand the question, "Where is the destruction we have caused in our astral body repaired?" We need a proper body when we are born again into a new bodily existence. Where are the forces that repair the astral body to be found in the universe? We might look for these forces on the earth with every kind of clairvoyance, yet we would never find them there. If it depended entirely on the earth, a man's astral body could never be repaired. The materialistic belief that all the conditions needed for human existence are to be found on the earth is utterly mistaken. Man's home is not only on the earth. True observation of the life between death and a new birth reveals that the forces man needs in order to repair the astral body lie in Mercury, Venus, Mars, Jupiter, Saturn, that is, in the stars belonging to the planetary system. The forces emanating from these heavenly bodies must all work at the repair of our astral body, and if we do not get the forces from there, we cannot have an astral body. What does that mean? It means that after death, and it is also the case in the process of initiation, we must go out of the physical body together with the forces of our astral body. This astral body expands into the universe. Whereas we are otherwise contracted into a small point in the universe, after death our whole being expands into it. Our life between death and new birth is nothing but a process of drawing from the stars the forces we need in order that the member we have destroyed during life can be restored. So it is from the stars that we actually receive the forces which repair our astral body.

In most if not all lectures, some preparatory remarks, such as above, are followed by a description of the experience of various human soul inclinations as they expand outward beyond the Moon sphere and through each of the successive planetary spheres. The period within the Moon sphere is one of purification, called kamaloca. It lasts approximately one third as long as the life just ended, being the time there spent in sleep, when the Ego and astral body were outside of the physical body. Once through kamaloca, the soul enters what is called the lower spiritual world, or lower devachan, as it passes through the successive planetary (including Sun) spheres. Once beyond the solar system, the journeying spirit enters the higher spiritual world, or higher devachan, though only advanced spirits are able to retain consciousness during this period. Once the zenith of the soul's journey, called its "midnight hour," is reached, the spirit begins its descent toward incarnation. On the descent it works with the hierarchies in the formation of a personality (soul), astral body, and etheric body for the next incarnation. What it has perfected of these components from prior lives it gathers for use in the incarnation ahead.

The astral body is thus restored in the astral realm in its journey through the Earth Condition of Consciousness in preparation for dwelling in the astral realm of Jupiter.

Lecture 11, Frankfurt, March 2, 1913, LBDR 209–210

You will gather from the foregoing that from a higher aspect life on earth really constitutes a special case. We live embodied within a special organism on earth between life and death. Apart from an earthly incarnation one can speak of an "embodiment" between death and rebirth, or rather of an "ensouling." What I have elaborated in connection with the spiritual world also applies to the earth. Consider that a human being living between death and rebirth may pass through the Mars sphere without entering it in the slightest connection with the beings who inhabit Mars. He does not see them, and they are not aware of him. This is true of the earth also. Beings belonging to other planets, just as man belongs to the earth, are continually passing through the earth sphere. The inhabitants of Mars spend the normal course of their life on Mars, and during their experience, which corresponds on Mars to the period between death and a new life but yet is different, they pass through the planetary spheres. So that in fact inhabitants of other planets are continually passing through our earth sphere. Human beings are unable to establish any contact with them because they live under quite different conditions and because they will in the main not have made the least connection with these beings on Mars.

What would be the conditions necessary in order to meet the beings from other planets as they pass through the earth sphere? One would have had to develop points of contact with them in their own planetary realms, but this is only possible if on earth one has already reached the stage of being able to contact beings other than those of the earth as a result of the development of supersensible powers.

Lecture 13, Munich, March 12, 1913, LBDR 249–250

This subject is full of complications. On the earth we live among the beings of the three kingdoms of nature, and among men. By various means we come into contact with the souls who in their life after death still retain some connection with the earth but we also encounter beings who are utterly foreign to the earth. The more an initiate is able to widen his vision, the more souls are found who are strangers on the earth, and the more it is realized that wanderers are passing through the earth sphere. They are beings who are not connected with earthly life in the normal way. This is no different for us as men of earth than it is for the moon dwellers through whose sphere of life we also pass between death and a new birth. When we are passing through the Mars sphere, for example, we are ghosts, spectres [sic], for the Mars dwellers. We pass through their sphere as strangers, as alien beings. But the Mars beings, too, at a certain stage of their existence, are condemned to pass through our earth sphere and one who possesses certain initiate faculties encounters them when conditions are favorable.

Beings of our planetary system are continually streaming past each other. While we are living on earth, often imagining that we are surrounded only by the beings of the different kingdoms of nature, there are itinerants from all the other planets in our environment. During a certain period between death and a new birth we, too, are itinerants among the other planetary "men," if one might speak in this way. We have to develop in our lives on earth the essentials of our particular mission in the present epoch of cosmic existence. Other beings are alloted [*sic*] to the other planetary worlds, and between death and rebirth we must contact these worlds, too. Therefore, when reference is made to one region or another of life in devachan, it is actually the case, although it is not expressly stated, that the happenings are taking place in some sphere of our planetary system. This should be borne in mind. Thus at a certain time in life between death and a new birth we pass [for instance] through the Mars sphere.

Excerpt from Good and Evil Spirits and their Influence on Humanity (CW 102)[3]

Lecture 3, Berlin, February 15, 1908, 37

So you have seen these different cosmic bodies develop from the nebula for inner reasons, brought about by spirits. You will have been able to see that if one stays wholly with the physical, it does go the way we are told in modern science; but we need to gain real insight into the spiritual background, why it has gone that way. Those spirits created their own dwelling places, where they were able to live, within the original nebula. They may be said to have existed side by side in harmony for as long as everything had not yet split off, and they have not lost the connection but are certainly acting on and through one another.

The implication, it would seem, from this brief snippet, as well as from the excerpts above it, is that we have here another example of fission, ongoing relationship, and eventual fusion. Will it be by the Jupiter Condition, in whole or in part, or will it be wholly or partially in a later Condition? To the extent that the nebula is in the form of the creative spiral, we might well imagine that the joinder will be by the correlative spiral in our own parabolic journey of descent and reascent, which the ancients saw as the intersecting spirals of Cancer, an image of the Crab, in the heavens. The fractal nature of the spiral may well suggest that this Cancer image encompasses all seven Conditions of Consciousness, at least before the joinder of the most

---

3   RSP (2014), formerly published by AP under the title *The Influence of Spiritual Beings Upon Man* (1961).

spiritually primitive of our solar inhabitants. The initial excerpt from *OES* suggests that the Saturn beings will only be joined in the Vulcan Conditions of Consciousness. One surmises that the beings that are more advanced than we on Earth may well be awaiting us at some stage, perhaps advanced, of the Jupiter Condition of Consciousness. In any event, we planetary beings will all have worked together to some extent on our journey to Jupiter, the Holy City, the new Jerusalem, which we will now ponder.

14

THE HOLY CITY, NEW JERUSALEM

Surely scarce is the heart that has not been comforted at a funeral service by the music and lyrics of the song "The Holy City." It is a glorious imagination stimulated by selected portions of Revelation 21. Yet, real understanding of what the chapter represents is hardly revealed, and one who comes to this point in the present writing might pause before accepting, in the last verse, "The gates were open wide, and all who would might enter, and no one was denied." It probably all depends upon what spin is put upon the words "all who would." Few to whom it is sung yet comprehend that the holy city is a state that no human being will reach for many ages and future incarnations, followed by subsequent journeys in higher Kingdoms of Life before leaving the Earth Condition of Consciousness for that of Jupiter, the holy city.

Interpreting the Text

To the extent that chapter 21 describes the Jupiter Condition of Consciousness as Steiner has said, it does not represent the end of the long human journey since two more Conditions of Consciousness will succeed it.

Though ultimately inspiring to the human mind and heart by being a part of such a spiritual journey, chapter 21 alone peeks into an odyssey that is dizzying in its immensity.

To contemplate the magnitude of the jump that Steiner makes from the "More Perfect Astral" Condition of Form to the Jupiter Condition of Consciousness, please observe what all humanity must first pass through.[1] It must go through two more Conditions of Form in the

---

1   See chapter 2, "The Grand Schematic (*BB's* chart I-1).

Mineral Condition of Life. This entails the equivalent of ninety-eight of our "cultural ages" (two times seven times seven), each of which, in our physical condition is approximately 2,160 years long. Then it entails passing through three more Conditions of Life (Plant, Animal, and Human Kingdoms), the equivalent of 1,029 cultural ages ([7 x 7 x 7] x 3). So, based on chart I-1 alone, it entails the equivalent of 1,127 of our cultural ages. For perspective, if each of these "cultural ages" (which is an inappropriate designation for that part of the journey) were 2,160 years in length, as in our conditions in material form, it would be 2,434,320 years before we get to Jupiter.

The important thing to remember, however, is that once we leave the mineral realm, time itself is no longer a factor (cf. Matt 24:22). This is doubtless part of what Steiner meant when he said about chart I-1 that it was "related to the full reality not even like the inner framework of a house to the complete building, but only [to] the outer scaffolding—that has to be taken down when the building is complete."[2]

In chapter 3 we took up the meaning of "soon" as it appears in several contexts in Revelation. That such translation was seriously misleading, particularly in the popular mind's understanding of the word *soon,* now seems clear. History has dispelled the possibility of any rational idea that such popular understanding was correct. That it served an evangelical purpose in the earliest part of the Christian era can hardly be denied. Beyond that it cloaked truer meaning, first as explained by Steiner, and then also by what "soon" must mean in the context of our long cosmic journey.

As we now attempt an understanding of chapter 21, a higher and more ultimate meaning of *soon* gives that word some meaningful substance. Jupiter is not comprehendible by our present earthly Condition of Consciousness. Particularly is this true while we have understanding only in the Mineral Kingdom. The primary purpose of Lazarus/ John's vision was surely to guide humanity during the thousands of years it would work its way through bodies of matter in preparation for entry into the More Perfect Astral realm—that is through the great Evolutionary Epochs of the Mineral-Physical Condition of Form. Revelation does not extend, with any meaningful detail, beyond the era of the one hundred forty-four thousand (144,000), the point at which we

---

2   *ASJ*, lect. 10; 179–180.

give up bodies of matter and live only in the More Perfect Astral Condition of Form. The blowing of the last trumpet constitutes this critical transition. This transition ends the last Evolutionary Epoch of the Mineral-Physical Condition of Form, the first and lowest of the four kingdoms we must pass through before we reach the holy city. Serious contemplation of Steiner's Grand Schematic in chapter 2 suggests that John's vision was not detailed or explicit on the holy city and that he expressed it in general terms that were in keeping with the structure, especially the numerological structure, that pervades not only his own apocalyptic vision but the entirety of the canon. To the extent that he may have been capable of perceiving our spiritual existence in the Jupiter Condition, he would have realized that it was so far ahead, and so dependent on human endeavor in the interim, that it would have been useless as any sort of a guide. Moreover, long before we arrive at Jupiter, *writing* as we know it, including our canon as *graven image*, would have passed away (1 Cor 13:8–9).

John tells us that the angel "who had the seven bowls full of the seven last plagues" carried him "to a great high mountain" whence the spirit showed him the holy city coming down out of heaven (21:9–10). It was radiantly clear, like jasper, and was described as follows:

> [12] It had a great, high wall, with twelve gates, and at the gates twelve angels, and on the gates the names of the twelve tribes of the sons of Israel were inscribed; [13] on the east three gates, on the north three gates, on the south three gates, and on the west three gates. [14] And the wall of the city had twelve foundations, and on them the twelve names of the twelve apostles of the Lamb...
>
> [16] The city lies foursquare, its length the same as its breadth; and he measured the city with his rod, twelve thousand stadia;[3] its length and breadth and height are equal. [17] He also measured its wall, a hundred forty-four cubits by a man's measure, that is, an angel's.[4] [18] The wall was built of jasper, while the city was pure gold, clear as glass. [19] The foundations of the wall of the city were adorned with every jewel; the first was jasper, the second sapphire,

---

3   About fifteen hundred miles (RSV) [about 1,400 miles (about 2,200 kilometers) according to Christopher C. Rowland, NIB, vol. 12; 719].

4   Rowland, NIB, 719, more properly, it seems, says "man's measurement, which the angel was using." He then gives the measurement as "about 200 feet (about 65 meters).

the third agate, the fourth emerald, [20] the fifth onyx, the sixth carnelian, the seventh chrysolite, the eighth beryl, the ninth topaz, the tenth chrysoprase, the eleventh jacinth, the twelfth amethyst.[21] And the twelve gates were twelve pearls, each of the gates made of a single pearl, and the street of the city was pure gold, transparent as glass.

The above description of the holy city is couched in terms used in the world of matter. Yet we know that we leave the world of matter long before we reach this Condition of Consciousness that is beyond our own Earthly Condition. To be sure, we are dealing, in such description, with symbols from our world of matter, so we must ask the meaning of this symbolism.

Perhaps the most dominant aspect of the symbols is their adherence to the numerological aspects of the canon. While within the world of numerology every integer has meaning, some numbers seem to have an overwhelming presence in scripture. They are the numbers three, four, seven and twelve. While the word *seven* appears only twice (both in 21:9) in the last two chapters of Revelation, and even there it is not part of the description of the holy city, we know that, like the Bible itself, Revelation begins with sevens and moves to twelves. But beyond that, seven is the sum of the first two numbers, three and four, and the city itself was three dimensional and four-square of immense size, with length, height, and breadth being equal (21:16), each dimension being about 1,400 miles. It had four walls, each measuring about 200 feet, with three gates in each wall for a total of twelve gates. It also had twelve foundations supporting the four walls, being three on each side.

The Mystery of the Wall's Height

Here we are pressed for an aside—the city and its wall is a hard imagination. The city is described in the form of a cube with each dimension, length, breadth, and height measuring 1,400 miles. In verse 17, the measurement of the wall is said to be 200 feet "by a man's measure, that is, an angel's." Strange that this standard of measurement—"a man's measure, that is, an angel's"—was not applied to the city itself. The man and angel aspect has been noted by commentators without coming up with a different measurement, in the end, than the 200 feet otherwise suggested by the text. That distance is probably what was intended by the writer. That it was the measurement of an "angel" would have been justified simply because at that point there would have been no "man" there in terms of material earthly embodiment.

The problem is that both height and thickness were important measurements of physical resistance offered by a city's wall, and we are not told which dimension the 200 feet represents. This has to be a problem for a modern reader, as it also was for me initially. One today who is told of "measurement of a wall," would normally think of two dimensions, height and length. That would not have been the case of walls around cities in ancient times. Those walls were protective, and thickness was then a factor as well as height. The proportions, as height, are unrealistic in a material mode of thinking.[5] As a measurement of height, 200 feet is dramatically out of proportion to the size of the city, suggesting that thickness is the intent. While a height or distance of 200 feet is meaningless for a city of that great cubical size, a wall's thickness of that measure seems appropriate.

Not only that, but right at the outset of the description of the city itself we are told, "It had a great, high wall." Words must be construed in context. The measurement is in thickness.

Returning from the aside, we may see this structure as representing the human being who has accomplished the goal of Earth evolution. Recall that such goal is the perfection of the Ego, the "I Am," following which, in the last three Conditions of Consciousness will be perfected, in sequence, the three spiritual aspects of the human being (see *BB* chart **I-9**). The human being during the Earth Condition of Consciousness involves four components (physical body, etheric body, astral body, and Ego) the last being threefold (sentient soul, intellectual soul, and consciousness soul).

Representing thus the accomplishment of such primary goal of Earth evolution, it seems appropriate that the predominant feature of the description of the holy city, the initial aspects presented in it, is

---

5   A wall of 200 feet would contrast with the city's height of 7,392,000 feet (1,400
     x 5,280 feet); it would only be .000027 times the height of the city, or a quarter
     of 1/100,000 [.25/100,000, or three inches for every 100,000 feet, or for every
     19 miles].

the fourfoldness of the city and the threefoldness, in gates and foundations, of each of its four walls. Embodied in this is, however, the twelvefoldness of the longer journey that continues to engage the "I Am," the Christ-imbued human. That the twelve is the thread of the future is evidenced by the 144 (21:17) in describing the dimension of the wall, and by the twelve jewels (21:19–20), and then by gold and pearls, there being also twelve of the latter.

What is the Holy City?

The holy city consists of four walls, each with three gates and three foundations (21:12–14). Shorn of adjective, quality, and adornment, that is it—both simple in metaphor, and complex in allegory, for the human being who has finished the journey through Earth evolution, the Earth Condition of Consciousness. The eleven verses before it are preamble, the thirteen following encomium. Lazarus/John describes his initiation in John 11, the middle chapter of his Gospel. Closely, in point in time, he here describes human attainment of the Jupiter consciousness in the middle of Revelation 21.

The four walls are simple metaphor for the fourfold human being of Earth evolution, the three bodies—physical, etheric, and astral, and the Ego. The three gates of each wall are allegory, inviting a greater search for meaning within the ubiquity of the number three.[6] We should probably be slow to assert that the three gates have only one meaning. Truth exists at different levels, and some possibilities may seem more powerful than others.

One with appeal seems to relate closely to the vision itself. In each of the units of the Grand Schematic (chapter 2, or *BB*, chart **I-1**), the human passed through three descending and then three ascending stages—this applied in each of the seven race (cultural age) cycles within each of the seven Evolutionary Epochs; then to the seven Evolutionary Epochs themselves; then to the seven Conditions of Form; then to the seven Conditions of Life.

The threefold element, the descending and ascending portions, joined in each level by the parabola's lowest, and turning, point, are

---

6   Nearly inexhaustible, it seems, is the source of the three concept within scripture, as well as Anthroposophy. See "The Three Bodies" in *BB*, including item 2 in the Preface to the Revised Edition.

part of the sevenfold nature of evolution portrayed in the Grand Schematic. However, while Revelation began with sevens, it moved into the twelves. The holy city comprises four walls, with each being threefold, collectively twelve. Each wall has three gates and each wall has three foundations, both the gates and the foundations numbering twelve. The names of the twelve tribes were on the gates and the names of the twelve apostles were on the foundations. While it does not state whether each gate or foundation had on it one name or twelve, the intent points to each one being given one name. Steiner indicated the twelve jewels that soon appear in the text (21:19–20) represent the zodiac, and he described the order of their assignment, one jewel to each foundation.[7] Moreover, Ezekiel describes the city that shall be for all the tribes. It also is to have four walls each with three gates, and he names each gate for one of the twelve tribes, identifying which wall each gate is on—on the north side: Reuben, Judah, and Levi; on the east side: Joseph, Benjamin, and Dan; on the south side Simeon, Issachar, and Zebulun; and on the west side: Gad, Asher, and Naphtali.[8]

It seems appropriate to ascribe the descending portion to the twelve tribes and the ascending portion to the twelve apostles. The ascent could begin only with the Mystery of Golgotha. It was in connection with the Ascension and Pentecost that Steiner gave us the basis for ascribing the ascending part to the twelve apostles. "In a way, the Apostles now had the soul content of the Sun Heroes of old. The spiritual power of the Sun poured out over their souls and from then on continued to be active in human evolution."[9]

---

7   See below, Benesch, *Apocalypse*, 236, citing unpublished Steiner lecture in Berlin, Oct. 9, 1906.

8   Ezek 48:30–34. While Reuben was the first born of Jacob's children, the order in which they are assigned to the gates is not that of their birth (Gen 29:31–30:24 and 35:16–20). The names of the twelve and the mother of each is succinctly given, again not in order, in Gen 35:23–26. Of particular note are the names on the east wall, since the east has special significance (see "Eden's Locus" in *SLJ*). Those assigned to the east wall are Joseph, Benjamin, and Dan. Joseph had special spiritually perceptive powers, consistent with the connotation of the east. Joseph and Benjamin were the beloved Rachel's only two children, and Dan was the first child of Rachel's handmaid Bilhah.

9   Steiner, *The Fifth Gospel*, RSP, lect. 3 (Oslo, Oct. 3, 1913), 35, concluding description 32–35 (CW 148).

The Twelve Jewels

Considering first the twelve jewels, we note that they are not structural but are merely *adornments* (v. 19) of the twelve foundations that are the structural supports for the wall.

Each of the twelve jewels is an item of great or considerable value in its material form, as is also true of gold and pearls which we will discuss separately below. We may ask ourselves how it can be that in the holy city, a spiritual state devoid of matter, we find items that without exception are cherished in our materialistic earthly state not only for their inherent physical beauty but also as items of monetary value indicative of wealth beyond basic human need in a world of need.

As I write, in early May 2015, I have in my hand a book, hot off the press in its English translation, that deals extensively with these precious items of matter and their relation to the non-material world.[10] The book is a challenge for one who would seek a quick and simple solution to the significance of these precious substances at the end of the Apocalypse. The challenge may be detected by the stated purpose of the book, elaborated in its preface (xii–xiv) as follows:

---

10 Friedrich Benesch, *Apocalypse, the Transformation of Earth*, Lindisfarne Books, in association with Goldstone Press, in English translation by Joseph Bailey; Lindisfarne Books is an imprint of SB/AP (2015).

Benesch (1907–1991), had a strong and dominant sense of German nationalism, a quality (dominant nationalism) essentially contrary to basic principles of Anthroposophy. Thus, as an anthroposophist, he presents for me considerable ambivalence, inasmuch as he was also, apparently until 1945, a leading Nazi in Romania. He was otherwise brilliant, holding doctorates in biology, theology, and anthropology. His prominence in Anthroposophy and in the related Christian Community seminary and priesthood developed after the war. For reasons mysterious, perhaps related to the dysfunctional state of the anthroposophical movement in the decades immediately following Steiner's death in 1925, Benesch's Nazi activities were not a matter of cognizance within the movement during his post-war anthroposophical activity nor, in fact, until thirteen years after his death. A "publisher's note" of some length about Benesch at the end of the book, presents an objective look at the facts, in the interest of transparency. In its conclusions, the enigma is stated there, however, as follows:

In the silence and solitude of his sickbed, one imagines he was able to review his life. Again, we do not know what passed within him; there is no record. Nor do we know whether he spoke (or confessed) to anyone either about his past beliefs and activities or about what kinds of radical change, if any, were taking place within him.

The actual mystery of this city-imagination [the holy city, Rev 21] is its "substance," its "construction material," the suprasensory mineral nature of which becomes the central question. The present book is an attempt to answer this question, which, in simplified form, reads as follows:

1. Are mineral substances pure matter or are they of spiritual nature?
2. Are there only material minerals that are perhaps also spiritual, or are there also "spiritual minerals" of non-material nature?
3. How are we to understand the concrete minerals used to build the Heavenly Jerusalem?

These three questions place us before [*sic*] the problem of an "esoteric mineralogy." For anything purely spiritual can only be the object of esoteric cognition, esoteric research, and science. Esoteric science presupposes, though, that not matter, but rather spirit is the actual, original, and essential reality of the world—hence of the mineral world as well. This fundamental question of knowledge, regarding our modern consciousness, can be structured into sub-questions in the following way:

The primacy of the spirit or of substance, of matter. Either the spirit is the origin and all that is material is densified or condensed manifestation of the spirit, or else matter is what comes first and all that is spiritual but a function of matter, a project of material processes of sublimation.[11]

One senses, I would assume, that by the end of the book of Revelation, the need is for the primacy of spirit over matter and that interpretation should lend itself in that direction. But Benesch differentiates above "esoteric mineralogy" and "esoteric science," and he calls his

---

11   This paragraph is the first of six "sub-questions" which, in the interest of brevity, I deem to essentially subsume the last five, which, condensed, are as follows: 2. The primacy of life or of death.... 3. The primacy of the gestalt or of the atom.... 4. Primacy of the meaningful and harmonious or of the meaningless and coincidental.... 5. The primacy of the essential or of the objective.... 6. The primacy either of natural law as the actual law of the cosmos, or of the ethical world order proceeding from a soul and spiritual world that...assumes higher meaning.

book "An esoteric mineralogy" that has to do with "The Transformation of the Earth."

A great deal of the body of the work goes into the mineral nature of these components of the holy city—and that mineral nature is extensively and scholastically detailed. He concludes his preface by suggesting that one gets to the "essence and future" on the path of "esoteric mineralogy."

An anthroposophist encountering the number twelve will probably assume the likelihood of some connection to the zodiac. Benesch helps by giving us an unpublished Steiner reference:

> In a lecture not yet published (Berlin, Oct. 9, 1906), Rudolf Steiner pointed to the connection between the entities of the zodiac and the twelve gemstone images in the Apocalypse and determined their affiliation in the sequence of the shift in the vernal equinox of the Sun, beginning with the image of heliotrope [jasper] in the sign of Pisces and proceeding backward through Aquarius, Capricorn, and so on (cf. Appendix 25).[12]

His section on the twelve jewels (21:19–20) approaches each of the twelve under five aspects, in the following order, 1. Name; 2. Scientific Research; 3. Origin and habitat; 4. Soul virtue; 5. Spiritual future.[13]

Of the twelve jewels, Benesch puts the greatest focus upon the first, jasper.[14] Before we consider it along with gold and pearls, it is well to note the collective appearances of these jewels in scripture. They are as follows:[15]

---

12 Benesch, *Apocalypse*, 236; the referenced appendix 25 is at 411–413 and the table showing the twelve zodiacal beings in the order stated in the text is at 412.

13 Ibid., 234–295.

14 Ibid., 176–195 (Jasper); 195–234 (Jasper Experience); 240–243 (Jasper as Heliotrope).

15 The order in which the jewels appear varies as do the different names given them in the respective lists. Each of the jewels appears in the Benesch text, to which reference is made for description.

Exod 28:17–20 and 39:10–13	Ezek 28:13	Rev 21:17–19
sardius	carnelian	jasper
topaz	topaz	sapphire
carbuncle	jasper	agate
emerald	chrysolite	emerald
sapphire	beryl	onyx
diamond	onyx	carnelian
jacinth	sapphire	chrysolite
agate	carbuncle	beryl
amethyst	emerald	topaz
beryl		chrysoprase
onyx		jacinth
jasper		amethyst

The Exodus passages prescribe the jeweled contents of the sacred breastplate of the high priest. Ezekiel lists only nine jewels, a number that may suggest the ninefold human being, especially when we consider it in its context:

> [12b] You were the signet of perfection, full of wisdom and perfect in beauty. [13] You were in Eden, the garden of God; every precious stone [listed as above]…and wrought in gold were your settings and your engravings.[16]

Jasper, Gold, and Pearl

Jasper, gold, and pearl have special meaning and emphasis. As items of precious matter they are uniquely different. One is stone, one metal, and the other animal product. Each seems to have its own message, and collectively they constitute a "threesome," reminiscent of the Peter, James, and John among the twelve.

---

16 The Lord, through Ezekiel, was here, and in what followed at length, laying the predicate to castigate the king of Tyre and cast him from the mountain of God. The Ezekiel passage may, in its context, relate to the appearance of the jewels in Revelation, for whenever the jewels might have taken their material form on earth, the human being had not yet entered bodily materiality on earth while in Eden (see "Eden's Locus" in *SLJ*, 195–204).

Two of the three, jasper and gold, are described in the twenty-first chapter as being "clear, or transparent, as glass" (21:11, 18) even though as precious materials they are not transparent. This transformation itself in the language of Revelation suggests their non-materiality, or spiritualized symbolism, at that stage of the human journey.

Jasper: Neither gold nor silver present a conceptual problem to the modern reader. Jasper presents an almost insurmountable conceptual problem, as it relates to the Apocalypse. Benesch elaborates on it at length but does not present a description that is as "clear as crystal." He says that "a survey ... shows the difficulties involved in identifying the mineral and the name definitively. What mineral should we associate the name jasper with if we want to understand the language of the Apocalypse? The matter becomes all the more complicated with [sic] one considers that not even in modern systematic mineralogy can the designation for jasper be clearly defined."[17] In short, the name jasper and its description in modern times is hardly compatible with its supernal qualities as described in the Apocalypse. We must attribute that use to something that came to the Apocalyptist from a now-faded hoary wisdom—in short, an ancient concept buried in obscurity for the modern mind.

Taking Jasper in that sense we read:

21:10–11: And in the Spirit he carried me away to a great, high mountain, and showed me the holy city Jerusalem coming down out of heaven from God, having the glory of God, its radiance like a most rare jewel, like a jasper, clear as crystal.

21:18: The wall was built of jasper, while the city was pure gold, clear as glass.

21:19: The foundations of the wall of the city were adorned with every jewel; the first was jasper.

Gold: Jasper appears in scripture only as cited above in this chapter. Pearl, in the singular or plural, is also cited sparingly, once in the OT (Job 28:18), twice in Matt (7:6; 13:45–46), once in 1 Tim (2:9), and four

---

17   Benesch, 180.

times in Rev (17:4; 18:12, 16; 21:21). Gold is cited extensively throughout the canon, especially in the OT.

Jasper is always used in reverence. Both gold and pearl(s) are used in both favorable and unfavorable contexts, the unfavorable speaking of them as ungodly spiritual burden of wealth.

In an early lecture Steiner spoke of gold as "solidified sunlight."[18] In his lectures Steiner related the seven bodies in our solar system to seven critical organs in the human body and seven well-known metals. Their representation is set out below:[19]

PLANET	METAL	HUMAN BEING
Saturn	Lead	Spleen
Jupiter	Tin	Liver
Mars	Iron	Gall Bladder
Sun	Gold	Heart
Venus	Copper	Kidneys
Mercury	Mercury	Lungs
Moon	Silver	Brain

"It is one of the greatest of world enigmas that, in all the old traditions, gold was always associated with the Sun."[20] In the insert above about Steiner's as yet unpublished lecture of October 6, 1906 (relative to the zodiac's appearance in the twelve jewels), the "jasper" is parenthesized following the word *heliotrope* as being related to the sign of Pisces. If Steiner used *heliotrope* as a name for jasper, while

---

18   Steiner, *Foundations of Esotericism*, 1st Eng. ed., RSP (1983); 207 (lect. 26, Berlin, Oct. 28, 1905).

19   This three-column tabulation came from the late Otto Wolff, *Anthroposophically-Oriented Medicine and its Remedies*, MP (1991), 30, which he correctly stated that Rudolf Steiner had presented. While presented in lecture form, all of the detail in the three columns is found in Steiner, *An Occult Physiology*, 3rd Eng. ed., RSP (1983), lect. 8 (Prague, Mar. 28, 1911) (CW 128). All of the information in all three columns, with the exception of the Sun-heart-gold connection, can also be found in Steiner, *Health and Illness*, vol. 2, SB (1983), lect. 9 (Dornach, Feb. 10, 1923) (CW 348). The seven planets and their related metals are also found in *BB*, chart **I-29** at page 598.

20   Benesch, *Apocalypse*, 317.

identifying the precious metal gold as "solidified sunlight," it must be that in the realm of precious stones, he perceived jasper, whatever it was, to represent the highest level, the sun level, within the twelvefold zodiacal belt of stones. The literal meaning of the word *heliotrope* is "turning toward the sun," which Benesch equates to "Belonging to the Sun."[21] So both gold and jasper have strong sun elements. In the case of gold, it is the sun in a materialized earthen form. In the case of Jasper, it is something that turns toward the sun, like a plant. It would seem that as high as jasper thus is among the precious stones, that gold as a precious metal is higher. The holy city was said, in v. 11, to have a radiance and a clarity like jasper, a simile, while in v. 18, the wall is said to be jasper but the city "pure gold," as in gold refined by fire.[22]

The Pearl: "Purified Pain"—these are the first words Benesch uses in his chapter on the Pearl, and not only so, but they are the first words in his subtitle at the start of that chapter. He develops these words by relating them to the role of suffering in the development of the higher "I Am" in the human being.

In concluding a lecture entitled "The Origin of Suffering" (Berlin, Nov. 8, 1906), Steiner said:

> This is meant to be only a sketch which is to point to the connection between earthly existence and pain and suffering. It is to show how we can realise the meaning of suffering and pain when we see how they harden, crystallize in physical things and organisms up to man, and how through a dissolution of what has hardened, the Spirit can be born in us again, when we see that the origin of suffering and pain is in the Spirit. The Spirit gives us beauty, strength, wisdom, the transformed picture of the original abode of pain. A brilliant man, Fabre d'Olivet, made a right comparison when he wished to show how the highest, noblest, purest in human nature arises out of pain. He said that the arising of wisdom and beauty out of suffering is comparable to a process in nature, to the birth of the valuable and beautiful pearl. For the pearl is born from the sickness of the oyster, from the destruction inside the pearl-oyster. As the beauty of the pearl is born out of

---

21 Benesch, *Apocalypse*, 240.
22 Rev 3:18; Mal 3:3.

disease and suffering, so are knowledge, noble human nature and purified human feeling born out of suffering and pain.[23]

Just over two months earlier, regarding the "mission of illness":

> Fabre d'Olivet, who has investigated the origins of the Book of Genesis, once used a beautiful simile, comparing destiny with a natural process. The valuable pearl, he says, derives from an illness: it is a secretion of the oyster, so that in this case life has to fall sick in order to produce something precious. In the same way, physical illnesses in one life reappear in the next life as physical beauty.[24]

We saw much earlier in this book that the crucifixion of the mineral-physical body is the price of human entry into the realm of the 144,000, the More Perfect Astral Condition of Form. The pearl is, ultimately, the symbol of that victory. The Apocalyptist's vision that each of the twelve gateways (21:12–13) was a pearl reflects the truth that suffering and sacrifice are the pathway to the perfection of the Ego and entrance into the holy city.

The River through the Holy City (Revelation 22)

The most critical portion of this chapter 22 is its first two verses, but within that brevity is a powerful vision into the distant future—a worthy conclusion to our long journey through the Earth, and into the Jupiter, Condition of Consciousness and beyond. It reads:

> [1] Then he showed me the river of the water of life, bright as crystal, flowing from the throne of God and of the Lamb [2] through the middle of the street of the city; also, on either side of the river, the tree of life with its twelve kinds of fruit, yielding its fruit each month; and the leaves of the tree were for the healing of the nations.

The river of living water: The holy city is the Jupiter Condition of Consciousness. It is the city of living water—water flowing down the middle of its "street," its way (via) of life. The water of Jupiter is

---

23 Steiner, *The Origin of Suffering, Evil, Illness and Death*, North Vancouver, Canada, Steiner Book Centre (1980), 15–16 (CW 55).

24 Steiner, *At the Gates of Spiritual Science*, 2d ed., RSP and SB (1986), 71 (lect. 8, Aug. 29, 1906) (CW 95).

the water of the Moon (the Ancient Moon Condition of Consciousness), enhanced in the upward retracement of what was prepared for the descending human on the Moon. Recall that the four classical elements are fire, air, water, and earth—or warmth, gas, fluid, solid—that had their origin, respectively, in the Saturn, Sun, Moon, and Earth Conditions of Consciousness. In the excerpt from *OES* in the early portion of chapter 13, we saw that Jupiter is to come about from a joinder of what comes from Moon and what comes from Earth. The elements from the Moon are even now undergoing evolution in its sphere but these are elements that "did not condense enough to be physically perceived by our senses." The living water on Jupiter will also not be water that we will perceive with senses as we have on Earth. While Moon water is enhanced by its own evolutionary journey during Earth evolution, on Jupiter it also picks up the life element that was enhanced by Christ on Earth, the living water—a water that is of the fluid nature of the blood of Christ, the home of the "I Am" in earthly life—from the pierced body of Christ from which blood and water flowed, as the Apocalyptist Lazarus/John wrote (John 19:34; 1 John 5:6). It is, after all, a river of *living water* that flowed from the throne of God and *of the Lamb* (22:1).

How easy it is to read these two verses (22:1–2) and quickly pass over the living water that flows through Jupiter without appreciating the weight of the power attached to that phrase from beginning to end in the biblical journey of humanity, especially as that power is enhanced by the insights of Anthroposophy. Water pervades the canon.[25] We cannot even begin to look at its many appearances. But let us ponder that water and river imagery as it flows through the canon:

> **Gen 1:2b:** Spiritual fire, air, and water had been prepared in the Saturn, Jupiter, and Moon Conditions of Consciousness. While in the early stages of the Earth Condition, the spirit of God was *stimulating the waters in the etheric realm*, before they took on their mineral nature.

---

25 It is found in 61 of the 66 books of the Protestant Bible. It is absent only in Esther, and four of the twelve so-called "minor" prophets (Obadiah, Zephaniah, Haggai, and Malachi).

Gen 2:10–14: This passage is in the Lemurian, the third, Evolutionary Epoch of the Mineral-Physical Condition of Form, the period of the Garden of Eden. Eden existed only in the supersensible world.[26] The Lemurian Epoch was a recapitulation, during Earth evolution, of what was brought over from Ancient Moon, where the fluid aspect of the four classical elements originated. In this passage we are told that four *rivers* flowed out of Eden to *water* its life-giving garden. Two of the precious items found in the holy city description (Jupiter), namely, gold and onyx, are mentioned in connection with these supernal "rivers."

Gen 7: The *water* of the great flood submerged Atlantis bringing about the Noah transition from the Atlantean to our present Post-Atlantean Epoch.

Gen 32:22–32: On the banks of the *Jabbok River* Jacob wrestled with God and reconciled with his brother Esau. It was on the banks of the Jabbok that Jacob asked for his *name*, a significant event in human evolution, leading eventually to the same question by Moses, to whom the name *I Am* was first given (Exod 3:14).

Exod 2:10: Moses *comes on the water*; like the Solomon Jesus child through the many Zarathustra incarnations in each of which he *"came on the water."*[27]

Exod 14:21–29: The *waters of the Red Sea are parted*, by Moses, who had come on the water. Just as he had parted the etheric waters to incarnate (like his predecessor Zarathustra), Moses parted the etheric waters for the birth of his Hebrew culture in moving away from that of the Egyptian, which he had to kill, both individually (Exod 2:11–15) and collectively (Exod 14:26–28)—and I prefer to interpret them both metaphorically.

---

26 See "Eden's Locus" in *SLJ*, 195–204.

27 *BB*, 92–93; also 38–40. The etheric realm is that of water symbolism. That the etheric body of Zarathustra was given to Moses indicates how spiritually accurate it was for Moses to leave, for later recording, the legend, that he had come in the same water mode as his benefactor Zarathustra. Recall that the only two places the term *tebah*, or *tevah*, was used referenced Noah's ark and the basket in which the infant Moses was placed.

Num 20:11: In the wilderness, Moses strikes the *rock*, bringing forth *living water*; Paul, the reincarnated Moses, recognizes that the Rock *was Christ* (1 Cor 10:4); Isaiah ("second Isaiah") says it was the Lord who cleft the rock to bring forth *water* (Isa 48:21).

Josh 3:14–17; 4:23: The *waters of the Jordan are parted*, as they had been at the Red Sea, followed in Joshua 4 by the placement of the twelve stones at Gilgal.[28]

Ps 1:3: The righteous person "is like a tree planted by *streams of water*, that yields its fruit in its season, and its leaf does not wither." The metaphoric symbolism in this first psalm is strikingly similar to that in Revelation 22:1–2.

Song 4:15: Speaks of "a garden fountain, a well of living water, and flowing streams from Lebanon," *a threefold living water imagery.*

Isa 30:25: Upon every lofty mountain and every high hill there will be *brooks running with water*, in the day of the great slaughter, when the towers fall (end of Earth evolution).

Jer 2:13: His people have forsaken *the Lord, the fountain of living waters* and hewed out broken, waterless cisterns. (Same language, "forsaken the Lord, the fountain of living waters," in Jer 17:13.)

Zech 14:8: On that day living waters shall flow out of Jerusalem... (Jupiter as the new Jerusalem).

John 4:10: (Jesus to the woman of Samaria at the well) "If you knew the gift of God, and who it is that is saying to you, 'Give me a drink,' you would have asked him and he would have given you *living water.*"

John 7:37b–38: "If any one thirst, let him come to me and drink. He who believes in me, as the scripture has said, 'Out of his heart shall flow *rivers of living water.*'"

Rev 7:17: "For the *lamb* in the midst of the *throne* will be their shepherd, and he will guide them to *springs of living water*; and *God*

---

28   For the significance of Gilgal and these twelve stones, see *SLJ*, 121–133, "Gilgal and the Whirlwind".

will wipe away every tear from their eyes." (Great similarity to Rev 22:1–2; rivers of running water often begin at a spring.)

Inasmuch as the goal of Earth evolution is the perfection of the Ego, the "I Am," a necessity to bring about the "living water" of Jupiter, it seems worth noting that a phenomenon during Earth evolution is that chemical processes can occur only in the element of water (fluid).[29] In an application of that, Steiner says (emphasis of *chemical* is mine):

> Anyone who accepts materialistic criteria will say that breathing is a physical process in the human being: a person takes in air and then, as a consequence of the breath, certain processes occur in the blood, and so on, all of this being physical processes. Of course these are all physical processes, but the forces on which the *chemical* processes of the blood are based come from the *I*.... The place where the *I* is really present is in the circulation of the blood...the most important thing in the blood is the *I*. Morality affects the blood... the physical blood is only there to occupy, so to speak, a position in space where the forces of the *I* can work.... Morality, therefore, affects the *I*. In the blood, the forces of the *I* encounter the forces of morality...there is a spiritual encounter between what pulses in [the] blood and the moral forces that radiate into it.[30]

The highest moral force to ever enter into the bloodstream of a human being was that which, through a divine chemistry, came into the blood of Jesus through the flowing waters of the Jordan River. The Incarnation of the Christ in the waters of the Jordan was the culmination of long descents of both the divine and the human. That of the human manifested in the three bodies of Jesus of Nazareth whose approach to this spiritually historic event is described by Steiner:

> Jesus of Nazareth had united himself intensely with the words in which he gave expression to all the pain he felt at the suffering of humanity. And it was as if his self had vanished from the shell provided by physical, ether and astral body, with the shell being again as it had been when he was a little boy, only that it was now also

---

29 See *DQWIM*, 157–162 (in its "Fire" essay) and 92 n. 22 (in its "The Four Elements" essay).

30 Steiner, *The Riddle of Humanity*, RSP, lect. 4 (Dornach, Aug. 5, 1916), 49–51 (CW 170).

filled with everything he had suffered from his twelfth year. The Zarathustra-I had gone, and all that remained in the shell was what survived of those powerful experiences. Now an impulse arose in the threefold shell. It drove him to take the road that would lead him to John the Baptist by the river Jordan. He went on his way as though in a dream, yet it was not a dream but a higher state of consciousness, and only the threefold shell was there, filled with the spirit and impulses of the experiences gained from his twelfth year. The Zarathustra-I had departed. The threefold shell guided him, and he was scarcely conscious of anything around him. With the I departed, he was wholly given up to his direct vision of human destiny and of human needs.[31]

The perfection of the Ego is the high attainment of moral perfection, the attainment of perfect love, the love of the Father (Matt 5:48). As the Moon is the planet of Wisdom, so the Earth is the planet of Love. God is Love (1 John 4:8). Blood provides the place for the necessary chemical change that can only be brought about by the highest morality of perfect love. The living water of Christ that flows through the holy city is the blood that flowed, and flows, from the Lamb, the Christ.

The Tree of Life with its Twelve Kinds of Fruit

The two trees, the tree of life and the tree of knowledge first appear in the account of "the fall" in Genesis 3. These are trees in the Garden of Eden, the tree of life being the etheric, or life, body, and the tree of knowledge being the astral, or sense, body, respectively. During Earth evolution the tree of life is related to the circulatory system and the tree of knowledge to the nervous system. The "garden" was still only in the spiritual realm, existing before the descent of the human

---

31 Steiner, *The Fifth Gospel/From the Akashic Record*, 3rd. ed., RSP (1995), lect. 12; 203–204 (Cologne, Dec. 17, 1913) (CW 148). Shortly after the initial publication in English translation (by Catherine E. Creeger) of his *Rudolf Steiner and the Fifth Gospel/Insights into a New Understanding of the Christ Mystery*, SB (2010), Peter Selg was the featured speaker at the annual SteinerBooks Seminar in New York City in March, 2010. Selg's impassioned and moving seminar lectures, followed by the reading of his book, brought home to this author, more forcefully than before, the depth of pathos in Steiner's soul as he lectured successively in Oslo, Cologne, and Berlin in late 1913 and early 1914.

Ego.[32] The setting of the Genesis 3 account is in the transition from the Lemurian Evolutionary Epoch to the Atlantean. It preceded the descent of the Ego into an earthly mineral-physical body.[33]

Recall that the etheric body does not exist in the holy city, in Jupiter, but only that part of it that the Ego was able to ennoble, with Christ's help, during Earth evolution, the part that took on the nature of buddhi, the "Life-Spirit" (see *BB*, chart **I-9**). The perfection of the astral body is the goal of Jupiter, while perfection of the etheric body is the goal of the Venus Condition of Consciousness (Venus). So, for purposes of understanding the reference to the "tree of life" in Revelation 22:2, we must consider it more and more to be the Christ Spirit, for it is that Spirit, the higher "I Am," that is the life (the living water) beyond Earth evolution (John 1:4).[34] So, when one enters into the "life" of Christ in the Earth Condition of Consciousness, that life continues through all the later Conditions. The tree of life in the 22nd chapter should be understood as surviving Earth evolution because it is the unity with Christ. In truth, the Christ is in all, working there for the bringing of life, even in those beings who remain to be redeemed up through the Venus Condition.

Having thus dealt with "the river of the water of life," how are we to understand the part of verse 2 that reads: "also, on either side of the river, the tree of life with its twelve kinds of fruit, yielding its fruit each month"?

Early in chapter 8, dealing with the opening of the seals, we spoke of the River Lethe (Roman name) or Styx (Greek name) as being allegorically portrayed in Ezek 47:1–12. Obviously, Ezekiel speaks of a river that as one moved "eastward" got deeper. We spoke of it there as the river that wipes out memory from one life to another in the long human journey. Then following his first six verses he tells us that on

---

32   "Eden's Locus," in *SLJ*, 195–203.

33   The Ego's progress in descending into its earthly body is described in *BB*, chart **I-35**, at pages 608 and 609 and in the "Naked" essay in *BB* on page 402. Both the chart and the essay cite Steiner's *The Influence of Spiritual Beings Upon Man*, SB (1961) (CW 102).

34   Beyond John 1:4, that Christ is the "life" source pervades the Gospel of John. It is found in every chapter except, perhaps, in chapters 2, 16, 18, 19, and 21, but even those cannot be read except in the context of the powerful Johannine umbrella of Christ being the life and the light of all.

the bank of the river there are "very many trees on the one side and on the other" (47:7), and then later, "And on the banks, on both sides of the river, there will grow all kinds of trees for food. Their leaves will not wither nor their fruit fail, but they will bear fresh fruit every month, because the water for them flows from the sanctuary. Their fruit will be for food, and their leaves for healing" (47:12). We may take the variety of fruits and the extensiveness of trees and healing in their leaves in that vision to relate to the healing effect in the karmic journey from life to life that leads toward perfection.

John's apocalyptic version speaks of only one tree, the "tree of life," which is on both sides of the river. Ezekiel has many kinds of trees producing fruit on each side of the river each month, but in Revelation one tree produces twelve kinds of fruit in each of the twelve months of the year. The motif of twelve times twelve is picked up. In Ezekiel the "all kinds of fruit" is not numbered by kind, though the division of the land for the twelve tribes that immediately follows it may import the concept of a single twelve into the account. In Ezekiel, the leaves are simply for healing, the type of healing that, in the context of that chapter's imagery, is involved in karma and reincarnation. In Revelation 22:2 it is for the nations. A scope beyond the individual is described. We may rightly infer, in light of what has been said about the increasing powers of healing that the redeemed will gain, they will continue to work up through Venus for at least a form of redemption for those who suffered the second death, and whose names were not found in the book of life (20:15), but are eventually brought to salvation.

Already in earlier chapters we were presented with the multiples of twelve, in the 144,000 to begin with, and then the cube in 21:16 brought in another multiple so that we have twelve times twelve times twelve. Now in chapter 22, on each side of the river we have twelve times twelve, that is, twelve kinds of fruit in each of the twelve months. We have a proliferation of twelves from the river bank. Conceptually we have at least five twelves in the line of multiplication. The first pair of twelves produced the 144,000 to get into the holy city, where we added another twelve in the threefold dimension (length, breadth, and height). Then through the river we get at least two more twelves in the twelve trees and twelve months. Perhaps we even have the suggestion that the twelves keep going on.

How may we conceive of this? I suggest that we go back to the spiral of creation near the end of chapter eight. The spiral that pervades creation reflects the golden mean and is charted by the numerical progression of what has come to be known as the Fibonacci ratio. The notable thing about that spiral is that it is only every twelfth Fibonacci number that is an integer, a natural number, a number without anything but zeros to the right of the decimal point, as demonstrated by the tabular calculation through the 48th Fibonacci number in chapter eight.

The remarkable thing is that the numerical phenomenon that produced a meaningful explanation of the 144,000 projects on out to show the evolutionary significance of a rather continuous sequence of twelves. Such a sequence seems implied by the string of twelves emerging in the last chapters of Revelation.

After concluding his description of the vision, John declares he is the one who "heard and saw these things" (22:8). He twice expresses the nearness of the apocalyptic events (22:10) and that the Alpha and Omega is "coming soon" (22:12–13). An immense sweep of spiritual journey is described, very little of it beyond the blowing of the last trumpet and the giving up of the material body. In that sense, the focus of the book bears most heavily upon the portion of the long journey that is to happen "soon," in a manner of speaking, or in relation to the immensity of the journey. With the exception, perhaps, of the short chapter 22, even everything up to Jupiter is the part that is "soon."

The canon ends with these words on *soon*. However, a final chapter is added to conclude our discussion. It deals with the significance of the canon's three rainbows, deferred until now since it bears upon the credibility of Steiner's insights reflected in "The Grand Schematic" of chapter 2 that has been the basis upon which this book is structured. Their unique significance is enhanced by the fact that the rainbow appears only in the first and last books of the canon, once in Genesis and twice in Revelation.

15

THE THREE RAINBOWS

HOW MANY RAINBOWS?

The word *rainbow,* sometimes simply *bow,* appears the following four times in scripture:

1. **Genesis 9:13:** "I set my *bow* in the cloud, and it shall be a sign of the covenant between me and the earth."

2. **Ezekiel 1:28:** Like the appearance of the *bow* that is in the cloud on a day of rain, so was the appearance of the brightness round about.

3. **Revelation 4:3:** And he who sat there appeared like jasper and carnelian, and round the throne was a *rainbow* that looked like an emerald.

4. **Revelation 10:1:** Then I saw another mighty angel coming down from heaven, wrapped in a cloud, with a *rainbow* over his head, and his face was like the sun, and his legs like pillars of fire.

While the rainbow appears in the four different scriptures cited above, only three rainbows are described, for Ezekiel is seeing the same future event or events John sees in one or both of the Revelation passages. The bow in Ezekiel 1:28 follows Ezekiel's vision of the four living creatures that are seen also by John in Revelation 4, but also precedes Ezekiel's vision of his eating of the scroll as did John in his own vision in Revelation 10. Many similarities in these respective accounts lead to the conclusion that Ezekiel was seeing the same future events seen by John.

The evidence preponderates, it seems to me, in favor of Ezekiel's vision relating to that of John in Revelation 4, if a choice has to be made between John's two visions. Note that Ezekiel refers repeatedly in chapter 1 to the four living creatures and sees that over their heads one who, like John's vision, was seated on a "throne" whose likeness was like the rainbow. Moreover, Ezekiel speaks in 1:22–23 of a firmament appearing over their heads that shined "like crystal," which could be the same as the "sea of glass, like crystal" that is before that throne in Rev 4:6 which immediately precedes the first appearance of the four living creatures in Revelation.

The only thing that might possibly relate to the third rainbow, the appearance in Rev 10:1, is the common discussion of the scroll that the prophet is told to take and eat (Ezek 2:8–3:3 and Rev 10:8–10). In Ezekiel it is merely sweet in the mouth, while in Revelation it is not only sweet in the mouth but bitter in the stomach. That distinction alone may suggest that the Ezekiel episode comes earlier than the imminent blowing of the last trumpet, as was the case in Rev 10. In any event, Ezekiel is not expanding the number of occasions on which a rainbow appears. But its appearance in Ezekiel seems to fit much more precisely with the rainbow situated in Rev 4:3.[1]

Ezekiel's vision occurred in Babylon during that captivity, and based upon the presence in his work of references to certain events and the absence of others, it has been placed between 593 and 571 BC, almost seven hundred years before John's vision on Patmos.[2] It is remarkable, though not surprising, that these two seers experienced such a similar vision, but the one in Revelation, in the light of anthroposophical understanding, seems to play out with a greater depth and distance of insight. It would be hard to make a case for Ezekiel's

---

1   Christopher C. Rowland's commentary recognizes that the vision of the rainbow in Ezek 1:28 was essentially the same as that of John in Rev 4:3, while the vision in Ezek 2:8–3:3 (which did not separately refer to a rainbow) was related to that of John in 10:1, but that the former of these comparisons (with Rev 4:3) was more direct and extensive than the latter (with Rev 10:1). *The Book of Revelation*, NIB, vol. 12; 591–592, 638.

2   Moshe Greenberg, *Ezekiel 1–20*, AB, vol. 22; 15, Garden City, NY, Doubleday (1963).

rainbow being associated with any other biblical scenario than these of John's rainbows, whether one or both.

RAINBOWS AND EVOLUTIONARY EPOCHS

We may now ask ourselves when these three rainbows appear in relation to the seven Evolutionary Epochs of the Mineral-Physical Conditions of Life and Form of the Earth Condition of Consciousness, as set out in the Grand Scheme. It is clear that they appear at the following transitional points:

1.　The rainbow in Genesis 9:13 is seen by Noah in his transition from the Atlantean to the Post-Atlantean Epoch, that is from the Fourth to the Fifth such Epoch.

2.　The rainbow in Revelation 4:3 is at the conclusion of the seven Cultural Ages ("Churches") of the Post-Atlantean Epoch, associated with the time of the War of All against All as humanity moves from the Fifth Epoch into the Sixth, that of the seven seals.

3.　The rainbow in Revelation 10:1 appears in the seventh Age of the Seventh Epoch at the end of which the seventh trumpet is blown ending the Physical Condition of Form of the Mineral Condition of Life, for the move of humanity into the More Perfect Astral Realm of the Mineral Condition of Life.

Thus, what we have is the rainbow symbol appearing at both the beginning and the end of our Fifth Evolutionary Epoch, the one that encompasses all of that Epoch's Cultural Ages ("Churches"); then it appears again at the end of the last Epoch when humanity leaves the Mineral-Physical Condition to live in the More Perfect Astral Condition of Form.

We will look at the profound symbolism of the rainbow, but at this point we note how these three, and only three, rainbows fit precisely with three major transitional points in the human journey as Steiner has described it in relation to the Grand Scheme. Steiner did not, to my knowledge, specifically call this out in his lectures or writings. It is, instead, incumbent upon us to note its strong corroboration of the accuracy of his General Scheme and his presentations on John's Apocalypse.

THE RAINBOW AS SYMBOL

Rainbow as Covenant

Genesis 6:18: But I will establish my *covenant* with you; *and you shall come into the ark*...

Genesis 9:13: I set my *bow* in the cloud, and it shall be a *sign of the covenant* between me and the earth. When I bring clouds over the earth and the *bow* is seen in the clouds, I will remember my covenant, which is between me and you and every living creature of all flesh; and the waters shall never again become a flood to destroy all flesh. When the *bow* is in the clouds, I will look upon it and remember the everlasting *covenant*...

The covenant in 6:18 is established with Noah when he "comes into the ark." The original meaning of the ark in that first covenant is the human body as it came over from Atlantis in the transition from the Atlantean to the Post-Atlantean Epoch.[3]

The phrase "ark of the covenant" appears often in the canon, but the *ark* and the *covenant* and the *rainbow* are connected in only two places. The first of these is in God's covenant with Noah and "every living creature of all flesh" in Genesis 9:13–17.

> [13] "I set my *bow* in the cloud, and it shall be a sign of the covenant between me and the earth. [14] When I bring clouds over the earth and the *bow* is seen in the clouds, [15] I will remember my covenant which is between me and you and every living creature of all flesh; and the waters shall never again become a flood to destroy all flesh. [16] When the *bow* is in the clouds, I will look upon it and remember the

---

3   From *BB*, "Overview," 21: "The human being, in its evolution, had expelled, one by one, the various animal natures that hardened into the animal kingdom. However, some residue of the astral nature of each animal remained within the human being, so that when Noah took into the ark the animals of all kinds, he was taking into the Post-Atlantean Epoch the human being filled with animal nature of all kinds, which would have to be purified over time. The dimensions of the ark, 300 by 50 by 30 cubits (Gen 6,15), are essentially proportional to the mineral-physical body the human being would carry over from Atlantean to Post-Atlantean times. This was the original 'ark of the covenant.'"

See also *BB*, "Three Bodies," 429, #6: "**Gen 6,16**: The Ark Noah was to build (whose three dimensions of 300 by 50 by 30 [vs 15] are in proportion to the physical body of the Post-Atlantean human being) was to have three decks, namely, a lower, second and third."

everlasting covenant between God and every living creature of all flesh that is upon the earth." [17] God said to Noah, "This is the sign of the covenant which I have established between me and all flesh that is upon the earth."

The covenant that God will remember is the one He pronounced to Noah in Genesis 6:18 in the passage (6:13–22) about the ark.

The only other place in the canon that this ark appears, being the second of the two places mentioned above, is in Revelation 11:19: "Then God's *temple in heaven* was opened, and the *ark of his covenant* was seen within his temple; and there were flashes of lightning, voices, peals of thunder, an earthquake, and heavy hail" (emphasis added). As in John's Gospel (2:21), the temple is the human body, or bears a strong relationship to it in its relationship to God.

A clear distinction must be made between the ark in the Noah account and the ark, the cultic box that was to house the testimony. This latter was a wood construction described in Exod 25:10. In contrast with the ratio of length, breadth, and height of 30 by 5 by 3 of Noah's ark, the ratio in Exodus 25:10 was 5 by 3 by 3. The Hebrew word for Noah's ark is *tebah*, or *tevah*, but for all other OT references to the ark, as in the "ark of the covenant," the word is *'aron*. The only other place in the canon that the Hebrew word *tebah*, or *tevah*, is used is for the basket into which the infant Moses was placed in the passage Exod 2:1–10.[4] The ark appears in the NT only in Matt 24:38; Luke 17:27; Heb 9:4 and 11:7; 1 Pet 3:20; and Rev 11:19. We noted above its use in Rev 11:19. The only NT usage to refer to the cultic box is in Heb 9:4, the rest all refer to Noah's ark. The NT Greek does not differentiate between the *tebah* and the *'aron*, calling them all *kibotos* (or *kiboton*).[5]

The "ark of his covenant" in Revelation 11:19 is connected with the appearance of the rainbow in 10:1. The rainbow appears after the blowing of the sixth trumpet (Rev 9:13) when the blowing of the seventh and last (11:1) is imminent. The end of the seventh and last

---

4   See the discussion of these terms in *BB*, "Three Days' Journey," 322–323.

5   The Greek word *kibotos* means "box, chest, coffer." It refers to both Noah's ark and the ark of Moses and also to the ark described in Exod 25:10; Liddell & Scott, *Greek-English Lexicon*, 9th ed., New York, Oxford University Press (1940), new supp. (1996), 950.

Evolutionary Epoch is at hand, when humanity would pass from the world of matter into the More Perfect Astral Condition.

The special covenant relationship between the rainbow and the ark that appears in the first and last books of the Bible, in each case at the end of one of the seven great Evolutionary Epochs, clearly suggests that the rainbow in Revelation 4:3 at the transition from the Atlantean to the Post-Atlantean Epoch was of similar nature to that in 11:19, especially since the latter also came with the voice like a *trumpet,* was observed by the twenty-four elders, and issued forth flashes of lightning and claps of thunder. Two of the three appearances of the rainbow frame the great Epoch so central to our canon that spans a period of approximately 15,120 years from Atlantis till the War of All against All—the Epoch of humanity's greatest enshacklement in matter, in the depths of the valley of the shadow of death (Ps 23:4).

The Rainbow as Major Transition

As if by divine wisdom, the symbol of the rainbow is withheld from our canon save at its beginning and end, always appearing as humanity moves from one of its Evolutionary Epochs to the next or, in the case of the last, from the Physical to the More Perfect Astral Condition of Form.[6] Our canon is devoted, essentially in its entirety, from Noah to the end of the Post-Atlantean Epoch, over fifteen thousand years, to our difficult journey through the deepest part of the valley of the shadow of death.[7]

We see from chart **I-19** that the Noah transition from Atlantis to the Ancient Indian Cultural Age falls within the zodiacal Sign of Cancer. That sign depicts two intertwining spirals, symbols of the marriage of the rhythmic march of seven through human evolution to the golden mean that promises ascent into and through the ever advancing divine realms of twelve—the sevens of our solar system as we move within the twelves of our zodiac—the marriage of light (clairvoyance) and sound (clairaudience) within that journey through the ethers, as we shall see.[8]

---

6   *BB*, chart **I-1**.

7   *BB*, chart **I-19**, page 573.

8   See *BB*, chart **1-81** ("The 'Seed,' the vortex, the zodiacal sign of Cancer, and the 'golden mean." The chart is based on numerous lectures by Steiner;

Lecturing in Berlin in early 1908, Steiner described the descent of the Ego from the spiritual realms as it penetrates successively the three human bodies during the Lemurian and Atlantean Epochs, but awaits the greater development of human spirit till the Golgotha Deed and its implantation of the I Am in earthly being.[9] For that to happen, Atlantis had to disappear under the ocean named for it and Noah had to bring the most advanced from Atlantis into our current Post-Atlantean Epoch—a transition accompanied by the first appearance of the rainbow.

The Rainbow as Symbol of Ether

While this book might eventually have been written anyhow, its most immediate catalyst was an invitation from the Southeastern Regional branch of the Anthroposophical Society in America to lead a weekend Saint John's Day seminar in Cartersville, Georgia in 2012.[10] Some focus upon Revelation was specifically requested. The two years that followed the seminar were devoted to fulfilling a promise to my wife Jo Anne.[11]

In anticipation of the seminar, I awoke shortly after midnight on Memorial Day 2014 with the three rainbow passages on my mind. The fact that they appeared at both the beginning and end of our Post-Atlantean Epoch and at the end of the last Evolutionary Epoch of the Mineral-Physical Conditions of Form and Life of the Earth Condition of Consciousness seemed deeply and powerfully significant. That it frames our 15,000+ years in the Post-Atlantean Epoch's deepest

---

Supersensible Knowledge, SB (1987), lect. 11, Berlin, 1906 (CW 55); *Old and New Methods of Initiation*, RSP (1991), lect. 3, Dornach, Jan 8, 1922 (CW 210); *An Esoteric Cosmology*, Blauvelt, NY, Garber Communications ((1987), lect. 11, June 7, 1906 (CW 94); *According to Matthew*, SB (2003), lect. 11, Sept. 11, 1910 (CW 123).

9   BB, "Naked," pages 402–403 and chart **I-35**, based upon Steiner's *Good and Evil Spirits and their Influence on Humanity*, CW 102, RSP (2014), lects. 3 and 4, Berlin, Jan 15 and Feb 29, 1908; published earlier as *The Influence of Spiritual Beings Upon Man*, SB (1961).

10 Saint John's Day, at the summer solstice, commemorates John the Baptist.

11 A few years earlier I made a promise to her to write an autobiography for our descendants. It turned into two books, a small "family" version, *Pathways: Ancestry and Memories from Childhood*, and a "public" version, *Pathways: An Autobiography,* both published by SB in late 2014.

enmeshment in matter, and then finally signifies humanity's eternal departure from the realm of matter, is a sobering contemplation. As we have seen, many higher realms and levels of consciousness remain for humanity in its timeless journey to ever greater perfection. The rainbow's arc is a visible arch through which we pass into that spiritual future.

The Grand Scheme (chapter 2; chart **I-1**) is simply a schematic of the sevenfoldedness of the human journey. But we see that the sevens move into the zodiacal realm of the twelves in Revelation's last chapters, and we see as we make that move that the mysterious 144,000 thousand is not a number of souls as such, but a sign describing the point where the sevens of creation in the mineral-physical realm of time move into the twelvefold timelessness of the More Perfect Astral Condition of Form and beyond. In short, the spiral of creation coexists with the sevenfoldedness of the mineral-physical realm. This is evidenced by how that spiral pervades the mineral-physical realm, as a study of the golden mean (Fibonacci ratio) clearly reveals. That the spiral extends beyond the realm of matter is suggested by the fact that every twelfth number in the charting of the golden mean, the Fibonacci series, intersects the spiral even as the spiral approaches a straight line from our earthy perspective (see chapter 8).

I suggest that we give up the etheric body in four significant stages before moving into the Jupiter Condition of Consciousness, the new Jerusalem, or Holy City. Observing the chart of the Grand Scheme, we note that there are four "kingdoms" we must move through; mineral, plant, animal, and human. Our first relinquishment of the etheric body is from the mineral realm at the end of the seventh Evolutionary Epoch, at the blowing of the last trumpet and the farewell appearance of the last rainbow. This interpretation seems to comport with Steiner's indication that there are four etheric stages we move through in order to incarnate or in our departure from an incarnation. These four stages are a progressive reprise of the Conditions of Consciousness we have moved through thus far, Saturn, Sun, Moon, and finally Earth.

To illustrate the principles of descent (fission) and reascent (fusion) through the etheric realm to incarnation on our earth, I derived in Chart **I-22** at *BB*, page 585 the following illustration of the four etheric realms to be traversed:

SATURN	SUN	MOON	EARTH
			Life
			/
		Sound	
		/	\
	Light		Light
	/	\	/
Warmth (Fire)		Warmth	
	\	/	\
	Air		Air
		\	/
		Water	
			\
			Earth

Let us consider the birth and death process for a single incarnation. After the soul-spirit (Ego or I Am) has passed through its "midnight hour" in higher devachan (spiritual world), it begins its descent back through higher and lower devachan, carrying with it all it has developed through many incarnations but resolved to carving out a portion of its massive karma needing perfection and thus creating its own destiny. The process is carried on as it passes down through the astral realm, picking up an astral body, including that part of its own astral body that has been sufficiently perfected in prior incarnations. It then begins its entry into the earth's etheric realms through the four ethers that are creative of the "four elements" in the mineral-physical world.[12] So, the soul enters the region of the fire ether first, on the left side of **I-22**, moving downward in the etheric realm, but upward on **I-22**, to the right, passing next through the light ether, then the sound ether (also called chemical ether), and finally into the life ether at birth. We must think that as the Ego passes downward through these realms, the mineral-physical counterparts that are produced by the etheric body, namely, fire (warm blood), air, water and flesh are developing in the selected mother's womb.

12　See the essay "Four Elements" in *DQWIM.*

The child is born, lives a life facing its chosen destiny, and at some point when its purpose has been served it dies. We know that it first lays aside its mineral-physical body, then after three days it lays aside its etheric body, entering the astral world for a period equal to the time it slept in the life just ended on earth after which it gives up its astral body. We should observe that the portion of the astral, etheric, and even physical bodies that have been perfected are treasures for it "laid up in heaven" that wait for it (and/or for others) in those realms, but that the portion, if any, of the three bodies that has been perfected becomes their higher counterparts, namely, Spirit-Self (manas), Life-Spirit (buddhi), and Spirit-Man (atma), respectively, collectively called "Spirit." The Soul (Ego)-Spirit, having passed through the astral realm enters into the lower, then higher, spiritual realm, nurtured by the hierarchies. It passes through its midnight hour there and repeats the process toward a new incarnation.

Note with interest what Jesus says to Nicodemus in John 3:5, "Truly, truly, I say to you, unless one is born of water and the Spirit, he cannot enter the kingdom of God." This must be pondered in under-standing what it means to be "born again." Whatever merit exists in the concept held by those who claim to be "born again" Christians, Jesus was teaching a "teacher of Israel." The term *spirit* comes from the Greek word that also means "air," so Jesus is pointing to the pro-cess of dying, passing upward through the etheric realms first of water (sound or chemical ether), air (light ether) and fire ether. On this latter, recall Christ's "I came to cast fire upon the earth" (Luke 12:49). One has to literally be "born again and again" until one has been able to pass through the realm of etheric fire, giving up the mineral body and moving into the astral realm at the blowing of the last trumpet (see *BB*, chart I-2).[13] The journey is thus quite long. Every living person has been "born again" many times and will be many more times before the last trumpet is blown ending the last Evolutionary Epoch.

What then may we infer as the meaning of the rainbow at the end of the last Epoch? Let us first consider that sound relates to the trum-pets, the last of which ends the Seventh Epoch, and that light relates to the colors of the rainbow. Let us then consider how both sound and light reflect both seven and twelve. There is much of vibrational

---

13   See the "Fire" essay in *DQWIM*.

physics in sound, but simply stated, the normal scale of seven notes is reflected by the seven white keys on the piano, while adding the black keys brings the total to twelve. The chromatic scale includes all twelve keys. But what is the significance of the word *chromatic?* The Greek "chroma" means "color." Modern theory is that the word *chromatic* came from the fact that both white and black colored keys were played in the scale. But this assumes that such keys were in existence at its origin—not likely! We are told that "The chromatic scale...was...ancient." Aristoxenus' view is that its origins "go back into the night of time."[14] Aristoxenus, a student of Aristotle, was a fourth-century-BCE Greek peripatetic philosopher, the first authority for musical theory in the classical world.[15] So somehow it seems that the origin of the twelve key scale had to do with color. But the connection to color is still mysterious as it pertains to the sound ether.

When we move to the light ether with its colorful rainbow the meaning becomes clearer in the light of what Steiner, with his Goethean Science, demonstrates.[16] When we look at the rainbow we only see seven colors, but the two colors at the extreme are only there in part, and above the rainbow is a second rainbow where the colors appear in exactly the reverse order of the first. The implication of these phenomena is that there are twelve colors that encircle a sphere, implying a continuation on the opposite side. The peach color of human skin is in the center of the back. In short, the light ether in its twelvefold aspect more clearly points us toward the human being.[17]

So in the last three Epochs we move in reverse of what we did in the first three Epochs, from life ether to sound ether to light ether, and then through the fire ether at the "last trumpet" to the point where it touches the twelvefold nature reflected at the end of the book of Revelation when we reach the Jupiter Condition of Consciousness. The point at which the spiral and the number twelve intersect, which is at every twelfth (Fibonacci) number (the first "twelfth number" being 144 at the last trumpet), points to and suggests the meaning of the

---

14 See www.dolmetsch.com/musictheory25.htm

15 See www.britannica.com/biography/Aristoxenus

16 See the "Fire" essay in *DQWIM* in the section subtitled "Heat and the Other Ethers," 145–166, immediately preceding the section subtitled "Fire, the Spiral and the One Hundred Forty-Four Thousand."

17 See also *BB*, chart **I-83**, 663–665.

three dimensional cube in Revelation—the measurement of the Holy City in Rev 21:15–17 (twelve by twelve by twelve).

But the last rainbow, standing as it does at the point of humanity's passing through the fire ether, reminds us of its appearance in Rev 4:3 at the end of our Post-Atlantean Epoch, to the last Cultural Age ("Church") of which the Lord says, "Therefore I counsel you to buy from me *gold refined by fire…*" (3:18, emphasis added).

The last rainbow stands at the point where humanity passes through the fire ether in relinquishing its body of matter in the Mineral Kingdom. But the rainbow also symbolizes both the light ether of the Plant Kingdom and sound ether of the Animal Kingdom through which humanity must still pass, giving up those ethers in such passage. The sevenfold and twelvefold composition of both the rainbow's colors and sounds, as discussed above, anticipates humanity's passage through both the light and sound ethers as it moves through the Plant and Animal Kingdoms. Similarly, we may see, as we leave the Earth, and move into the Jupiter, Condition of Consciousness, our passage through the life ether of the Human Kingdom. We may ponder that the life and light in the prologue of John's Gospel (1:4) subsume all four etheric states implied in the rainbow's symbolism.

CONCLUSION

In closing, while there are scientific explanations for the appearance of the rainbow in our world of matter, may we be grateful that its appearance in the sky always brings into our heart the sense of spiritual mystery. And may such gratitude extend to Lazarus/John for his placement of that rainbow mystery at such important transitions in our long journey, and, in the end, for his priceless Apocalypse itself.

BIBLIOGRAPHY

Allen, Paul M. and Carlo Pietzner, compilers and editors, *A Christian Rosenkreutz Anthology*, rev. 3rd ed., Blauvelt, NY, Rudolf Steiner Publications (Garber) (1981).

Bamford, Christopher, *An Endless Trace*, New Paltz, NY, Codhill Press (1993).

Benesch, Friedrich, *Apocalypse: The Transformation of the Earth; An Occult Mineralogy*, SB (2015).

Bock, Emil, *The Apocalypse*, Edinburgh, Floris Books (1957).

———, *Kings and Prophets*, London, Floris Books (1989).

———, *The Three Years*, London, Christian Community Press (1955).

Brown, Raymond E., *An Introduction to the New Testament,* ABRL (1997).

Buchanan, George Wesley, "To the Hebrews," 2d ed., AB, vol. 36, (1983).

Collins, Adele Yarbro, *Revelation, Book of,* sec. H, "Relation to Other Ancient Literature," ABD, vol. 5 (1992); 74.

Craddock, Fred B., *The Letter to the Hebrews,* NIB, vol. 12 (1998).

Culpepper, R. Alan, *The Gospel of Luke*, NIB, vol. 9 (1995).

The Ethiopic Book of Enoch, Oxford, Clarendon Press (1978).

Fitzmyer, Joseph A., *The Gospel According to Luke 1–9*, AB, vol. 28 (1981).

Ford, J. Massyngberde, *Revelation*, AB, vol. 38 (1975).

Frend, W. H. C., *The Rise of Christianity*, Philadelphia, Fortress Press (1984).

Greenberg, Moshe, *Ezekiel 1–20*, AB vol. 22 (1963).

Hess, Richard S., "Abel" in ABD, vol. 1 (1992); 9–10, esp. 10.

Jones, Brian W., "Domitian," ABD, vol. 2 (1991); 221–222, esp. 222.

The JPS Torah commentary, Genesis, vol. 1, JPS (1989); 32.

Kirchner-Bockholt, Margarete and Erich, *Rudolf Steiner's Mission and Ita Wegman*, RSP (1977) (CW 238).

Koester, Craig R, *Hebrews,* AB, vol. 36 (2001).

Kovacs, Charles, *The Apocalypse in Rudolf Steiner's Lecture Series,* Edinburgh, Floris Books (2013).

Liddell & Scott, *Greek-English Lexicon*, 9th ed., 1996 Supp. New York, Oxford University Press (1996).

Marshall, Alfred, *The Interlinear KJV-NIV Parallel New Testament in Greek and English*, Grand Rapids, Zonderman, 1975.

Mathews, Kenneth A., "Boaz," ABD, vol. 1; 765.

Mirecki, Paul Allan, "Manichaean's and Manichaeism", ABD, vol. 4 (1992).

Nickelsburg, George W. E., "Enoch, First Book of," ABD, vol. 2 (1991).

——, *Son of Man*, ABD, vol. 6 (1992); 137–150.

Pagels, Elaine, *Revelations*, New York, NY, Viking (2012).

Plümacher, Eckhard, "Luke," trans. Dennis Martin, ABD, vol. 4 (1992).

Powell, Robert, *Chronicle of the Living Christ*, SB (1996).

——, *Hermetic Astrology*, vol. 1, Kinsau, West Germany, Hermetika (1987).

Prokofieff, Sergei O., *Eternal Individuality*, 1st English ed., TL (1992); German ed. *Ewige Individualitat*, Dornach, Switzerland, Verlag am Goetheanum (1987).

——, *The Mystery of John the Baptist and John the Evangelist at the Turning Point of Time*, TL (2005).

Querido, René, Introduction to Steiner, *The Book of Revelation and the Work of the Priest*, RSP (1998) (CW 346).

Rist, Martin, exegesis to "Revelation," *The Interpreter's Bible*, New York/ Nashville, Abingdon Press (1957), vol. 12; 443–444.

Rowland, Christopher C., "The Book of Revelation," NIB, vol. 12 (1998).

Selg, Peter, *Rudolf Steiner and the Fifth Gospel: Insights into a New Understanding of the Christ Mystery*, SB (2010).

Smith, Edward Reaugh, *The Burning Bush (BB)*, rev. ed., AP (2001), orig publ. AP (1997).

——, *David's Question: "What Is Man?" (DQWIM)*, AP (2001).

——, *The Incredible Births of Jesus (IBJ)*, AP (1998).

——, *Pathways: Ancestry and Memories from Childhood*, SB (2014).

——, *Pathways: An Autobiography (PWA)*, SB (2014).

——, *The Soul's Long Journey (SLJ)*, SB (2003).

——, *The Temple Sleep of the Rich Young Ruler (TSRYR)*, SB (2011).

Smith-Christopher, Daniel L. , *The Book of Daniel*, NIB, vol. 7 (1996).

Steiner, Rudolf, *According to Luke*, trans. Catherine E. Creeger, AP (2001) (CW 114).

————, *According to Matthew*, SB (2003) (CW 123).

————, *Ancient Myths, Their Meaning and Connection with Evolution*, N. Vancouver, Steiner Book Centre (1979) (CW 180).

————, *The Apocalypse of St. John (ASJ)*, 4th ed., var. translators, AP (1993) (*CW* 104).

————, *At the Gates of Spiritual Science*, 2d ed., RSP and SB (1986) (CW 95); now available as *Founding a Science of the Spirit,* RSP (1999).

————, *Background to the Gospel of St. Mark*, 3rd ed., AP (1968) (CW 124).

————, *The Bhagavad Gita and the West*, CW 142, SB (2009).

————, *The Book of Revelation and the Work of the Priest (REVP)*, RSP (1998) (CW 346).

————, *Building Stones for an Understanding of the Mystery of Golgotha (BSU)*, 2nd ed., RSP (1972) (CW 175).

————, *Christianity as Mystical Fact (CMF)*, SB (2006) [1902], CW, vol. 8.

————, *Cosmic Memory*, New York, Harper & Row (1959) (CW 11).

————, *The Effects of Spiritual Development*, RSP (1978) (CW 145).

————, *Egyptian Myths and Mysteries*, SB (1971) (CW 106).

————, *Esoteric Christianity and the Mission of Christian Rosenkreutz*, 2nd ed. RSP (1984) (CW 130).

————, *An Esoteric Cosmology*, Blauvelt, NY, Garber Communications (1987) (CW 94).

————, *The Fall of the Spirits of Darkness*, RSP (1993) (CW 177).

————, *The Fifth Gospel/From the Akashic Record*, 3rd. ed., RSP (1995) (CW 148).

————, *Foundations of Esotericism*, 1st Eng. ed., RSP (1983).

————, *From Jesus to Christ*, RSP (1973) (CW 131).

————, *Genesis*, rev. ed., RSP (2002) (CW 122).

————, *Good and Evil Spirits and Their Influence on Humanity*, SB (2014) (CW 102); formerly *The Influence of Spiritual Beings Upon Man*, AP (1961).

————, *The Gospel of St. John (GSJ)*, rev. ed., AP (1962) (CW 103).

————, *The Gospel of St. John (GOSPSJ)*, November 1907 cycle at Basel, unpublished English transcript (CW 100).

——, *The Gospel of St. John and Its Relation to the Other Gospels*, rev. ed., AP (1982) (CW 112).

——, *The Gospel of St. Mark (GSMk)*, AP (2001) (CW 139).

——, *The Gospel of St. Matthew (GSMt)*, 4th ed., AP (1965) (CW 123).

——, *Health and Illness*, vol. 2, SB (1983) (CW 348).

——, *How Can Mankind Find the Christ Again?* 2nd ed., AP (1984) (CW 187).

——, *How to Know Higher Worlds*, AP (1994) [1904] (CW 10).

——, *The Influence of Spiritual Beings Upon Man*, AP (1961); new trans. *Good and Evil Spirits and Their Influence on Humanity*, RSP (CW 102) (2014).

——, *The Inner Aspect of the Social Question*, RSP (1974) (CW 193).

——, *Intuitive Thinking as a Spiritual Path*, AP (1995) [orig. ed. 1894] (CW 4).

——, *Karmic Relationships*, vol. 3, 2nd ed., RSP (1977) (CW 237).

——, *Karmic Relationships*, vol. 5, 2nd ed., RSP (1984) (CW 239).

——, *Karmic Relationships*, vol. 6, 2nd ed., RSP (1989) (CW 240).

——, *Karmic Relationships*, vol. 8, 2nd ed., RSP (1975) (CW 240).

——, *The Last Address*, RSP (1967) (CW 238).

——, *Life between Death and Rebirth*, SB (1968) (CW 140).

——, *The Lord's Prayer*, SB (1970) (CW 96).

——, *Man as Symphony of the Creative Word*, 2nd ed., RSP (1945) (CW 230).

——, *Materialism and the Task of Anthroposophy*, AP (1987) (CW 204)

——, *Occult History*, RSP (1982) (CW 126).

——, *The Occult Movement in the Nineteenth Century*, RSP (1973) (CW 254).

——, *An Occult Physiology*, 3rd ed., RSP (1983) (CW 128).

——, *Occult Seals and Columns*, lect. Munich, May 18, 1907, unpublished English transcript (CW 285).

——, *Occult Signs and Symbols*, AP (1972) (CW 101).

——, *Old and New Methods of Initiation*, RSP (1991) (CW 210).

——, *The Origin of Suffering, Evil, Illness and Death*, N. Vancouver, Steiner Book Centre (1980) (CW 55).

——, *An Outline of Esoteric Science (OES)*, AP (1997) (CW 13).

——, *The Principle of Spiritual Economy*, AP (1986) (CW 109).

——, *Reading the Pictures of the Apocalypse*, AP (1993) (CW 104a).

———, *The Reappearance of Christ in the Etheric,* AP (1983) (CW 118).

———, *The Riddle of Humanity*, RSP (1990) (CW 170).

———, *Rosicrucian Christianity*, MP (1989), 6 (CW 130).

———, *Rosicrucian Esotericism*, AP (1978) (CW 109/111).

———, *Rosicrucianism Renewed,* CW 284, SB (2007).

———, *The "Son of God" and the "Son of Man"*, unpublished English typescript, lect. Munich, Feb. 11, 1911.

———, *Spiritual Beings in the Heavenly Bodies & in the Kingdoms of Nature*, AP (1992) (CW 136).

———, *The Spiritual Guidance of Man*, ed. Henry B. Monges, AP (1950) (CW 15).

———, *The Spiritual Hierarchies and Their Reflection in the Physical World*, AP (1970) (CW 110).

———, *Supersensible Knowledge*, SB (1987) (CW 55).

———, *The Temple Legend (TL)*, RSP (1985) (CW 93).

———, *Theosophy*, AP (1994) [1904] (CW 9).

———, *Theosophy of the Rosicrucian*, 2nd ed., RSP (1966) (CW 99).

———, *True and False Paths in Spiritual Investigation*, 3rd ed., RSP (1985) (CW 243).

———, *Turning Points in Spiritual History*, SB (2007) (chs. 1–4 in CW 60; 5–6 in CW 71).

Watson, Duane F., "Seven Churches," ABD, vol. 5, citing W. Ramsay. *Letters to the Seven Churches*. London, 1904.

Wellburn, Andrew, *The Book with Fourteen Seals*, RSP (1991).

———, *From a Virgin Womb: The Apocalypse of Adam and the Virgin Birth*, Leiden, Brill (2008).

Witherington, Ben III, *Revelation*, New York, Cambridge University Press (2003).

Wolff, Otto, *Anthroposophically Oriented Medicine and Its Remedies*, MP (1991).

Yonge, C. D. (trans.), *The Works of Philo*, Complete and Unabridged, new updated ed., Peabody, MA, Hendrickson (1993).

Zajonc, Arthur, "Manichaeism—Religion of Light," in *Catching the Light*, New York, Oxford University Press (1993).

INDEX OF SCRIPTURES CITED

GENERAL INDEX